THE THEATRE OF URBAN

Youth and Schooling in Dangerous Times

Because of its powerful socializing effects, the school classroom has always been a site of cultural, political, and academic conflict. In an age in which terms such as 'hard to teach' and 'at-risk' permeate our pedagogical discourses, and anti-immigrant, anti-welfare, 'zero-tolerance' rhetoric is commonplace, how we frame and understand the dynamics of the classroom has serious ethical implications and practical consequences. Using theatre and drama education as a window into life in four urban secondary schools in Toronto and New York City, *The Theatre of Urban* examines the ways in which these schools reflect the cultural and political shifts in North American schooling policies, politics, and practices of the early twenty-first century.

Resisting facile comparisons of Canadian and American school systems, Kathleen Gallagher opts instead for a rigorous analysis of the context-specific features – noting both the differences and similarities – of urban cultures and schools in the two countries. Gallagher re-examines familiar 'urban issues' facing these schools, such as racism, classism, (hetero)sexism, and religious fundamentalism, in light of theatre performances of diverse groups of young people and their commentary on their own creative work together. A profoundly challenging and innovative work, *The Theatre of Urban* not only provides new insights into the conflicts that often erupt in these highly charged school spaces, it also explores the potential of drama as a powerful medium for personal growth and social change.

KATHLEEN GALLAGHER is an associate professor and Canada Research Chair at the Ontario Institute for Studies in Education of the University of Toronto.

D1566506

KATHLEEN GALLAGHER

The Theatre of Urban

Youth and Schooling
in Dangerous Times

UNIVERSITY OF TORONTO PRESS
Toronto Buffalo London

© University of Toronto Press Incorporated 2007
Toronto Buffalo London
Printed in Canada

ISBN 978-0-8020-9291-5 (cloth)
ISBN 978-0-8020-9483-4 (paper)

Printed on acid-free paper

Library and Archives Canada Cataloguing in Publication

Gallagher, Kathleen, 1965–
    The theatre of urban : youth and schooling in dangerous times / Kathleen
Gallagher.

    Includes bibliographical references and index.
    ISBN 978-0-8020-9291-5 (bound)
    ISBN 978-0-8020-9483-4 (pbk.)

    1. High school students – Ontario – Toronto – Social conditions – Case
studies.   2. High school students – New York (State) – New York – Social
conditions – Case studies.   3. Urban high schools – Ontario – Toronto –
Case studies.   4. Urban high schools – New York (State) – New York – Case
studies.   5. College and school drama, Canadian (English) – Ontario –
Toronto – History and criticism.   6. College and school drama, American –
New York (State) – New York – History and criticism.   I. Title.

    PN3171.G34 2007   373.18'09713541   C2006-906270-6

This book has been published with the help of a grant from the
Canadian Federation for the Humanities and Social Sciences, through
the Aid to Scholarly Publications Programme, using funds provided by
the Social Sciences and Humanities Research Council of Canada.

University of Toronto Press acknowledges the financial assistance to
its publishing program of the Canada Council for the Arts and the
Ontario Arts Council.

University of Toronto Press acknowledges the financial support for
its publishing activities of the Government of Canada through the
Book Publishing Industry Development Program (BPIDP).

To the brilliant teenagers with whom I have spent the better part of my teaching and research life: 'Thank you for the fire.' (Dr Rank, *A Doll's House*)

CONTENTS

Foreword   ix

Acknowledgments   xv

Prologue   3

1. CONTEXT   9
Discourse, Space, and Competing Narratives   9
Space and Subjects: Security, Surveillance, and 'Zero Tolerance'   26
Photo Essay   39

2. IN THE FIELD   54
An Ethnographic Critique   54
The Situated Character of Ethnography   60
Disenchanted Youth, Falling Test Scores, Rigourous Curriculum and
    other Prevailing Myths   73

3. SUBJECTIVITIES   84
The Social and the Artistic   84
Social Dramas: Relations of Power, Gender, and Race   91
Imaginative Trespassing and Ethnographic Artefacts   97
The Gay Other Not among Us: Sexuality and Its Guises   109
Dark Dramas: The Occupied Imagination   128

4. URBAN OBSESSIONS   140
Pedagogies of Conflict   140
Alternative Literacies and the Sociology of Aesthetics   155

5 CONSTITUTING CULTURE AND CO-RESEARCH
   WITH YOUTH   172
A Problem-Posing Ethnography   175

References   183
Name Index   197
Subject Index   203

FOREWORD:
BEARING WIT(H)NESS

The lights are flickering, signalling that *The Theatre of Urban* is about to begin. Author Kathleen Gallagher promises us, in the words of Deborah Britzman, a performance that 'disturb(s) the impulse to settle meanings.' Situated in four distinct schools, in New York and Toronto, the scene is neoliberal urban North America. The photo essay vivifies this now familiar site of schooling for alienation, colonizing minds and bodies, eerily stretched across national borders. Poor urban youth, usually of colour, cast as 'dangerous' in the larger culture tossed into schools of last resort. Their teachers' moods swing from earnest to beaten down.

The historic timing of the performance is politically charged: 'In the current political moment of *homeland* and *otherland* safety and security, there is unprecedented attention being paid to the containment, movement and dispersal of people in public spaces; the manifestation of fear and the priority of 'security' has never before been so acute in public schools.' *The Theatre of Urban* opens a window onto the contentious global politics in which youth of poverty and colour marinate.

Just after 9/11 Martin Ruck, Anita Harris, and I combined research efforts to interrogate how teens across Toronto, Canada; Melbourne, Australia; and New York City, USA, were experiencing the proliferation of state-sponsored strategies of surveillance on youth, particularly youth of colour and poverty (see Ruck, Harris, and Fine, 2006). With street and school surveys, participant observations and ethnography, conducted by adult and youth researchers, we documented across continents spikes in surveillance, suspicion, and arrests of native, Black, and immigrant youth. In parallel, we gathered evidence of a seething subterranean erosion of youth belief in and commitment to state-sponsored democratic institutions and practices.

Our findings of racialized and classed surveillance among youth were confirmed by a chilling analysis of adolescents involved with the juvenile justice system. Drawing on U.S. Department of Juvenile Justice data, Poe-Yagamata and Jones (2000) report that African Americans account for 15 per cent of young people in the United States and 26 per cent of those who are arrested. At every point in the criminal justice process thereafter, being African American increases the likelihood of adverse outcomes. Most chilling, a full 58 per cent of the youth who end up in state adult prisons are African American, more than doubling their original over-representation in the arrest rates. Data from Toronto track similar racial and ethnic discrepancies, and in Australia, Aboriginal and Torres Strait Islander youth make up 36 per cent of the total numbers in juvenile detention centres, but comprise only 2.6 per cent of the 10- to 17-year-old Australian population. They are 21 times more likely to be held in legal custody than non-indigenous youth.

Politically and developmentally, the consequences of such targeted surveillance and criminalized scrutiny are devastating. Public authorities that are *supposed* to protect and public institutions that are *supposed* to educate have been transformed into sites for the criminalization of youth. As urban zip codes gentrify and elite interests and families occupy long-neglected neighbourhoods, carpenters and real estate developers are joined by police and security who constitute the first line 'troops' ordered to clear out 'what is' in order to reclaim 'what will be.' Neither streets nor schools are exempt from the massive infusion of state power, watching and targeting youth, remaking the urban United States, Canada, and Australia.

The Theatre of Urban exposes these geopolitical dynamics in the micro-relations of schooling, drama classrooms, and participatory research with youth and academics. Creating conversation between critical scholars and equally brilliant youth from among the North American urban landscape, Gallagher accompanies us into this territory through the window of the drama classroom. She intends to 'provoke imagination,' insisting that the audience 'bear witness ... [and] carry a heavy load that eventually must be shared.'

Relations of educational devastation and hope compress in the tiny corners of drama in these four urban schools. Drama class wedges open a sweet space where educational possibilities flourish; here creative conflicts are engaged and critical inquiry is embodied. Students are invited to appreciate difference, play with multiple identities, try on their many hyphenated selves and resist identity calcification.

The youth, educators, and the ethnographers are cast brilliantly, bust-
ing open the fossilized roles they are meted out in urban North America.
Choking on the toxic winds of symbolic violence, surveillance, and
oppressive mis-recognitions, and threatened by the symbolic and enacted state violence of police harassment, high stakes testing, and
underfunded mis-education, the young people are asked simply to act.
Gallagher has waged her life's work on the belief that 'if we hold a
mirror up to the various policing measures inflicted upon a fictional
group of workers (the youth in role), [we might] see how this kind of
theatre pedagogy and analogous thinking might explore our sense of
the imagination as *occupied space* in the current criminalizing of youth
in and out of schools.'

The drama classroom is a construction site designed for desire, bodies, and voices to speak. The space of performance invites urban youth,
so fiercely cast as dangerous and fixed, to engage in performances of
self that are 'incomplete fiction, with profound moments of discovery,
resonance and truth.' Lorelei (Black, female, new immigrant, born in
the former Congo, moved from South Africa to Belgium to Canada,
grade twelve) reflects this shift in a poignant question, 'When drama
students walk out of this class, why is it that it is a different story when
you walk out of that door?'

You will meet Jin, an immigrant youth who remains relatively silent
during much of drama class, morphing language issues into social
alienation, who nevertheless tells us about the openings created through
the drama space, despite his 'peripheral participation.' You'll meet
Jake, a confident White boy who volunteers to role-play a pregnant
teenage girl, and pulls it off eloquently. Dion, who refuses to perform
gay, explains his homophobia, 'That's just plant inside of me, Sir, I can't
get rid of it, you know what I'm saying ... it grew up ... into a big tree.'
And Tanisha, a biracial (Black and Hispanic) twelfth grader, narrates
how she exports drama class to the streets, 'When I go into job interviews, I'm so like, up there, and they're looking at me, like we were
expecting this shy little girl to sit in the corner and just merely answer
the questions. No! I'm in theatre, I'm going to answer the questions, you
know, I'm going to elaborate on those questions. When I'm on the street,
and guys are like, 'hey, mommy, how you doin?' they don't expect how
I react ...'

This class may be the one space in school where students are invited
to risk, articulate, embody the range of emotion, speak in varied dia-
lects, all in the presence of adults who will catch them if they fall. Yet

even here, in this relatively protected space of performance, psychic ghosts of hatred linger, racist stereotypes, xenophobia, and homophobia contaminate, flashbacks of social neglect invade – none of these left easily at the door. Within this space a stunning struggle ensues between the polarized identities that racism, classism, surveillance, and schooling can impose on youth, and the hyphenated, elastic, and malleable identities young people yearn to engage in drama.

Educators, stretching and moving and dancing and trying to hold the space open for what could be, tire as they try to buffer the weight of oppression that festers in the twenty-first-century North American city, unsure if they can/should challenge students' sense of experience and authority, when everywhere else they have been demonized, trivialized, silenced, and ignored. Ethnographers watch and labour alongside, with exhaustion and empathy, the not-yet-sufficient attempts by Ms S. to engage the young people in their roles, 'because their performances *as students* were so overpowering that they could neither physically nor intellectually enter into the possible dramatic interpretations or personas available.'

Drama, born in the writings of Augusto Boal and theatre of the oppressed, transforms the space. Even in tired spaces of urban schooling, bad lights, graffitied desk, broken chairs and dreams, 'there is always the possibility of both identification with and distance from the drama.' Indeed, the drama class offers 'an aesthetic experience that resides in the connection between what a person already knows (of herself and her community), feels, and desires with what a new experience might offer.' This contrasts so fundamentally with the everyday praxis of schooling and social life, where urban youth are cast routinely as dangerous or invisible. You will leave thankful for the recuperative space of drama, but worried that the rupture may not be sufficient in a world dedicated to toxic representations. You will worry – if you stay present, with all pores open – that these youth are being encouraged, perversely, in almost all of their lives to develop hard skin, masks, refusals; that saying No and opposing are increasingly the only open spaces for agency. And then you will worry that hard skin will penetrate deeper, as is the case with the 'real' embodied condition of hard skin, *scleroderma*:

'The term "scleroderma" comes from the Greek words for "hard skin",' says M.E. Csuka, MD, Associate Professor of Medicine at the Medical

College of Wisconsin. 'Its most obvious manifestation is thickening and hardening of the skin, and that's how we usually make the diagnosis.' Although it's the most obvious sign of scleroderma, skin hardening is by no means the most dangerous symptom of this baffling disease.

'Patients who have this thickened, hard skin experience decreases in physical functioning and limits in the activities of daily living. But for the most part this skin problem is not what causes them their most serious morbidity and mortality,' says Dr. Csuka. In fact the disease can run much deeper and cause life-threatening problems in the lungs, heart, esophagus, gastrointestinal tract and kidneys. (health.mcw.edu/article/1031002255.html)

I write this foreword to warn you, the audience: if you think you are out for a relaxing evening, to watch, enjoy and leave, you're wrong. The brilliance of the text lies in Gallagher's seductive pen. You will be distracted by a haunting question ... how much is enough? Can one class keep a young person from hardened skin? There will be moments when you'll want to bolt as you take in ... 'a 76 minute class on reasoned, justified hatred of gays. For this session, gay had to be the other. Gay had to be outside "our" space. Gay was banished. So where did we go? I retreated into the chalk brush, the important task of delivering it to the person who was speaking, blaming, hating, imploring, defending ... after class we instinctively brought the five chairs together, emotionally drained, each in our own turmoil but collectively carrying the burden of witnessing.'

And you will soon come to realize, for these students, these teachers, and for you, there is no exit. We are all implicated.

The Theatre of Urban captivates and thrusts fundamental questions of public and collective responsibility onto our laps. As you watch, and note the discomfort in your body, you will have to answer – are these young people your children or somebody else's babies? Is this their tragedy or ours? And you will remember that Gallagher quotes James Baldwin as saying, 'The purpose of art is to lay bare the questions which have been hidden by the answers.'

In the end, you – as audience – can, of course, leave. Indeed, exit is the signature move of elites when we are discomforted.

But many of these young people, and their most devoted educators, are cemented into this theatre. Tattoos of disinvestment are branded into their souls, as a desire for something radically different burns in their hearts. While you can leave, they can't. Indeed, Jean-Paul Sartre would say, ultimately, even for you: 'There's no escaping each other and there's no escaping the truth.'

The Theatre of Urban is a brilliant, moving, compelling, empathic, funny, and sad invitation to join urban youth, educators, schools, and radical social movements – to bear wit(h)ness.

Michelle Fine
The Graduate Center, City University of New York

ACKNOWLEDGMENTS

No one knows alone, I once heard Madeleine Grumet say.

I would like to acknowledge the vast community of scholars who research and write about urban schools. Their conviction that a body of work can change people's material lives and further our always incomplete understanding of the powerful socializing forces of schooling is very sustaining to me. For this book, scholars of 'youth,' 'race,' 'art/ theatre,' 'sociology,' and 'schooling practices,' in particular, have contributed to this complex arena of analysis and importantly extended the boundaries of knowledge production.

My gratitude also extends to colleagues at the Ontario Institute for Studies in Education at the University of Toronto for their support of my work and for creating an intellectual environment in which 'education' is always writ large. I have so greatly benefited from this. I appreciate as well the funding support I have received from the Social Sciences and Humanities Research Council of Canada. And I am thankful for the privilege that academia affords, for the sabbatical time that has allowed such an immersion into my thinking and a needed reacquaintance with my creative impulses.

Thank you Caroline for turning me onto 'space,' for your profound understanding of spatial theory, your inventive spatial ethnographic research, and your always generous sharing of the ideas that fuel you. I am truly grateful.

Thank you John for our discussions about the theatre, about performance, about art and education and life. You expect much of the theatre and never settle for less.

Everyone needs a cheerleader. Thank you David for always being in my corner and for the many conversations that comfort and assuage worries.

Finally, I would like to acknowledge the teachers in schools who resist the forces of fear and bureaucracy so ubiquitous today. These teachers continue to open spaces for students to explore and play, and then to get on with the business of changing the world.

THE THEATRE OF URBAN: YOUTH AND SCHOOLING IN DANGEROUS TIMES

Drama ... is not life described but life imagined, it is possibility and not reproduction.

Howard Barker, *Arguments for a Theatre*

All the world is not, of course, a stage, but the crucial ways in which it isn't are not easy to specify.

Erving Goffman, *The Presentation of Self in Everyday Life*

They're researchers, they don't know what answers they want yet. They want to see if they can find it. If they wanted it on acting then they would go straight to the point and say, 'Okay I want to see you act.' But it's about students and how they act in Drama class ... They don't know what they're looking for, that's why they're doing all these activities and exercises, just to see our reaction and how we act towards it ... in Drama class.

Ari, grade twelve, Middleview School

PROLOGUE

This is a book about youth in public, urban North American high schools. This is also a book about the artistic theatre as a special window onto the larger theatre of school life. In other words, I have been very interested in the contemporary social, political, and artistic meanings of drama in schools. And like improvised theatre, schools operate in the 'here and now.'

The ethnographic study upon which this book is based was called *Drama Education, Youth, and Social Cohesion: (Re)constructing Identities in Urban Contexts.* It centred upon the work, the relationships, and the ideas that developed over three years in four public high schools. Two schools are located in Toronto, Canada, and two in New York City, USA. To be precise, one school is in downtown Toronto, the other in North York. In New York, one school is located in midtown Manhattan, the other in Queens. The rationale for selecting the four schools is both conceptual and geographic. In each city, I imagined working in one 'inner-city' school and one 'inner-suburbs' school. I also selected these schools because they either had teachers or principals, or both, who supported drama as a discipline and would understand and support the research. In Toronto, I wanted one school from each of the two publicly funded boards, and I selected a single-sex Catholic school from among the possible public Catholic schools because I have done research in single-sex environments and am still strongly persuaded that this structure opens up interesting ways to examine the question of gender. In New York, a very large public co-educational school in Queens and a small alternative 'last resort' school in midtown Manhattan seemed interestingly different from one another. In both cities, I was ultimately searching for schools that operated in challenging urban circumstances and understood themselves to be working with diverse and complex populations of students.

The schools are unique, each one of them. They are Canadian and American. But they are also similar in the ways in which they reflect cultural and political shifts in 'big city' North American schooling policies, politics, and practices of the early twenty-first century. As an ethnographer, I did not set out to compare these sites, nor to measure differences in practices or outcomes. Rather than adhering to measures of comparison, I wanted this multi-site ethnography to hold me to robust examinations of context and specificity.

And so the title, *The Theatre of Urban*, refers to the performances of 'student,' 'teacher,' and 'urban' in public school space that demand close scrutiny at a time when education is urgently called upon as a social force for good. Looking at the theatre that is invented by young people alongside the theatrical turns and performances of the everyday has been particularly revealing. The subtitle, *Youth and Schooling in Dangerous Times*, is ominous, yes, but it is also an expression of just how important I think it has become to take a hard look at our educational institutions and make clear decisions about what young people need to know and how they need to know it. The times are dangerous because of a range of political and social crises: global economics, global politics, social unrest, and cultural experiments have forced a point of reckoning: Are 'the children' 'our future' or are they not? Will they thrive in the years to come or will the next generations only know war and social malaise, either up close or at some muted distance? Will we continue to distrust youth? Will our cultural and media productions of urban youth, in particular, persist in criminalizing them? Will social and economic divides worsen? Will we continue to measure and commodify learning in ways that seriously disregard the arts and the social contexts of schooling?

Colette Daiute's interesting study (2000) of narrative sites for youths' construction of social consciousness provides evidence to support the idea that those youth who do well enjoy discursive consistency across home, school, and community, while the stories of urban youth, those more like the youth in our research sites, who do not enjoy such mainstream narrative coherence, call on other histories and logics in their stories and storytelling (p. 213). Based on our research, then, I might also boldly assert that drama as research with/by/for youth does not privilege such discursive cohesion and linearity, but demands, instead, that a different kind of attention be paid, that a different kind of story be told.

In an age where terms such as 'hard to teach,' 'at risk,' and 'behavi-oural' students (as though other students are without behaviours en-tirely) beset our pedagogical discourses, where students have grown up in systems all over the globe plagued by anti-immigrant, anti-welfare, 'back-to-basics' rhetoric, how we frame and understand the dynamics of classrooms has serious ethical implications and powerful conse-quences for praxis. Lather (1991) has described this as 'doing praxis-oriented intellectual work in a post-foundational context' (125). Moreover, notions of global education continue to identify 'diversity' (still, more often than not, implying low-achievement or declining stan-dards) and other 'inner-city challenges' as the greatest obstructions to healthy, safe, and high-achieving (or competitive) classroom communi-ties. The ideologies that help to constitute the phenomenon of being 'at risk,' a pervasive term in urban schools, too often carelessly link failure with identity difference. Conceptions of multicultural classroom com-munities desperately need to push beyond the narrow confines of iden-tity politics. Most 'democratic' classroom spaces hide behind an illusion of neutrality and fairness. They are crying out for what Sawicki (1991) calls a 'radical pluralism.' It is from here that my idea of sustained research in drama classrooms originated; I wanted the specificity and intimacy of these classrooms to create a counterpoint to the broader, more generic school context. How do, for example, the dialectics of self and other, of local and global, of democracy and domination play out in drama's pedagogy? Further, how do we come to understand the dialec-tical relationship between the performative and the non-performative, or the fictional roles enacted in the drama classroom and the so-called 'real' ones?

There have been many uneasy moments over the three years of this sociological study of schools and the young people in them. There have been conceptual shifts, methodological manoeuvres, and pedagogical challenges. There have also been moments of stunning clarity, moments of pure poetry in interviews and exchanges with young people. And there have been performances – of both the social and artistic kind – that will remain with me for a very long time. The youth in this study, I came to learn, use their words and stories not only to reflect their realities but to reconstitute them. At the risk, yes, of romanticizing youth, I must say that I gain immeasurably from their wisdom and their storytelling.

School is a site of cultural, political, and academic conflict because of its powerful socializing effects. There is no blueprint for the perfect school, to be sure, but the small narratives of individual schools presented here may point us in important directions. In the four schools where our team of researchers spent the better part of three years, we focused especially on the drama classrooms in these schools. Drama is unique among school subjects and the drama classroom is a space unlike others in a typical high school. It is a space that can be more permissive of the distinctive expressions and contributions of young people, a space in which speaking out of turn is the norm; a space that is the crossroads of students' performances as 'students' – socially positioned by gender, race, class, ability, sexuality, as they are – and as artists, young people improvising performances and identities out of thin air. The empirical nature of this work is central, therefore, to all aspects of the study, from participating in the classrooms to coding data and writing this book.

As I tell the story of this empirical research, I have endeavoured to share, as thoroughly as possible, the rich contexts, the diverse characters, and the marginal practices, that we encountered. And a story it is. Some may think that calling it research elevates its status, but there remains the fantastical; it seems clear to me that I am making decisions about which story to tell and how to tell it at every turn. That is the role of the witness. As Ann-Marie MacDonald says:

> There may be unhappy endings to stories, but all stories are happy, because as long as there are stories, there is hope. If even one person – or indeed, creature – is able to emerge from the rubble of our own making to say, 'I remember what happened. Listen, and I'll tell you,' that's a happy ending. Bearing witness can be just that: the carrying of a heavy load that eventually must be shared. (2005, 155–6)

As principal researcher of this study, I had the great fortune of working with an astounding team of graduate research assistants over the course of three years. Philip Lortie, Dominique Rivière, Isabelle Kim, Adam Guzkowski, Masayuki Hachiya, and Kentaro Miyamoto brought incalculable insights, expertise, and research savvy to this project. Their field notes and interview instincts lent great depth to our activities; our vibrant research meetings illustrated their enormous commitment to this project. When I say 'we,' I am referring to my cherished students/co-researchers.

What I would like you, dear reader, to get from this book is some of the thrill and foreboding that I experienced daily while working on this study. I have intended to pay attention to the discursive, spatial, and artistic practices at work in these classrooms. As I set the context, I have paid close attention to theorists and researchers of urban school space and offered insights from our rich documents of field notes and other artefacts that the team produced as we encountered, and came to know more thoroughly, the schools, neighbourhoods, and cities in which we were working. I have also paid special attention to the many interesting contradictions of schools; what they set out to do is often not what they accomplish.

It has furthermore become clear that greater research attention ought to be paid to more informal learning, the ways in which young people learn from one another, and what many refer to as the 'hidden curriculum' of schools. When I turn my attention to the youth – their words, actions, and performances in the classroom and in interviews – I am really speaking about the politics of knowing and being known. The study received ethical clearance and all research participants have given their informed consent; nonetheless, difficult issues of representation remain. I endeavoured, methodologically, to include the students in the production and analysis of data and invited them into the conceptual terrain of our work. I have also turned my eye towards the art that they make in drama classrooms, the darkness and the light that I found there, and am aware that my 'interpretations' of this work are privileged.

Through these encounters, I also came to know teaching in a new way; I learned immensely from four teachers through what they did and what they did not do, and express, here, my gratitude to them for generously opening their classrooms to us and tolerating our many intrusions. I thank them especially for their commitment to young people, to drama, and to the production of knowledge about education. As a teacher myself, I often recognized – viscerally – the small victories and the failures of communication, unavoidable in the act of teaching. I began to think about the craft as a marginal set of activities that beautifully coheres in some moments and staggeringly falls apart in others.

Finally, I will tell a story of methodology – a porous methodology – that I hope does justice to the exceptionally nuanced activity of social science research. This *situated ethnography*, as I came to call it, confirmed for me the all-consuming nature of research with human subjects and on decidedly human (although not always humane) contexts. The questions of imperialism and the effects of colonization served as a signal throughout this research to keep in check the researcher's goals, hopes for, and commitments to doing emancipatory work mindful of Tuhiwai

Smith's conviction that research is a humble and humbling activity (1999, 5). What she terms 'decolonizing methodologies' seemed especially important for research with a diverse population of less privileged youth who have been previously studied and commodified in ways that potentially reinforce positions of marginality or frame 'their world' as one that the expert outsider, with her/his hero narrative, can 'liberate.' Postcolonial and postmodern theories have turned a critical gaze upon traditional ethnography in particular, wherein 'field research often replicated the oppressive effects, if not the material conditions, of colonization, in which the Other found herself not only at the wrong end of the colonial gun but at the short end of the imperial pen' (Brown 2004). These urban communities are often referred to as the 'silenced' (Lincoln 1993). The temptation, then, as researcher, to make 'them' 'heard' is a potentially dangerous and myopic position of power that demands diligent attention throughout any research activity. On this count, I can only hope that I have remained true to my convictions: I was most interested in making practical Spivak's (1988) notion of listening to the plural voices of those normally Othered, and hearing them as constructors, agents, and disseminators of knowledge.

Both the sensations of disquiet and the fleeting flickers of light recounted here will further tell a story of school-based research by someone who continues to stubbornly believe in the educational and cultural importance of schools and teaching.

1 CONTEXT

Discourse, Space, and Competing Narratives

Middleview Technical High School (Toronto)[1]

Dominique (Black, female, first-generation Canadian, of Caribbean descent, research assistant): Okay. I wanted to take a little bit of a different direction here, because you have talked a lot about the differences between city and rural; you talked about this as a 'downtown school' vs. your other school, which I guess was not 'downtown.' When you hear the word 'urban,' what does that mean to you? When you hear the word 'suburban,' what comes to mind for you? When you hear those words ... what do you think of, what do you see?

---

1 All names of schools and research participants are pseudonyms. We invited students to invent their own pseudonyms and to offer any other 'descriptors' of their identity that they wished us to include in the writing of our research. We have included all descriptors, where available, that students chose for themselves. The social descriptors included in parentheses when speakers are introduced throughout the text are, by no means, meant to express fixed, unitary categories of identity. How bodies are marked, socially, matters immensely, although no such list of descriptors can ever capture the dynamic interplay of these markers and their relationship to a given context. I have elected, nonetheless, to include the social markers of speakers at the risk of fixing identities in ways I do not intend and with the proviso that their two-dimensionality is a convention of writing, which always confines the multiplicity of subject positions that we occupy in any given circumstance. Further, since no students, themselves, chose to signify their social class, these markers are absent in our descriptions too. In schools, social class is often an invisible marker of identity. The students in these schools range from lower middle class to those living in poverty, with most coming from what would be traditionally referred to as 'working class' or 'working poor' families.

Ari (Bi-racial [Jamaican and French Canadian], female, first-generation
Canadian, grade twelve student): I will give you a generalization of what
everybody else thinks, and then I'll give you mine ...
Dominique: That's totally cool.
Ari: Urban, Black. Suburban, White.
Dominique: Uh-huh ... Okay ...
Ari: For me – me and my friends we actually had a little – it wasn't really
a debate, we just got fed up with, like, people saying 'Well, that girl's
acting Black,' and blah, blah, blah. And so we changed it to 'She's acting
"urban."' [Does finger-quotes here.] Meaning like, she's just – you have to
do the quotes!
Dominique: You do, yeah. I get that.
Ari: Yeah. And so we just ... Basically, urban is just ... young people, or even
old people that like the trend, the trend, what's going on now. And subur-
ban is ... rich people ... that live in these amazing houses, and like ... they
go to work 9–5, and come home and cook dinner and like ... have 2.5 kids
and a dog ... and a white picket fence ...
Dominique: The whole shebang ...
Ari: The whole ... With their inside problems.
Dominique: Oh, okay.
Ari: Yeah. Behind closed doors.
Philip (White, male, American-born, research assistant) [interrupting]:
Um ... what? Sorry, go ahead.
Ari: Um, suburban is ... you keep your problems inside. Urban is like ... you
lay it all out on the street. You want to get into an argument, do it on the
bus; you do it right there. But, suburban people, they keep it to themselves,
they're so scared of what other people are gonna think, and judging them
and stuff.

Urban schools are lively labyrnths of discursive and physical space. As
we hear in this interview excerpt from Middleview High School, in
downtown Toronto, the discursive space is often marked with double
meaning for young people. The rhetoric of urban schools, what teachers, principals, researchers might call 'urban' or 'multicultural' or
'diverse,' is generally read by students as poor, non-White, and unruly.
In Ari's eloquence, above, we hear the perpetual binaries of urban/
suburban, rich/poor, sophisticated/savage. Her understanding invites
us, as researchers, to pay careful attention to the problems and ideas
that we bring to the surface in our study and also forces us to address
our assumptions, face our prejudices, and admit our euphemisms.

   In this chapter, I would like to increase the conceptual range of the term 'context,' particularly as it relates to empirical inquiry. To this end, I will make use of research on youth and urban classrooms, and particularly the work of ethnographers who have thought through some of the complex terrain of ethnographic methods like participant observation and interviews. I say complex because, in my study, were I to enumerate, I would have conducted approximately fifty formal interviews with students, two interviews with each of four teachers, and four focus-group interviews, and participated in an infinite number of informal conversations in the classroom, in the hallways, and outside the school. Over three years, we would have spent hundreds of hours, the better part of whole semesters, in these sites. To write an ethnography, then, is to also capture the complex contexts and time spans in which such discussions occurred.

I will borrow from spatial and critical theorists to understand better the social contexts of the research sites. The physical space of a school, for instance, is profoundly shaped by, and shaping of, the bodies that live in it. The signs on the corridor walls draw our attention to the life and shadows of the space: 'Crimestoppers: Call 323-TIPS. It's your school. Make it Safer!' Lefebvre (1991) introduced the concept of 'social space.' Social space 'incorporates social actions' (33). Social space is not just space in itself, it is not a frame or a container that is designed simply to receive whatever is poured into it (93–4). On the contrary, for Lefebvre, social space 'is at once work and product – a materialization of "social being"' (101–2). And significantly, such spaces are ideological. They produce ideas, transmit messages, contain fears. Early on in the research, it became clear that a probing of the spatial texts in our urban schools would be important. This move denotes a shift in our concern from the 'generalizability' to the 'contextuality' of ethnographic research, such that the goal of 'universal generalizability' is replaced by our emphasis on contextuality and heterogeneity of knowledge (Kvale 1996). Angrosino and Mays de Perez (2000) insist that social scientists are observers both of human activities and of the physical settings in which such activities take place. During our first visit to Middleview, I asked the students what they would do if they were themselves researchers and wanted to understand what life was like at Middleview. In other words, what advice did they have for us? 'Stay a long time,' one boy said. 'Yeah, don't just observe us for a short time. Watch us and listen to us for a long time,' a girl piped in. Woods (1994) agrees. An empirical study of the social world of schools focuses on

> how understandings are formed, how meanings are negotiated, how roles are developed, how a curriculum works out, how a policy is formulated

and implemented, how a pupil becomes deviant. These are processual matters, not products. Social life is ongoing, developing, fluctuating, becoming. It never arrives or ends ... This again emphasizes the need for long and sustained researcher immersion in the field in order to cover whole processes and produce 'thick description' (Geertz 1973) that will encompass this richness. (5)

Middleview: The Official Story[2]

Middleview Technical High School is the largest technological school in Ontario offering a comprehensive selection of Academic and Technological study programs. In response to the enormous industrial boom in the early 1900's the 'Dominion government' set up a panel of experts to address the need for technical training of its future laborers. But by 1912 the city of Toronto had already chosen the present-day grounds of Middleview Tech and the building was built entirely with civic funds.

Current population: 2450 students
Semestered school
Students:

As of Spring 2003, the most recent statistics

	Number	Per cent
Total number of students	2223	
Gender		
Male	1403	63
Female	820	36
Primary language other than English	957	43
Students born outside of Canada		
Students living in Canada for 2 years or less	139	6
Students living in Canada for 3–5 years	200	9

Note: The calculation does not include students for whom language information is missing.

The school has a tradition of teamwork, individual achievement, fair play, and exellence. We are proud of our multi-ethnic, multicultural student population and the services we provide our students. Our attendance program ensures that we maintain regular contact with parents, our partners in the education of our students.

---

2 The following information is taken from the Toronto District School Board website and the Middleview Technical School website.

We believe that each student's personal, intellectual, and social growth can be accomplished by a shared interaction with other students, staff, and the community. Middleview is committed to developing personal discipline, caring, and a respect for the rights of others. An active Students' Council adds to the excitement at Middleview, supporting varied co-curricular programs in physical education, music, art, and student clubs.

In addition to this official website introduction, it is important to know that Middleview has not scored well in the provincial literacy and numeracy tests. They also provide a 'breakfast club' for students in need.

Redmount Public School (Queen's, New York)

Ricky (Latino, gay, male, grade twelve student): We get a lot of stuff just because we're in Redmount. 'What, you go to Redmount? What?? Are there any stabbings?' and, I'm like, 'No!'

Leroy (Dominican, male, grade twelve student): When we went to the Shakespeare Festival, we decided to do our scene very simply, you know, different colours to show the different variety of groups and everything in the scene. And everybody else, like all the other schools, they had a whole bunch of different Shakespeare costumes, and they were like, 'Oh my god, they're doing Shakespeare in Tims and T-shirts?'

Steven (Bi-racial [Black and White], male, grade twelve student): And the judges were also, like, they liked that we didn't upstage it with costumes, that it was really simple, and they could tell, like, Orsino's court is all in blue.

Isabelle (Bi-racial [Korean and French Canadian], female, research assistant): That's brilliant.

Steven: And Olivia's court was red, and they liked that we kept it simple, 'cause other schools had, like, extravagant set designs.

Isabelle: That's sometimes a cover-up.

Philip and Steven: Yeah.

Ricky: Because Mr M is like one who believes we should show respect when acting.

[THE BELL STARTS RINGING. VOICE OVER THE PUBLIC ADDRESS SYSTEM: 'THIS IS OPERATION CLEAR SWEEP']

Philip: We're OK, right?
Ricky: Yeah. It's just the sweep.

I arrived at this Queen's New York school site after a complex process of background checks and fingerprinting. As I approached the school, I read hanging banners outside the school: 'New York School of Excellence' and another 'Theater and Education Award for Excellence.' There are no windows at this main entrance and so I enter through the metal doors with the pack of kids. Each of us, teachers, students, and Canadian visitors, lines up to proceed through the security process, carefully placing our bags on conveyor belts, passing through the metal detectors, and being frisked by the wand scanner on the other side. Once I am admitted, I must check in with the police officer on the other side of the door. It is here where I will show my picture ID and sign in, as a visitor. I am granted a visitor's pass from the 'Office of Security and Discipline,' signed by the 'Principal and Assistant Principal Security.' It reads: 'Dear Visitor: You have been given a pass which indicates a specific room number. You are not permitted to be anywhere else in the building. Thank you for your cooperation.'

Foucault prophesied: 'A whole history remains to be written of spaces – which would at the same time be the history of powers (both these terms in the plural) – from the great strategies of geo-politics to the little tactics of the habitat, institutional architecture from the classroom to the design of hospitals, passing via economic and political installations. It is surprising how long the problem of space took to emerge as a historico-political problem' (1980b, 149). In the current political moment of *homeland* and *otherland* safety and security, there is unprecedented attention being paid to the containment, movement, and dispersal of people in public spaces the manifestation of fear and the priority of 'security' has never before been so acute in public schools.

While I am waiting, droves of young people are swiping their identification cards and I am watching their faces appear on a large computer screen, authenticating their identities. Suddenly, a loud computer-animated voice exclaims: 'THIS STUDENT IS SUSPENDED. STOP THIS STUDENT.' A young Black girl gets pulled aside by a teacher and is loudly interrogated. I am amazed by the efficiency of this system. And by how unremarkable it all seems to the young people.

I meet the teacher whose classroom I will be observing this day. 'That's quite a welcoming committee in the foyer,' I quip. 'Well, you wanted an urban school,' he replies in all seriousness. And then further explains, 'At least we know we're safe in here. Normal fights but no weapons and the kids are totally used to it.'

Later, the teacher introduces me to the student 'spokesperson' for the school. I ask her what she is called on to speak about and the teacher explains that she has recently represented the school very well when the media decided to do a piece about how this school had turned its violence problem around through the installation of the 'scanning system.' Well, that and 'Operation Clear Sweep,' also known as 'The Sweep.' This, he explains, is a drill whereby the principal randomly calls for an 'operation clear sweep' over the public address system and ALL students must clear the halls immediately or be taken down to the office for 'disciplinary measures.' 'It really makes us feel safe,' he explains one last time.

I use the washroom before I leave; a security guard unlocks it to let me in. The grafitti in the stall reads: 'Jesus is the true Jehovah. King of Kings. Lord of Lords.'

Redmount: The Official Story[3]

Redmount is a progressive, standards-driven school with a proactive approach that prepares all of our students to meet the New York School Standards and Regents Diploma Requirement. At Redmount, you will find a commitment to excellence, innovative instructional approaches, a diverse student body and educational community, along with an active and supportive parent body who are focused on building the skills of our students to embrace high standards.

Redmount offers an individualized mini school program for each student, honors and advanced placement courses, College Now! Program, CISCO Certification center, Pre-Teaching Institute, Pre-Med Institute, Project Arts and partnerships with St John's University, Sophie David, CISCO and Theater Institute. Redmount is a recognized New York State School of Excellence. We, at Redmount, accept the responsibility for guaranteeing the right of every student to an education that helps to develop their own talent. Our mission is to provide quality education, which meets the needs of all students to live rich and productive lives. This occurs at Redmount through the collaborative efforts of all constituents – school staff, students, parents, community businesses and academic institutions.

Our school of 3000 students is a true microcosm of New York City divided into one of our six mini schools. Students develop into young men and women by

---

3 The following information is taken from the New York City Department of Education website.

focusing on the following areas: Pre-Med, Health Careers, Law and Commu-
nity Aid, Theater, Entrepreneurship or Teaching. A wide range of club and
sport activities contribute to the 'small town' atmosphere of Redmount.

Mini Schools – Theater Institute
Our Mission: To give the Theater student a well-rounded education with
specific and intensive training in theater related knowledge and skills. The
program is designed to prepare students for college, the new standards and
English Regents exam while at the same time exposing them to the vast
cultural resources associated with theater in New York City.

St Bernadette's High School for Girls (Toronto)

My first glimpse at the space of the publicly funded Catholic school in
the north-east end of Toronto conjured images of traditional schools of
the early part of the last century. From the outside, the school looked
forbidding, but like other schools it came alive in the corridors, with an
effervescent and diverse student body; girls from many different parts
of the globe, all wearing the kilts and blouses that constitute the 'school
uniform,' Muslim and Catholic, Black and White, Eastern European,
Filipino, East Asian, South-east Asian, Syrian, and so on.

In the classroom, I see 'Smoke Weed Everyday' in Magic Marker
graffiti scrawled into the back of the teacher's chair. She seems not to
have noticed. At one point, one young woman asks for the 'crown.' The
teacher gives her a plastic crown of thorns that she puts on her head
before she leaves the classroom. I ask what this is and the teacher
explains that she has the girls wear the crown as a 'hall pass,' figuring it
would be embarrassing and act as a deterrent, so they might ask to
leave the classroom less frequently. These first few moments in the
drama classroom, where we would spend the next year, tell us much.

Field-note Excerpt, St Bernadette's, November 6, 2002
The teacher 'briefs' me: 'There are "resource," "esl" and "good students" in
this class,' she explains. The room has desks and chairs, unusual for a drama
classroom. There is a small stage at one end but it is in terrible disrepair. The
students are working at their desks from a textbook called 'The School and the
Stage,' or as my research assistant Phil dubs it, 'How to suck the life out of
drama.' The 'resource kids,' she explains further, clean up the room. 'They like
that' ...
Ms G wants me to introduce the research to the students by telling them

that their participation in it will be 'for marks.' Of course, I explain that I cannot do this.

More explanation: '... she has problems – you know, a single mother ... she's Polish, very smart ... there's three groups in the class – the good group, the problem group, and the resource kids ... those girls just look in the mirror and play with their hair ...' I cringe. We will have work to do here. We must have impact on the praxis, that much is clear. We cannot simply 'observe' this. Teacher, students, researchers, we all have an opportunity to grow here. Much of it is difficult to observe. I can feel already the philosophical, political, and ideological tensions; I am situated as much as she is. That is why I must think carefully about methodology. This is not a simple story of good and bad teachers and teacher practices. I am remembering the explanation of the principal during our meeting: Ms G has agreed to teach drama in the absence of the usual drama teacher. She is not completely comfortable with it. Clearly, I will need to discuss with the others how we will approach this.

Once again, I asked these grade eleven students what advice they might have for us if we wanted to understand them better, understand their school and their drama classroom. 'Join in our conversations. *Really* listen to us,' one girl called out.

St Bernadette: The Official Story[4]

History and Tradition
St Bernadette's High School is a school for young women and is attached to the Motherhouse of the Sisters of St Bernadette of Toronto. In September 1960, St Bernadette's High School opened with an enrollment of 147 girls and a staff of nine sisters and one lay teacher.

Today the school is operated by the Toronto Catholic District School Board. The school is organized on a semester system. Resource assistance, a gifted program and English as a second language are also offered for our students. The student uniform consists of the MacKinnon plaid kilt, black slacks, green vest/pullover, white blouse, green or brown socks/leotards and brown or black shoes.

Our motto 'The love of Christ has gathered us together' is expressed as a school community committed to the continuing educational process of developing

---

4 The following information is taken from the Toronto Catholic District School Board website and the St. Bernadette's High School website.

unique persons in an environment where Christian faith is translated into action. In order to be integral members of the school community, students are strongly encouraged to participate in co-instructional activities such as sports, committees and clubs.

How We Meet the Diverse Needs of our Students
The chaplaincy team helps to develop within the school a community of faith. It plans and facilitates a variety of celebrations and activities, and encourages outreach to those in need. Chaplaincy is at the service of staff and students in need of guidance, support and direction.

To complement the guidance program and add another dimension, the peer helper club is an integral part of the school community. It includes peer tutors, peer ministers, conflict mediators, peers against drugs, career room helpers and Big Sisters. Special events are also organized by the counselors such as healthy lifestyle week and career week.

Mission Statement
As a Catholic school, we wish to continue the tradition of a Christ-centred community inspired by the Sisters of St Bernadette, fostering in students academic excellence, the desire for lifelong learning and personal growth, while inspiring them to be respectful, just and socially responsible citizens of the world.

Unauthorized Absence from Class
If a student misses a class without a parental permission, she will be considered skipping and disciplined accordingly. Suspension may result. Subject credit(s) may be withheld due to excessive absenteeism.

Punctuality and Lates
- *Students are expected to be in their period 1 (homeroom) class at least five minutes before the first class begins*
- *Students arriving late for school must sign in at the Attendance Office and receive an admit slip*
- *These steps will be followed for Period One lates:*
  - *Five lates – Letter to Parent/Guardian*
  - *Ten lates – Student/Parent/Vice-Principal Conference*
  - *Fifteen or more lates – Subject to Disciplinary Measures*
- *Lates for all other classes will be dealt with by subject teachers. However,*

if a student arrives more than ten minutes late, it will be considered a skipped class.
- *When excused during a class, a student must carry a hall pass.*

A male guidance counsellor made the following remarks on the website (circa January 2003):

- *The good thing about an all girls school is that there's 'one less temptation' (i.e. no boys; therefore, there are not any appearance worries)*
- *In class, the girls don't 'dumb down' their answers; generally, they're not afraid to show their intelligence*
- *The bulk of St B's graduates get accepted into university*
- *The average population 'reflects North York and Scarborough'*
- *There are 'no diversity issues' at St Bernadette's*

Amor Alternative School (Manhattan, New York)

Fieldnote Excerpt January 15, 2004, Midtown Manhattan
I'm waiting in the office at Amor. I'm 30 minutes early. Perfect. I can sit in the office and get a sense of things. It's a terrific place to get the sense of a school. Amor is on the 4th floor of a nondescript office building. And yes, I did have to sign in with a police officer on the first floor. Not a security guard, an NYPD officer. And yes, the signs warned me of grand larceny if I didn't keep my eyes on my possessions. How is this alternative space different? People affably call the principal 'the boss.' The secretaries are kept busy; there seem to be three of them. One always answers the phone with, 'how ya doin baby?' Yes, this is an alternative school. I hope I'm not concerning anyone with my furious typing. They carry on and seem altogether unaffected by my presence. That's good. Wonder what the school population is? A student came in to ask whether she could photocopy something. 'No. Your teacher has to do it for you.' Some things aren't different I guess.

There are photographs on the walls in the halls. Of teachers. Of kids. I'm looking at the cork board with staff names for messages and guessing that there are about 17 staff members. Casual dress by those teachers passing through seems to be the norm. I'm overdressed but at least a little funky. It's amazing to me that I am sitting in the middle of everything here. I can see that they are unaccustomed to 'outsiders' arriving for meetings; not set up for it.

A student has just arrived to 'write an exam.' They're setting her up in the hallway to write some kind of test. This is obviously not a totally unusual request. Ah, maybe she's come from a classroom and needs a quiet place to write a test.

The cop from the 1st floor just came in and asked if she could use a computer, because she's 'bored.' Now, she's playing solitaire on the computer. Must be on a break.

A few of her phrases remain with me after I spend some time that afternoon with the dynamic teacher who runs the drama program at Amor: 'Don't mistake my fatigue for lack of interest. I didn't sleep all night with my 11-month old.' She has two children. She's from Brooklyn, is Italian/Irish. Her husband is a musician, Spanish/Italian. 'Hand to mouth, you know?'

'Don't mess with Carm, man. She's gangsta.' That's what she says the students say about her. 'I'm strict but about things that matter. We have a no hat rule here now. We never used to. This was a school with maybe one fight a year, which is unheard of in New York City. But with the new amalgamation, we're forced to enforce the "no hat" rule. I'm one who doesn't. I say: "You know you're not supposed to be wearing that, don't you?" They say yeah. And I go on teaching.' During my time there, four students came in from her 'family group.' 'We're their foster mom, stepmom, adviser, good cop/bad cop, teacher, friend ... It's really exhausting,' she explains. These four kids all had crises they wanted her to solve. One of them needed Carm to read her fifty-page paper before tomorrow. It was crucial!

Another said she was quitting. Couldn't do it any more. Couldn't find all the work she'd done. It was lost, accidentally deleted on a computer. Carm said: 'Come here. I want to touch you.' The girl tried to slink away but Carm pulled her in and spoke intimately in a whisper: 'You need to be squeezed. (Pause.) Don't worry. You'll find your stuff. I'll help you. You can't quit. OK?' Finally, unable to squirm away, the young Puerto Rican girl melted into her embrace and laughed.

Much has been written in recent education research about the 'ethic of care.' Critiquing the prevalent 'school effectiveness' research, an alternative approach contends that 'care' (see Noddings 2003), or 'practice-with-hope' (see Riele 2006), are concepts that recognize teaching as a caring profession and address openly the emotional dimensions of schooling. At a place like Amor, these alternative discourses also importantly interrupt the 'normalizing' effects of the school-effectiveness discourse. At Amor, the discourse of caring is explicit and permeates every conversation with staff and students.

❅

The students come to the school (known by the board as a 'second chance' school) because they have just had a child, or just got out of jail, or couldn't 'cut it' in another school for whatever reason. They are mainly Hispanic and Black. The school is called Amor Mid-Town. It is one of four related alternative schools in the New York area. While interviewing a group of sixteen-year-old students during one visit, I remember asking one young man what he thought of the school. 'I hope if I ever had a kid that he can come to this school,' he said. He wanted Amor to be a 'first resort' not a 'last resort' school, as it is colloquially known. On my last visit to the school, in the final year of the project, I sat in on a staff meeting where the teachers were despondent about news that their alternative forms of testing and evaluating students – which had enjoyed such success and helped many students achieve a high school diploma – would be eliminated by new education policy that would enforce the 'Regents' (standardized) exams for all students, including those in alternative schools:

Carm (White, female, Italian descent, teacher): Because, they come to us after they've been in at least one other school, they're older, they have less credits ... So, in two years, we try to get them to a place where they can graduate, and still go off to college. You know? We know that tests don't prove whether you're gonna be a failure or a success at college. We know that. And, so we found ways that the State approved it. And now, the Bloomberg administration came in and said 'No.' They want this cookie-cutter model, where every single student, regardless of age, or, or learning ability, is – are going to take the Six Regents. So, we're slowly having to move over to a Regents-based school, and of course, what's happening is that we're trying not to let go of our ... creativity ... and not have to be – not have to teach the test (Kathleen: Right). And, my feeling is that, because the students are gonna have to take a certain amount of courses to lead up to the Science Regents, a certain amount of courses to lead up to the U.S. Regents, a certain amount that lead up to the Global Regents, a certain amount that lead up to the Math Regents ... We're talking about ... the kids are completely consumed. There will not be a space for drama.

An interesting notion of trust is put forward in the recent research of Ennis and McCauly (2003). They are asking what an emerging theoretical framework of educational trust might look like. In urban classrooms, they insist on a 'culturally relevant pedagogy' — culturally relevant to the particular classroom community. This 'cultural relevance' approach is, of course, often seen to be the enemy of the standards movement. It is also edged out by a realist-technicist curriculum. In philosophical terms, it is the difference between the technical-instrumental and the critical-humanist paradigm. The work of these researchers, nonetheless, speaks of the importance of 'second chances' with urban youth, the importance of disrupting student expectations of the oppressive practices they may have experienced in previous educational settings. They assert that building shared expectations and jointly constructing curriculum are essential in the context of 'educating other people's children' (Delpit 1988):

Martina (Latina, female, 17 years old): I love this school. I came in here, I seen the people were so nice to me. They made me feel comfortable because in my old school – oh my God – it was horrible. I mean, I knew a lot of people and it was hard for me concentrate, go to class, and everybody would be like 'oh let's go cut,' and I would go and I wouldn't focus. So I came here and you know Carm (the drama teacher) helped me. And my Strat (Family group like a home room), they love me, and you know every time I have a problem I go and talk to them. They made me feel comfortable. And this school is a very small school. I mean, it's good in a way, but then in a way sometimes it's like bad because you know everything gets around quickly. You have to be careful sometimes. And like lately in the interviews people come and they usually lie.

Torrie (Bi-racial [Black and White] female, 16 years old): I lied out my asshole.

(laughter)

Kathleen (White, female, first-generation Canadian, of Scottish descent, researcher): What interviews? Oh you mean to come to the school you have to have an interview?

Salvador (Latino, gay, male, 18 years old): In the interviews they act like real perfect, like angels, little angels.

Joseph (African American, male, 17 years old): I was myself.

Kathleen: You were yourself?

Salvador: I was myself too, but there's other students that act like 'I wanna do better, I wanna do this, I wanna do that,' and half of them didn't accomplish –

Kathleen: But that may be true. They may want to do better.

Isabelle: If you think they lie, why do you think they would lie?

Salvador: Since they have problems, like oh they probably threw them out of their old school, so they had no other choice. They view this as a last resort. If I don't make it here, where am I going after? [General consensus]

I am happy to be coming to the drama classroom of such a school of 'second chances.' The artistic space in drama's pedagogy is a space of many chances, many possible directions, many aborted plans, many reconsidered choices. Pragmatically speaking, it is a space where co-ownership of artistic projects requires second, third, and fourth chances. The dogmatism of 'getting it right,' and even the sometimes repressive political correctness of some progressive classrooms, can be replaced with a flexibility and an openness that remain focused on the experimentation and creation of the work.

Although the purported goal is often a kind of openness and flexibility, the results in drama do not always bear this out. At times, the exigencies of the institution or the individual teacher overwhelm the pedagogical inclinations or impose certain ideological frameworks on the devised dramatic work. In this study, I was less concerned, however, with the actual curricular choices in drama or the skill of individual teachers and more interested in how the students came to understand the modes of working and ideas raised in drama classes.

During my first ninety minutes with Carm, we were interrupted by four students and one teacher at different times. The four students all excused themselves when they interrupted us. I told her she had courteous students. She said, 'Yeah they are, and they're rude at times too. They're all of it.' And she was right. The teacher who interrupted our meeting wanted to check Carm's 'files' of one of her 'family group kids' because he thought this boy had maybe plagiarized a final paper. After chatting with Carm, he conceded that it might have been possible that the student had written the paper himself. But why hadn't he participated all term? 'Because he's got LBS,' says Carm. 'Lazy Boy Syndrome. It should be called something like that. Cause he can do it but he doesn't want to. Look, can I share something with you? He's bright. He's got a bright mother. They live in a house in Brooklyn. He gets fed every day. You know what I'm saying?'

I knew what she was saying. We all knew. Assumptions abound in the description and yet I felt some affection for this teacher who is obviously dealing with stories much worse than this one, with kids who cannot expect the very basic necessities and who turn up at school anyway. Part of me felt beleaguered by the 'profiling,' the 'short-hand' that goes on in school as a means of communication among educators. We all know what we mean when we say, 'He's got a smart mom.' We know the moms we are thinking of who wouldn't warrant that description. We also know what it means for kids to be fed. It matters.

Towards the end of my visit, Carm wants to tell me – I suppose, based on how I have introduced myself, my own work, my commitments – that she doesn't have 'white liberal guilt.' She 'expects more of these kids.' She doesn't let them 'play victim.' 'It doesn't help. I know they face discrimination every day. No doubt about it. But what are you going to do? Get angry. Yeah. But get moving too.' There was a Black woman teacher who had just retired who liked Carm a lot, she told me. Because Carm doesn't patronize the kids: 'Expects a lot from them,' she would say of Carm. 'And we should. That's right. None of that victim stuff and the white guilt.'

I left this space exhausted and thinking about what it takes to enter into the world of school, feel the exhaustion of the teacher, the liveliness and complexity and the troubles of kids; the autonomous world that it is.

Amor Academy High School: The Offical Story[5]

Amor Academy

Grade levels: 9 to 12
Class size: 24–29
Enrollment: 899
Free lunch eligible: 74.7%
Ethnicity %: 4% White 50% Black 44% Hispanic 4% Asian
Graduation rate: 14.5%
7-year graduation rate: 51.9%
Attendance: 77%
Neighborhood: Various
Admissions: Interview

What's special: A demanding curriculum for students who have failed else-where. Downside: No Gym at Midtown site. Mid-Manhattan is one of four sites in the Amor Academy school group, an alternative program for students who need a smaller school and more attention than most high schools provide. Each site is locally administered. The main site is in Midtown Manhattan. All are members of the Center for Collaborative Education and the New York City Performance Standards Consortium, which is pressing for relief from Regents test requirements for high school graduation. The group would like to see

---

5 The following information is taken from an independent online guide to New York City public schools, Insideschools.org.

multiple forms of assessment, including essays and oral exams, instead of the Regents tests.

After many years near City Hall, and then housed in temporary space, Midtown Amor moved in 2000 to the nicely renovated floors of an old office building. The school lacks a library and gym, but does have a multi-purpose community room. It shares a video library with Educational Video Center, which maintains an onsite office.

Students are older (the average age is 17¼) and seem serious and focused, having found a nurturing yet rigorous school after a number of false starts. Students and faculty are on a first name basis. The atmosphere is calm; very little in the way of conflict was visible when we [the online guide's authors] visited.

Students, who must have attended another high school and be at least 16 years old, apply to the site they wish to attend. All newcomers enroll in a semester-long orientation program with one or two classes a day. About 60% of graduates apply to college, and while most get accepted to two-year institutions, a few go to four-year CUNY colleges. Often students become the first high school graduates or college students in their families.

Classes are un-graded, 90 minutes long, and interdisciplinary. An advisor helps kids develop a program to complete the 40 credits required for graduation. Each semester is divided into two cycles, so students can get partial credit even if they do not complete the whole course. Students have the most catching-up to do in math and science, according to the principal.

About 10% are special education students. A small number of them also have emotional disabilities. There are no self-contained classrooms, but there is resource room service.

Classes use a variety of teaching techniques: directed instruction, student-led discussion, cooperative learning. A math class we saw was led by a student, with the teacher adding information as needed. Computer room students were developing data to make projections. In one science class, students were preparing posters – complete with charts, drawings, and lengthy written explanations – describing the natural life associated with various environments. The posters were to be included in portfolios to demonstrate the student's competence to a committee of peers, faculty, and family members. (November 2002)

One parent writes that her daughter is happy and successful at Amor Academy after an 'awful' experience at another high school. 'I see she wants to get a high school diploma,' she writes. 'The teachers are so helpful and encourage the students.' (June 2004)

A former student writes, 'Amor helped me realize my love of education. The caring environment and wonderful faculty inspired me to consider teaching as a career. My first few years of high school were spent wasting my days anywhere but in the classroom. Amor got me back on the right track.' (April 2003)

When I was first at Amor, I learned from teachers that, in local argot, Amor is known as a 'SINI' school, pronounced 'sinny.' This means it is a 'School In Need of Improvement.'

Space and Subjects: Security, Surveillance, and 'Zero Tolerance'

The discursive spaces that mark schools (codes of conduct, profiles, mission statements, philosophies ...), along with the virtual ones available for public consumption on websites, stand in as official introductions to the schools and together with architectural designs conspicuously mediate power in schools. I am using the term discourse in the sense of a conceptual terrain in which knowledge is produced. I have found the work of Foucault appropriate in analyses of school spaces because he clearly speaks to practices of inclusion and exclusion in historical contexts and the relationships between the margins and the centre, and most often examines institutions in his analyses of these concepts. In the study of schools, creating just such a wider frame, a theoretical frame, around routine and everyday experiences is indispensable. Foucault himself explained the impulse in this way: 'Each time I attempted to do theoretical work, it has been on the basis of elements from my experience – always in relation to processes that I saw taking place around me. It is in fact because I thought I recognized something cracked, dully jarring, or disfunctioning in things I saw, in the institutions with which I dealt, in my relations with others, that I undertook a particular piece of work, several fragments of an autobiography' (in Rajchman 1985, 35–6).

Goffman (1959) works with the theatre metaphor that I have found useful in my own work. He does this in his sociological studies through viewing all behaviour as performance. But his work on asylums (1961)

is especially instructive here as there are some striking parallels between the routines, architecture, and layout of contemporary urban
⋆ schools and those of asylums. 'Scanning,' as a relatively new school
practice, forces students into particular relationships with guards and
with other students, often, as McCormick found in her study (2003),
leading to their humiliation. After two school shooting deaths in New
York in 1992, scanners were installed in forty-one schools and by 1995
there were three thousand uniformed 'safety officers' in New York
schools. Politicians and educators gained support for high-tech weapons searches by appealing to the public's concern for safety: 'The city
cannot do business as usual,' said Sandra Feldman, president of the
teachers' union, 'We're losing our kids' (Berger 1992, cited in McCormick
2003).

   Other critical theorists have examined how both buildings and architectural practices are articulations of political, social, and cultural ideologies (Hollier 1992; Foucault 1977, 1980b, 1997; Grosz 2001; Markus
1993; Rendell, Penner, and Borden 2000). In fact, cultural studies of
architecture have recognized that it continues after the moment of its
design and construction: architecture is experienced, appropriated, perceived, and occupied, and plays, therefore, a significant role in the
processes involved in coming to know oneself as a subject (Dovey 1999;
Lahiji and Friedman 1997; Markus 1993; Whiteman, Kipnis, and Burdett
1992). Architecture can be 'read,' then, as a form of cultural documentation that contains representations of gender (Rendell 1998; Wigley 1992),
sexuality (Foucault 1978; Colomina 1992; Ingraham 1992), class (Markus
1993), race, and Western formal aesthetics and ideologies of empire
(Apter 1998; Burns 1997; Çelik 2000; Nalbantoglu and Wong 1997;
Wilson 1998).

   In some cases, school spaces become the purveyors of ideologies in
overt and disturbing ways:

*Mr M (White, male, drama teacher at Redmount): We're fortunate that we
   do have – it's really a theater. There's an extensive wing space, there's an
   extensive green – there's a green room, two dressing rooms. So, we're
   fortunate that we can also use that space. Unfortunately, the school has
   used that space for other things, non-theater related ... as a holding place
   for students, in the morning ... because of the number of students that have
   to come in, they need a place to go, um, because of the scanning. I mean,
   you can imagine the backlog, if ... if we couldn't stagger that. So they
   stagger it by having, kind of, an open entrance in the morning, but the kids*

*that don't have a class at that time, they need a place to stay. They can't go
in the hallway. So, now they put them downstairs, in the theater. Which
has been, kind of, a battle that I fight (Kathleen: Yeah, I'm sure) because,
you know, it's getting destroyed. You put kids that don't really care about,
you know ... but they're sitting in the theatre, you know ... and they, you
know, break this chair, or they're ... frustrated or restless ... and ... [trails
off]*

Kathleen: *Everyone arrives at the same time, but some of them don't have
class?*

Mr M: *Well, they arrive ... Like, they have ... the doors open, say at 7:00, for
the first class starts around 7:25–7:30. But the doors are open at 7:00. But,
they don't want students ... wandering the building, if they don't have
class. So, they put them downstairs for that 20-minute period. But, but,
you know, it's like ... it's a holding area, basically. But, it's my theater, or
our theater. It's the theater. So, it's kind of ... that's the negative side of,
like, having this big space, in a big school ...*

In *Discipline and Punish* Foucault (1977) argues that school buildings
have been scrutinized in the past because it was important that 'education space function like a learning machine' (147). From all accounts,
the scanning process at Redmount operated like a well-oiled machine,
that is, until anything out of the ordinary occurred. In the *History of
Sexuality* Foucault (1978) suggests that the architectural layout of schools
has demonstrated a preoccupation with children's sexuality: the classroom spaces, the planning of lessons, the distributions of partitions and
tables have been 'largely based on the assumption that this sexuality
existed, that it was precocious, active, and ever present' (28). What I
have identified as 'dangerous times' in schools, however, have much
less to do with eighteenth- and nineteenth-century European bourgeois
concerns for discipline, learning, and sexuality than they have to do
with the ideology of fear that disparages youth and deems public
(school) space inherently dangerous. Scanning systems, holding cells,
and other security procedures are based on the assumption that criminality is active and ever present. To paraphrase Foucault (1978), pedagogical institutions have multiplied the forms of discourses on the
subject of security; they have established various points of implantation
for criminality and danger; they have coded and (dis)qualified
(un)worthy persons. Such pervasive discourses of risk and safety operate with school architecture – the long corridors and contained classrooms – and produce social spaces that instruct particular codes of

behaviour. In our least 'dangerous' school, in the conventional sense, that we observed, because it was a girls' school, there was still a greatly heightened awareness of rules of conduct pertaining to safety:

Adrianna (White, first-generation Italian Canadian, grade ten student at St Bernadette's): Well you really can't be in the halls without a pass, and your teacher has to be notified. And, if a teacher's off, they're usually walking around the halls. So, like, you know nothing's gonna happen. And, people can't come into the school from other schools. And, if they do, they need to get a visitor's pass. And, if you see somebody that you don't know in the school, like, it's really easy to identify them. Especially in uniforms, so it makes it safer. And, if you're not in uniform, then you know that you don't belong here, and you're shooed out of the school. And there's always the cops around. So, if there is an issue, cops are called right away (Kathleen: Right). So, it's always safety first.

Foucault (1977, 1978) made many observations about the operation of power in educational institutions. In relation to schools, he argued that buildings are not just concrete spaces for organizing individuals, but that buildings, architectural arrangements, and spatial organization (in corridors, hallways, classrooms, locker bays, offices, theatre auditoria) are mechanisms of power reduced to their ideal (spatial) form. What I have seen over the last few years in the schools of my study are spatial arrangements no longer governed merely by physical architectural boundaries, but by sophisticated systems of electronic surveillance and embedded discourses ('It's your school. Keep it safe. Call 323-TIPS') that physically and psychically produce new and ever more threatening youth identities. Giroux (2003) sees it this way:

Youth have become the all important group onto which class and racial anxieties are projected. Their very presence represents both the broken promises of capitalism in the age of deregulation and downsizing and a collective fear of the consequences wrought by systemic class inequalities, racism, and 'infectious greed' that has created a generation of unskilled and displaced youth expelled from shrinking markets, blue collar jobs, and any viable hope in the future. (xvi)

This fear or state of alarm that Giroux points to is perfectly illustrated on the New York State's Department of Education website homepage, which offers various colour-coded levels of 'alert.' These levels can change daily. New York State is, at the time of writing this book, at a Yellow Alert Level (Elevated). According to the website, 'All New York State schools outside New York City should follow the guidance for Yellow Alert Level (Elevated) in the *NYS Homeland Security System for Schools*. New York City remains at an Orange Alert Level (High). Guidance on that level is also contained in the Homeland Security Document.' There is also a 'Color Coded Risk Level System and Recommended Actions for Schools Flowchart.' The level Blue (Guarded), beneath both levels Yellow and Orange, calls for increased security. At 'Normal' (Green) we are advised to 'continue normal operations,' and 'Severe' (Red) warns that we must 'close down the school, follow lockdown procedures, and transfer to an emergency shelter.'

In the case of the young Black woman at Redmount who was accused of returning to school while under suspension, it may be a matter of malfunctioning technology; the girl may be perfectly entitled to return to school, as she was claiming. If she is lying, however, her only real crime, it strikes me, is attempting to return to school prematurely. In the current state of alarm, it would seem that the system scarcely discriminates between 'real' crimes and minor infractions. There is also an important gender analysis to be made in this case. In McCormick's study (2003) of an urban school in New York, she found that young women regularly experience the 'twin abuses' of sexism and racism during these kinds of 'security' activities that both criminalize and sexualize the female subject. Participants in her study felt that security guards 'can get closer than they can ever get in a normal way' and that young women often build up a 'shield' to protect themselves from these routine procedures. McCormick's school, too, had routine 'sweeps,' a term she notes has been borrowed from police lexicon (117). The undiscriminating technology and perpetual sense of deviant activity skews our perspective, puts us on high alert, and commonly criminalizes otherwise 'normal' behaviours.

Here is what we know about students and handguns in Ontario: a recent (2006) study conducted by the Centre for Addiction and Mental Health reported that 2.2 per cent of students in grades nine to twelve, in response to the question 'How often (if ever) in the last 12 months have you carried a handgun?' reported carrying a handgun at least once over that period. This percentage represents about 14,800 high school students in Ontario; the sample of students surveyed in 2005 represents about 663,500 students in grades nine to twelve across the province. Carrying a handgun is significantly more likely among males (3.8%)

than females (<0.5%) and, interestingly, when data were examined by rural (2.9%) versus non-rural residence (2.0%), there was no significant difference. The researchers conclude that their data are useful in establishing a conservative estimate for gun carrying among a mainstream population, given that underreporting, even in an anonymous survey, is likely. A 2003 American school survey conducted by the Centers for Disease Control and Prevention found that 6.1 per cent (with a 95% confidence interval) of students in grades nine to twelve reported carrying a gun in the past month.

While there are, undeniably, real material consequences to violence and weapons in schools, the ever-present anticipation of 'risk' has resulted in increased surveillance, security-guard presence, and vigilance on the part of those who inhabit, and are inhabited by, this increasingly privatized space. There is both symbolic and real violence in schools in Canada and the United States and weapons in schools lead to serious, sometimes fatal, consequences for youth. Schools need to be safe for young people and teachers, free of violent incidents. They also need to be free of the structural violences of institutional racism and sexism. How we go about making safer *and more humane* school corridors and classrooms remains, therefore, the central question. Current punitive measures and systems of alert lack the language of ethics and social justice that schools desperately need; they do not represent a social investment in youth.

Youth have very few avenues of recourse in schools, and very limited ways to register their dissatisfaction with policies and procedures. At Middleview, over 50 per cent of the students in a grade twelve English class had a 0 per cent grade going into the final exam. They had 0 per cent, according to their teacher, because they were never there. The chronic absenteeism in this school might be a sign of student apathy, as is often suggested, but it might also be the result of increased efforts to keep 'undesirables' out. One student at the school explained that she felt safe at the school because 'most of the people who make it unsafe never come.'

Foucault (1977) proposes that the maintenance of discipline and order (in modernity) requires that individuals be distributed in space; he calls this 'the art of distributions.' Foucault's examination of prisons, schools, and other public institutions concludes that 'the art of distributions' requires that spatial techniques, like enclosures and partitioning, create functional sites that can be employed to organize the new economies of bodies and spaces. These help 'to establish presences and absences, to know where and how to locate individuals, to set up useful communications, to interrupt others, to be able at each moment to supervise the conduct of each individual, to assess it, to judge it, to calculate its qualities or merits' (143). The *New York Times* reported on a performance artist who has developed a tour of all the disguised surveillance cameras lurking in New York neighbourhoods. By his count, the number of such cameras has tripled in the last five years, driven by an increase in the use of private cameras (Tavernise 2004). His form of protest is to perform in front of these cameras, along with his group, known as the 'Surveillance Camera Performers.' He claims these cameras have turned us all into performers, so perform they will. The Surveillance Camera Performers are resisting 'the art of distributions' with their own distribution of the arts.

When I arrived at Redmount (*Dear Visitor: You have been given a pass which indicates a specific room number. You are not permitted to be anywhere else in the building. Thank you for your cooperation*) I understood immediately that 'each individual has his own place; and each place its individual (Foucault 1977, 143). And in the case of 'Operation Clear Sweep,' 'safe' space is also produced by removing, on command, all individuals from common, open space. 'Operation Clear Sweep' imposes a kind of curfew on students, and the open, more public spaces of the school must not be transgressed. All movement is monitored; violators are subjected to disciplinary procedures. In addition, the scanning system itself, and the identification tags that are becoming increasingly common in Canadian schools, not only operate as systems for supervising and identifying individuals; they also reward those who can pass through the gates, the reward being freedom to enter and not be picked out, 'ratted on,' by the scanning computer. Each student, staff member, and researcher who successfully negotiates the scanning system is then limited and governed inside the school. But as Rose (1996) suggests, disciplinary technologies not only control, subdue, and discipline individuals, they also make virtuous, productive, healthy, safe, enterprising, and empowered individuals. In other words, the architecture, safety measures, and spatial arrangements of schools separate out those who are suspect (potentially criminal) from those who are not and who gain unimpeded access, creating a system that effectively denies complex individuality. Most current researchers of urban schools have found, as Fine (2003) has in her work, that such artificial dichotomies abound: 'right and wrong answers, appropriate and inappropriate behavior, moral and immoral people, dumb and smart students, responsible and irresponsible parents, good and bad neighborhoods' (27).

The new 'high-security' school, in the new 'high-security' society, sets up, in the public imagination, an ever more dangerous class of youth as perpetual potential wrongdoers. The ideology of crime is sustained by new school security measures and enhanced reporting systems that clearly mirror the Bush administration's proposed Total Information Awareness System, renamed the Terrorist Information Awareness System after congressional and public protest (McGrath 2004), and the somewhat more benevolent-sounding Canadian version of Homeland Security known as the Emergency Preparedness Program. Two important ideas put forward by Michael Apple in his third edition of *Ideology and Curriculum* are instructive here. First, in describing what he calls *conservative common sense* in post-9/11 school policies, he makes clear that common sense is complicated, that it contains both 'good sense' and 'bad sense' and that, most disturbingly, a form of 'conservative modernization' is engaged in a social/pedagogic project to *change our common sense* (157). Second, he insists that 'any serious understanding of the actual results of September 11th on education needs to widen its gaze beyond what we usually look for' (170). His own examples point to the hidden effects of racism, in particular, in such new norms of security and unchallenged assumptions.

It was significant that the young woman pulled aside at Redmount was Black. The 'zero tolerance' policy, however, like the 'at risk' label itself, evokes a 'colourblind' or race-neutral vocabulary, which is then inscribed with racial meanings, and particularly meanings of blackness, in its various practices. 'Zero Tolerance' is an American concept that has been adopted in parts of Canada. Ontario's provincial Safe Schools Act, however, does not use the term, but the 'safe school policy' developed by the Toronto District School Board (TDSB), for instance, has imported it. The policy's intention was to create a uniformity of discipline with respect to students, but the ensuing widespread expulsion of Black children over what some insist are minor infractions, has resulted, in the case of Toronto, in a task force struck to examine the disproportionately high numbers of Black students affected by the policy. In November 2005, the TDSB struck a deal with the Human Rights Commission to remove the term 'zero tolerance' from the policy and keep future lines of communication open with the commission.

Using a policy analysis framework, Dunbar and Villaruel (2004) reveal data in the United States that show how the 'zero tolerance' policy adversely impacts a disproportionately higher number of students of colour in urban districts. Omi and Winant's work (1994) argues that for an institution or policy to become a racial project, it does not need to invoke race explicity, and that meanings and structures are often created in the absence of explicit racial categories. One need only look at the sizable populations of students of colour in the schools 'in need of improvement' by every measure in almost any urban district in Canada or the United States to see that 'race' is overrepresented as a 'problem' for ostensibly race-neutral policies to tackle. In other words, race-free discourse, often unwittingly reproduces racial categories. This is why Staiger (2005), along with many anti-racist scholars, argues in favour of racial statistics: 'Not having racial statistics, rather than reproducing a colorblind society, will at best lead to concealing race as a critical variable in social policy, and at worst, to racial inequity as an untrackable and intractable problem' (46).

A conversation between Dion and Phil probably best illustrates a student's perspective on the kinds of policies that exacerbate the 'culture clash' between 'home' and 'school,' especially when 'home' does not reproduce norms of mainstream, White, culture:

Phil: If you could change anything about Drama class or your school what would it be?

Dion (Black, male, Jamaican-born, grade eleven student at Middleview): Sir ... in the school I would change the Principal.

Phil: Oh really, what's wrong with the Principal?

Dion: Oh Sir, a lot of stuff. Principal ain't doing his job, we need to send back the old Principal.

Phil: How's he different from –?

Dion: Sir he's just different, Sir. He came up with some law like he's kicking kids out of the school like that. And where are they supposed to go, yo? They're gonna go home and look for a job, you know? They're kicking out, like I see, like, ten parents like a lot of parents come bring back their kids to school, try to put them back in Tech, you know what I'm saying? They kicked out everybody. This school is kind of empty right now, trust me.

Phil: Why is he kicking them out?

Dion: Sir, I don't know. Some of them don't go to class for like 3 days, like you know? But he don't even want to hear the situation about what kids got, like you know? Kids got situations too. They got problems, they're humans, you know? Something could be wrong and they don't come to school. Cause Sir sometime I sick I don't even go the Doctor to get a note. I can't even move, Sir. My Grandma, because she's from Jamaica, she just give me bush tea, and I drink it and I don't even got a Doctor's note. When I came to school I can't say nothing. You know, I can't say I was sick because they're going to ask me for a Doctor's note and if I don't give them a Doctor's note ....

Phil: So it sounds like this new Principal doesn't really care what the background is, he just has the rules and that's it.

Dion: Sir, the teachers too. The majority of the teachers do not want the Principal you know. But they think when you sick you have to go to a Doctor because they go to a Doctor, but I don't have to go a Doctor, my Grandmother got a lot of bush that she always get from Jamaica, she could give you, you got the flu or you know bellyache or headache, you know what I'm saying, and then you would get better in like two days, with some strong bush, you know what I'm saying? And when you come to school and say that, they don't even believe that you were sick because you don't even got a Doctor's note.

Phil: And they won't take a note from your Grandmother saying you were sick?

Dion: They don't, Sir. But you see, Sir, I could write my own notes, now cause ...

Phil: Oh that's right; you're over 18.

Dion: Right. I turned 19 on Friday.

What is implicit in Dion's explanation of his experiences at the school, especially with respect to his attendance problems, is that he feels he must renounce his cultural values and embrace ones that are incongruent with his 'home' culture. Many would suggest that this is a necessity for those who choose to make a new home in a different culture; there is a level of 'assimilation,' or at least adaptation, that is necessary. Critical race theorists, however, would argue that this popular view masks the prevailing deficit model of 'Communities of Colour as places full of cultural poverty disadvantages' (Yosso 2005). There is, for Dion and many other students, a very real problem of competing cultural models: school versus home. The French philosopher Lyotard (1988) argues, using his notion of 'différend,' that when a conflict arises between dominant and subjugated parties, the stories of the latter group are incommensurable with those of the former and are usually not taken into account in decision-making processes; quite literally, they cannot be heard in terms the system will understand. Although it is a great challenge, schools may need to work towards a more historically situated understanding of difference when working with multicultures; that is, they may need to decentre whiteness in their policy design and implementation and create practices that more openly address unequal power relations among racialized and ethnic groups. Gaudio and Bialostok (2005), in their study of everyday racism in White middle-class discourse, argue that the concept of 'culture' was once evoked by anthropologists for progressive social purposes, but that it is often used, in contemporary contexts, as a means to justify racial inequalitites.

You may now, for better or worse, have a clearer understanding of this book's subtitle, *Youth and Schooling in Dangerous Times.* The data from our schools point to the glaring problems of communication, the systemic barriers, and the kinds of challenges urban schools must come to grips with. In the upcoming section on 'The Occupied Imagination' (chapter 3) I will attempt to demonstrate how young people often 'talk back,' in this case through drama, to the imposition of increased documentation of their private lives, prying weapon-searching wands, and scanning machines. These counter-narratives can powerfully interrupt taken-for-granted assumptions about youth, especially those who are most frequently labeled 'at risk' or who are 'marginalized students,' a term that at least focuses on students' relationships with schooling rather than on their personal characteristics. But there are also students who are comforted by the discourses of security and safety, grateful for the increased surveillance, and fully participating in the very ideological frameworks and incarcerated thinking that limit their freedoms and – as Yon's critical ethnography (2000) of one Toronto school puts it – 'spoils' their identities. In one of our early classroom discussions about the subject of school security at Middleview, Misha, a young White, Serbian boy, exclaimed that he liked the new surveillance and record-keeping systems because that way if anyone was going to get up to no good, the school would be able to anticipate their actions and stop them. To this suggestion, a young Black girl named Sabicca indignantly replied, 'How does knowin' my business make you any safer?' It was a question that would haunt us for the duration of the study.

What is different about this study, which took place primarily inside drama classrooms, is that here was a space where peer relations took a different form, where home, cultural, and subcultural knowledges interacted relentlessly with the formal curriculum and where many of the usual classroom protocols were suspended. It was indeed a privileged space in which to work over three years and one that, more often than not, stood in opposition to trends gaining momentum in the rest of the school environment and in society more broadly:

Lydia (White, Eastern European, female, second-generation Canadian, grade twelve student at Middleview): Well, I think, uh, I don't know, I think you get a chance to talk to people you normally wouldn't talk to [in the drama classroom], and I also think it's a more open environment, like, there are no chairs and desks and they're not like the chairs upstairs, where they're, like, joined to the desk and you can't move around or turn to the side. Here you can sit on the ground, you can lie down ... I don't know, you can sit however you want; you can talk to whom you want to; you can move around ... and, that's definitely, uh ... it changes the way you relate to people.

The British Broadcasting Corporation website (www.bbc.co.uk) reports (1 December 2005) that there are between four and seven million closed-circuit television cameras in Britain. It has also been reported there were a mere 60,000 in all of France. This number, the BBC site speculated, is likely to dramatically increase because of the 'youth riots' of winter 2005 in France. In their critique of government policies regarding violence in schools and representations of young people in France and England, Osler and Starkey (2005) propose that both countries offer 'universalist' rather than 'targeted' policy responses. Proliferation of surveillance cameras is one clear example of how, in the Western world, video surveillance has become our first line of defence, our first and most comprehensive response to perceptions of escalating crime or danger. In his interesting study of performance, privacy, and surveillance space, McGrath (2004) claims that the expression 'You are under surveillance' is no longer an announcement made to a selected individual. It is a description of our culture: 'You are under surveillance. Not many years ago, this statement could not have been made in a generalized form to an unknown addressee. Today, assuming that you are an urban dweller in a developed country, to be "under surveillance" is a general condition' (19). Today, assuming you are a high school student in an urban public school in North America, you can expect that most areas of the school will be monitored by video cameras, most washrooms will be under lock and key, most lockers will be closed permanently, and most teachers / guidance counsellors / administrators will have access to your and your family's personal information regarding such things as health, immigration status, and education and employment history. In the world of public education, is it not time –

before we go any further down this precarious road – to listen to young people speak about their experiences of 'urban' in and outside schools and to re-evaluate our policies and practices? Is it not time to ask, simply, what kind of (public school) communities we are creating?

Ari: People – adults, they always say, 'Oh, I know how it's like to be a student' and blah, blah, blah, 'I was at that age once,' but it's different. It's not the same situation. Like, my mother's from ... somewhere else, she's from up north. And she lives in the city now, and she's like 'Oh, I went through that,' and I'm like, 'No you didn't!' [we laugh] 'It's different.' Up north is like, everything's so safe up there, you can do whatever you want. But, like, the city's different. And besides, people from my school come from a lot of different places so there's a lot of different personalities and backgrounds and stuff. And we clash sometimes.

Front entrance, Redmount, Queens (New York), Spring 2004

Signs from school hallways

NO **HATS**
NO **WALKMAN**
NO **RADIOS**
NO **HEAVY GOLD**

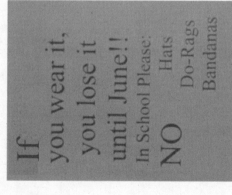

If you wear it,
you lose it
until June!!

In School Please:

NO

   Hats
   Do-Rags
   Bandanas

COATS
HEAD GEAR
CELL PHONES
PAGERS

Signs from school hallways

Newspaper article in hallway, Redmount, Queens (New York), Spring 2004

Video surveillance camera

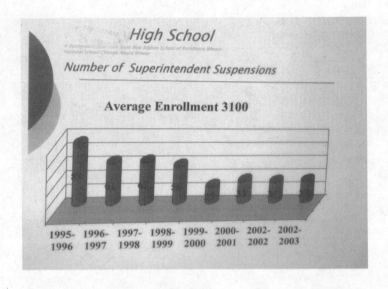

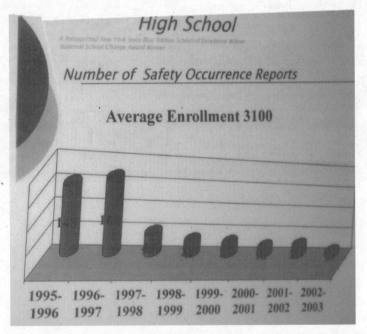

Reports posted in main hallway, Redmount, Queens (New York), Spring 2004

Blackboard in drama classroom, Amor Alternative, mid-town Manhattan, Spring 2004

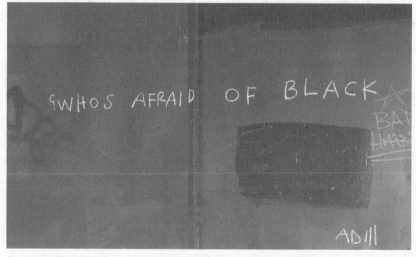

Street graffiti, Manhattan, Winter 2003

Hallway, Middleview, Toronto, Winter 2004

Grade 12 drama class, Middleview, Toronto, Winter 2004

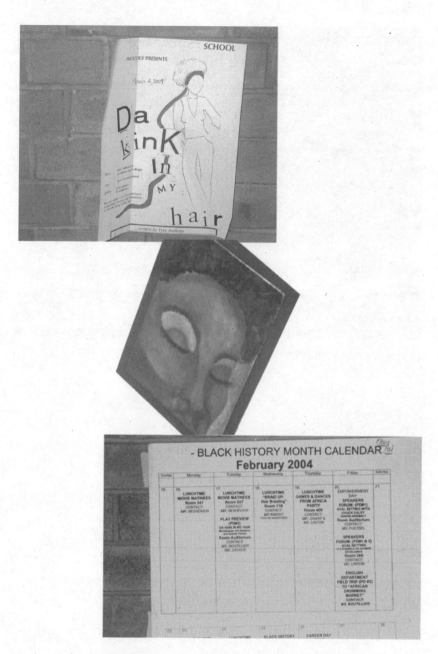

Hallway posters, Middleview, Toronto, Winter 2004

Drama classroom, St Bernadette's, Toronto, Spring 2005

'Twilight' monologue performances, Middleview grade 12 drama class, Toronto, Spring 2004

Students watching each other perform, Middleview grade 12 drama class, Toronto, Spring 2004

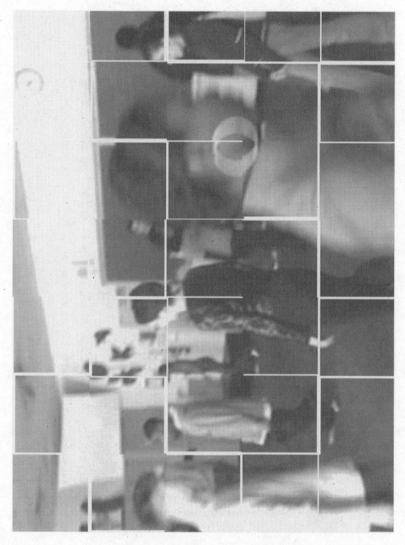

Movement exercises, Middleview grade 12 drama class, Toronto, Spring 2004

Whole class discussion, Black History Month, Middleview grade 12 drama class, Winter 2004

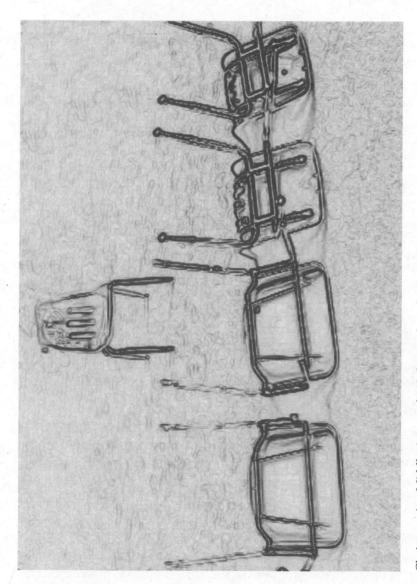

Chair exercise, Middleview grade 12 drama class, Spring 2004

2 IN THE FIELD

An Ethnographic Critique

The critique of what we are is at one and the same time the historical analysis of the limits that are imposed on us and an experiment with the possibility of going beyond them.

Michel Foucault, 'What Is Enlightenment?'

Ethnography is a kind of qualitative research that seeks to describe culture, or parts of culture, from the point of view of cultural insiders (Hatch 2002). In more critical terms, ethnography, as both a process and a product, provides the researcher with an opportunity to 'disturb the impulse to settle meanings,' as Britzman argues (2000). And the writing of ethnography, Tedlock proposes (1991), is the continuation of 'field-work,' rather than a transparent record of past experiences in a field. As this study looked primarily at school culture from the point of view of young people, the ethnography made particular use of participant observation and interview methods, along with the analysis of texts, scripts, and pedagogy particular to drama classrooms. The qualitative interviews in this study, for instance, created a special kind of open-ended speech event that aimed to pay close attention to the perspectives of youth on the issues discussed and to the clues they provide that reveal the meaning structures exploited in their understanding of their world. What is additionally important to note, and different from other forms of research, is that data collection, the tasks of analysis, and theorizing often happen simultaneously throughout an extended ethnography such as ours.

The interviews were undertaken with an eye towards at least two theoretical frameworks: feminist and post-structural. The feminist imperative shaped our activities as opportunities to co-construct meaning with participants and define the kinds of actions that might bring about desirable social changes. Also central were feminist concerns with the ethics of representation, and with questions of agency and emancipation. I wanted specifically to develop research practices designed to encourage inclusion, facilitate dialogue, and sponsor creativity and a courageous philosophical imagination (Cole 1993, 21). The post-structuralist notions embedded in our methods reminded us that it would not be possible to 'know' the world through our participants, but that 'truths' would be local, temporal, and provisional. Rather than proceeding from classical notions of truth, our research methods observed instances of situated knowledges in deeply heterogeneous contexts. Emerson et al. (1995) write that the popular notion – from grounded theory research – that theory is supposed to emanate from the data 'dichotomizes data and theory [and] avoids seeing theory as inherent in the notion of data in the first place' (167). Ours was, therefore, not only an exercise in making conceptual and theoretical coherence from a vast well of 'evidence,' but an activity that self-consciously aimed to transform culture rather than simply observe it. Brooke and Hogg (2004) submit a useful definition of critical ethnography: 'We understand critical ethnography as a research practice, primarily related to education, whose purpose is to use dialogue about a cultural context to develop critical action, while remaining highly attuned to the ethics and politics of representation in the practice and reporting of that dialogue and resulting actions' (117). Critical ethnography, therefore, has a desire for the 'results' of the research to be theoretical, rhetorical, creative, and pragmatic.

Oriented by such theoretical frameworks in the research encounter, we might see why our educational ethnography teetered so precariously on the brink of participatory action research, largely borne of Paulo Freire's work in education. Critical ethnographic work can sometimes feel like action research precisely because of its participatory nature and the explicit goals of change. Our *porous methodology*, as I came to call it, was driven often enough by the explicit and immediate needs in the field. The feminist ethics of this study also work well with action research's agenda for change. In education, action research has been primarily concerned with activity and change; it is usually undertaken through explicit partnerships with practitioners or those whose behaviours and actions most directly affect and are affected by the context under study. For this reason, the youth and their teachers moved in and out of co-researcher modes, both identifying problems and imagining ways to address them. Unlike the often practitioner-led action research in classrooms, however, our work did not determine, in advance, what specific changes were required. Instead, we found ourselves immersed in the (un)usual dynamics of the classrooms by, more often than not, following the instincts and interests of the students and then engaging them (and sometimes their teacher) in a negotiated understanding of what was happening, what it told us about life in classrooms, and how we might like it to change. I was concerned to build a research foundation that might leverage change for those students who would most benefit from a challenge to the status quo. In short, the study demanded a porous methodology because it is of human, as well as scientific, interest; improvement of human welfare remained central.

I shall continue, accordingly, to call this work ethnographic, with the proviso that the theoretical and political imperatives embedded within the project and the desire for reciprocity between us (the researchers) and them (the youth) often demanded a more critical and less traditional approach. In fact, it was often the case that we would break entirely from traditional modes of research and participate in fictional performances with students. This seemed, instinctually to me, to be the best place to begin a conversation with them about change.

Critical ethnography, marking an important evolutionary moment within the field of educational ethnography, provokes a particularly apt research modality for examining the social and artistic relationships and performances inspired by drama work. As I have argued elsewhere (Gallagher 2004), the 'critical' nature of critical ethnography, as it has come to be termed, is profoundly interested in the relationships of power (re)produced in spaces, as marked by differently positioned subjectivities. A critical epistemology for drama research is especially fitting because the activity of drama itself is about taking up positions (characters) and creating spaces in order to examine the worlds they produce. If drama is, indeed, 'a man in a mess,' as celebrated drama pioneer Dorothy Heathcote once proclaimed, then critical ethnography becomes one fascinating way to deconstruct and understand how it all came to be so. The dramatic world has infinite stories to tell the actual world; it is both informed by it and fleeing from it. In return, critical ethnography offers the dramatic world rich theoretical scaffolding in order to help the researcher interrogate both the situatedness and the agency of the drama's (and the classroom's) 'characters.'

In our study, the adolescent participants are both 'informants' about (and therefore witnesses of) and 'representatives' of (and therefore actors within) the 'topic' of the research. Their multiple selves become central, as do the particular constellations of identity of the researchers. Knowledge is both 'out there' and 'in here' for participants and researchers alike. The classic, realist ethnographic text has been productively revisited in this postmodern moment. A critical ethnographic inquiry of drama observes the phenomena that allow people to function in a particular drama-education classroom culture while taking account, also, of the researcher's impact on the context under study. The traditional account of the ethnographer's gender/race – neutral self within a realist story about 'the other' (Spivak 1990; Trinh 1989) – is replaced by the multiple truths, identities, and discourses that operate in a social and aesthetic space. The social categories of identity, therefore, are always included when excerpts of interviews and classroom discussions are cited. This is not because I take social identity markers as some fixed set of characteristics, as I argued at the outset. On the contrary, these descriptors mark the bodies and performances and tell us something a little more about who the characters are and how they might relate dynamically to others.

Some ethnographers (see Ball 1990, 43) have attempted to systematize the ways in which the critical ethnographer can remain self-reflective in her/his processes by urging the researcher to become a 'reflexive analyst.' This would involve a continuous weighing of the impact of their presence, and of the participants' perceptions of them, against the usefulness and limitations of the data recorded. These self-reflexive processes also help to keep researchers vigilant about the ways in which their research methods might be implicated in the reproduction of systems of oppression. As Sanjeet (South Asian, first-generation female, grade twelve student at Middleview) pointed out in her reflection on our research process:

I find that a lot of research projects that involve teenagers are centred on negative things. Big research issues that involve teenagers nowadays are dropout rates, drug use, and involvement in gangs. Such projects seek to make teenagers 'more intelligent,' and act more maturely. While these issues are valid things to research, they are not encouraging and do not make teenagers think very highly of themselves. What's effective about the research project being conducted in our class is that it focuses on our interactions as individuals, not potential gang members, or students at risk of using drugs or dropping out of school.

According to critical epistemology, the subtleties, and the invisibilities, of oppression must be resisted.

The challenges put forward by critical ethnographic research ask how we represent, how we evaluate the legitimacy of our representations, and whether it is possible to effect change in the world. I would also ask of such research in *drama classrooms* the extent to which research of dramatic worlds and relationships can offer a special leverage on our understanding of actual worlds and relationships; and, further, whether the study of these 'improvised' worlds might offer possibilities or suggest actions to help us redress issues of social injustice more broadly. In other words, I am suggesting that through studying how drama teachers and students work in role, with each other and through theatre genres, these non-linear and narrative modes of drama education might, indeed, productively interrupt our traditional qualitative accounts of classrooms and theatre studios, and of the actors/people who enliven them. The new ethnography, as Denzin (1997) describes it, has crossed that liminal space that separates the scholarly text from its subjects; we are all co-performers in our own and others' stories. Denzin's use of theatre/performance metaphors is not accidental, I should think, if, as I am suggesting, we are each both the stars of our own performances and the secondary characters in a range of developing plots surrounding us.

Because conducting educational research, I would argue, is about both studying and creating culture, as critical researchers we entered 'the field' on the first day with some particular questions about the kind of culture we were poised to encounter. First, keeping alive the tension between our use of critical theory and our deployment of ethnographic methods – like participant observation and interviewing – we began by asking what happened in our observation of the drama activities we observed on day one that made concrete the various critical theoretical frameworks we were discussing. In other words, we were interested, first, in asking how culture is contested terrain rather than a set of shared patterns (Quantz 1992).

Because the critical tradition in education is always changing and evolving, being constantly informed by new (inter)disciplinary practices, there was the opportunity to develop flexible research methods for the drama classroom that did not limit the creativity and transdisciplinarity that so often energizes these classrooms. Critical social research has not produced a tight methodological school of thought. Designs, field techniques, and interpretations have enjoyed a proliferation, rather than a narrowing or refining, of possibilities. Furthermore, the tension of the individual and the group, the self and other dichotomy of drama worlds, helps researchers to pay exacting attention to the ever-present theoretical tension between structures and agency at the core of critical ethnographic epistemologies.

Finally, it is both philosophies and their related theories that ready one for 'the field.' These philosophies support the ways that we mediate the truths we 'encounter' in the field. Philosophies and theories are not in a culture-free zone, separate from the embodied experiences of people. Practical issues of method grow from philosophical and epistemological questions about the nature of knowledge. In our case, phenomenology, dialectics, and postmodern frameworks predisposed us to our activities. While it is often tempting to start with a certain theoretical naivety – presuming one will then be most 'open' to the phenomena one encounters – the linguistic and social construction of reality is marked, well in advance, by the presuppositions of a basic material and disursive world and the plurality of understanding one might expect to encounter using a postmodern lens.

In qualitative studies, a phenomenological approach has widely influenced ethnographic work. Kvale (1996) asserts that phenomenology elucidates both that which appears and the manner in which it appears:

> It studies the subjects' perspectives on their world; attempts to describe in detail the content and structure of the subjects' consciousness, to grasp the qualitative diversity of their experiences and to explicate their essential meanings. Phenomenology attempts to get beyond immediately experienced meanings in order to articulate the prereflective level of lived meanings, to make the invisible visible. (53)

However utopian, perhaps impossible, an approach this may seem, it was, nonetheless, useful in our case as it compelled us to pay particular attention to the detailed descriptions of events and contexts, the prior knowledge, understanding, and experiences of our youth participants, within and beyond school. 'Home,' 'peer,' and 'sub' cultures came to the fore in many of our interactions. The participants' imagery and descriptions of these other contexts gave us fuller and more complex pictures.

The postmodern affiliation further creates particular possibilities and challenges for both participant observation work and interview methods. Britzman (2000) argues that it disturbs the ethnographer's confidence in 'knowing' experience, that 'being there' does not guarantee access to the 'truth': 'Thus, the tradition of ethnographic authority derived from participant observation becomes a site of doubt, rather than a confirmation of what exists prior to representation. These positions undermine the ethnographic belief that 'reality' is somehow out there waiting to be captured by language' (32). Perhaps the most overstated postmodern concept is the notion of multiple truths. But the postmodern ethnographer, nonetheless, continues to ask, Which book do I write? For research, like art, is always about choices.

Finally, such a study of human 'subjects' engaged in making drama does not allow me to elide the persistent tension between art and scientific enquiry. This was a tension that, for the most part, remained productive. Nonetheless, an interesting anxiety remains. Madeleine Grumet (1990) encapsulates well the disquiet that many qualitative researchers feel, particularly those who see their work as more allied with art than science:

> For some time many of us have been arguing that qualitative inquiry is an art rather than a science. Having made that assertion, we quickly crawl into it for comfort. No longer radically disassociated from the object of our inquiry and subjugated to the epistemological loneliness that plagues the scientist, we bring together that which science has separated and declare our connectedness, our continuity with our world. The problem of validity – ascertaining a concept's adequacy to the phenomenon to which it corresponds – is relegated, we think, to the skepticism of the Cartesians who must struggle to assert connections they have denied.
>
> The artist, on the other hand, admits the relation to the object that the scientist represses. That is the message of Henry James's artist in 'The Real Thing' ... After struggling in vain to illustrate a text on the aristocracy by working with authentic models, the artist finally has his servants pose, and it is their perception of class difference that strikes the gestures he draws. His canvas depicts a relationship to the phenomenon rather than a display of the thing itself. (101)

The Situated Character of Ethnography

Participant Observation

Powers of observation heightened beyond the normal imply extraordinary disinvolvement: or rather the double process, excessive preoccupation and identification with the lives of others, and at the same time a monstrous detachment ... The tension between standing apart and being fully involved: that is what makes a writer.

Gordimer, *Selected Stories*, 4

The tension between standing apart and being fully involved is also the tension that typifies ethnographic research. The process and character of our participant observation in our drama classrooms over three years might well be more fittingly described as the 'observation of participation' (Tedlock 1991). The question to be asked was, 'What is it we are all participating in?' in these sites marked by personal and theoretical tensions. Our notes from the field come from the sensual experiences and the different readings of the researcher and, in most instances, three research assistants. We related to the world differently, positioned by our differences of gender, race, class, and sexuality. Britzman (2000) concludes that ethnography is always about a second glance. So what might this second glance imagine? In the different imaginaries of four researchers in a field the 'question of belief' (Phelan 1993) becomes a highly unresolved point. Each of us is involved in our own self-other experience, overburdened with expectation, paying particular attention to the details that strike us, engaged in close and protracted interactions with people, and experiencing different emotional responses. Participant observation is, for each one of us, a profoundly intersubjective method, and our memories of it – some recorded, some merely inscribed on the banks of our memory – cannot be separated out from other social processes. We were, each of us in the field, led in our own way to the question What is school?

A Room with Four Views: Notes from Day One in the Field, Middleview Technical School, 30 October 2002

I include the following uninterrupted and lengthy field notes from day one of our study, day one of our participant observation; that is, our observation of our own and others' participation in a complex inner-city high school in downtown Toronto. I do this in order to dispel any myths about the dispassionate observer and to take up Gearing's call (1995, 211) for an 'emotionally aware inter-actor engaged with other actors.' This is, on the one hand, an introduction to the research team. It is also, however, a stark picture of the many complexities of one class period in an inner-city high school and of the various ways that different researchers might relate to, describe, and interpret what they see. It is the way I came to understand what it might mean to work with a team of researchers, and how I became interested in Butler's question: How is it that we become available to a transformation of who we are, a contestation which compels us to rethink ourselves, a reconfiguration of our 'place' and our 'ground'? (1995, 131)

Adam (White, male, first-generation Canadian, of Polish descent, research assistant) writes:

First Impressions
Walking down the main hall, the glaring White faces in the photos of the guidance department staff are contrasted by the diverse faces of the students.
The proud old architecture is at odds with the litter, gum and gobs of spit in the stairwells.
The massive, echoing hallways are reflected in rounded mirrors at every corner, the same mirrors that are used as surveillance tools to monitor shoplifters.

Class Begins
There is constant chatter while Ms S [the teacher] is trying to get permission forms and money. They are listening, you can see it in small ways – subtle body language, eyes tracking Ms S, reactions to what she's saying – they just appear like they're not.
I feel intense internal pressure not to laugh, even when they're funny – but they're also being disrespectful – but funny – but I can't laugh!
Boys sit on one side of the circle, girls on the other, with the exception of Jeremy and Carlin, the two football players in the class. Jeremy is busy 'flirting' with Lila, though she doesn't appear to welcome this interaction with him. Nate is obviously something of a class clown.
Kathleen just laughed, so it must be OK. But it wasn't disrespectful, just honest – a 'woah miss' reaction to the possibility of being in the hot seat for the drama convention 'Interviews in Role.'
Two guys sit outside the circle, but are listening. Isaius sits slumped, while Samuel sits with arms and legs crossed, but their eyes are tracking who's talking, and they're both reacting in small ways that show they're listening.
The room's not that cold, but a number of students sit with jackets on, a few with gloves, and two with headbands.

An insightful comment by Carlin, to which Ms S responds with 'Excellent!'
This is greeted with mocking and derision.
They aren't even making a big deal out of guys taking on a woman's role (is
there some of that to come?).
The clock, door, and blackboard are all labeled as such with rectangular pieces
of cardboard and magic marker – why?
The students are told that any inappropriate questions during the in-role
interviews will result in an automatic zero – and that they should know
what's 'inappropriate.'
The ones who will be answering in role are told to sit individually, and read
over their scripts. The remainder of the class is broken into smaller groups
to come up with questions to ask the people in role.
The clock fast-forwards over an hour in under a minute. This clock never
seems to have the right time, and does strange things – runs backwards,
zooms forward, and stands still.
Phil and Dominique are sitting in on groups, but I've decided not to. Though
supposedly separated and sitting individually, the individuals who will be
answering in role are still talking to each other. One of them doesn't even
have a script, and their conversation is most definitely not about the play. I
can only catch snippets of what they're saying, but don't want to move
closer for fear they'll stop talking. They're talking about trying drugs, and
who among them has smoked, had a joint, and even tried cocaine (though it
seems none of them has ventured into the latter). There's pressure to both
be cool and be honest: 'Have you tried it? Don't lie man' (Jeremy).
The group's conversation also wanders into the following exchange:
Jeremy: Are you going to the dance?
Sam: No, no one's going.
Jeremy: A lot of the teams are going.
Sam: Well maybe ...
Ms S, in her lead-in to starting the in-role interviews: 'Everyone knows
getting up there is difficult. Staying focused is difficult.'
Jeremy, while in role as the Matron, says, 'You have to be tough on them. It
gets them through life.' A short while later, he says, 'You have to be tough
on them. It helps them be tough later in life.' (Is this just a reading of the
character's motivation on his part? – I doubt it ... I think he's probably
drawing from authority figures – parents? coaches? – who have used those
words to justify 'being tough' on him – but what form of 'being tough'
have those experiences taken?)
Carlin, while in role as Mr Adams, answers Isaius's question 'What do you

mean by becoming a man?' with a long answer, of which I only managed to record these snippets:

'I mean being able to support yourself and your family. Being able to do things right.'

'I had a rough childhood. I tried to walk in my father's shoes.'

'I wish I could have spent more time with my dad.'

'I like to hunt.'

'If I found out some guy had gotten my daughter pregnant, I would shoot the guy and beat my daughter with a belt.'

Close to the end of class, when someone looks at their watch, Ms S responds with 'Eh! No watches!' She gets a mumbled apology in reply. It's obviously accepted as one of the rules of her classroom that you're not supposed to keep checking when it will all be over. (But the clock in here doesn't work right – I would be looking at my watch too!).

Phil (White, male American-born, of French Canadian descent, research assistant) writes:

First class – working on 'Be My Baby,' a play about teen pregnancy

- Apparently quite a bit of negotiation/socializing goes on just outside the room. The teacher (hereafter, Ms S) engaging with students in an informal manner, at times apparently coaxing them into entering class.
- Students hang coats on rack, or lay them on table. They place bags under the table, which is located to the left of the door and in an area filled with cabinets, tables and cubbyholes for theatre-related props.
- Chairs set up in a circle in the middle of the room.
- In this class, rough count is 6 girls, 15 boys. The girls mostly grouped together.
- Ms S asking for names of characters from play and a short description of them.
  Queenie: 'bad girl,' 'gangster,' and she smokes
  Mrs Adams: 'She's old school'
- Mostly boys shouting out answers to questions, even when questions are about pregnancy.
- Quite a few side comments among students, Ms S has to talk over these to keep answers coming in.
- Ms S's face appears flushed, her voice a little hoarse. She drinks water a couple times while getting a tell-back from students about the play they have read. She wears her keys around her neck on a 'Roots Canada' loop. At times I sense a fatigue in her facial and vocal expression.

- *10:55 a.m. – A girl enters (late) and Ms S makes eye contact, but there's no spoken interaction.*
- *Boys immediately volunteer for female roles. Ms S accepts this easily.*
- *A flare-up occurs between two boys, Ms S moves to stand between them to calm them down, after asking each of them to move and they refuse.*
- *In small group: Only one of them has a pen. They begin to write questions separately on the slips of paper Ms S gave each of them to form the question-making groups. Later, when Ms S distributes writing paper to them, one student takes on responsibility for coalescing their individual questions as well as writing down additional ones the group develops.*
- *Several times Ms S incorporates into her descriptions of activities the fact that it is being evaluated. She tells them what she is looking for both from the actors in the Hot Seat and from the interviewers.*
- *Strikingly little is made of the fact that boys are playing female roles.*
- *Student, in praising Jeremy's portrayal of Matron, says that 'he didn't think about his answers.'*
- *Mr Adams (Carlin):*
  His father 'didn't baby me; let me figure it out for myself; had to bring myself up.'
  'I'm a farmer; I kill animals and humans (nah, just kidding). I grow whatever's in season, wherever the money is.'
  'If my daughter were pregnant, I'd beat her, and I'd kill the guy.'
  'I wish I could spend more time with my father. I wish I could've told him I loved him.'
  (About his daughter) 'I want to get an education, so she doesn't have to be a housewife.'
  Interviewer-student: Like your wife?
  Mr Adams: Yeah, but she's frustrated. She says 26 years is a long time. She's bored.
- *Ms S stops to talk about what came up during Carlin's role play. Wants them to discuss the difference between the role portrayed and the person portraying it.*
- *In the midst of asking about the above, Ms S sees a student checking his watch and says, 'Hey, no watches!' He apologizes.*
- *Mary (played by Sam)*
  Abuse and violence a big theme.
  Distant or absent fathers – student interviewers ask a lot of questions about fathers.
- *As class draws to a close, Ms S tells them they will continue with the interviews tomorrow. She requests that each group return their questions*

*to her with the names of each group member written on the page. One stu-
dent hands her the page rolled up into a tight cylinder and she says, 'What
are you doing? Don't give me a sheet like that, please.' He attempts to flatten
it out and hands it to Ms S.*

- *Realization: there's an implicit lesson here about the importance of relationships in drama. The interviews were dependent upon both parties doing
their best, i.e., good questions resulted in good answers. As an interviewer
your goal is to help the performer. Sets up a positive, non-competitive
ethos.*

Dominique (Black, female, first-generation Canadian, of Caribbean
descent, research assistant) writes:

- *So far, this seems to be a really typical high school class: students are
trying to assert themselves, challenge the teacher ... they seem to be 'deliberately nonchalant,' like they're 'too cool' for class.*
- *Teenage boys are so typical!*
- *Some of them look bored with Kathleen's speech ... Do they understand
what she's trying to say?*
  - *Now, there's some interest – some students have answered her questions ... good points made.*
- *I think the script that they're working on is the one about the 'common'
girl who gets pregnant by her employer's son ... I think we discussed that
in 'Foundations of Curriculum' oh-so-long ago.*
  - *Oops! I was wrong – it seems that this script is about a young girl in a
home for unwed mothers-to-be.*
  - *Students seem to be responding to Ms S's questions in 'contemporary'
language – is this because they can link the story to their own 'contemporary' lives?*
- *Now that the class is doing 'their' work (and no more boring admin stuff),
they're much more lively, much more 'turned on.'*
  - *They're making value judgments, and giving their opinions about the
characters (e.g., 'That's messed up man!' – Dion).*
  - *There's much use of slang (e.g., the matron is 'old-school').*
- *Some students' body language reeks of attitude ... They're way too 'cool' for
this.*
  - *E.g., 'Spike' seems to deliberately keep himself apart from his classmates – it's like he resents having to be in the same space as people who
aren't as 'cool' as he is ... I wonder what his story is? ... He's definitely
one student whose head I'd like to get 'inside' of.*

- *Interesting 'switch': when Ms S starts asking more 'official' questions about the characters, the students' language becomes more 'official,' too ... Reminds me of the 'language switch' I noticed in my own thesis work.*
- *There are a lot of volunteers for the group exercise: they're eager and excited about it – cool!*

Group Work: Interviewing in Role
- *One group of students plays each of the main characters.*
- *Rest of class divides into smaller groups, and comes up with ten questions to ask each character.*
- *'My' question group ('Mrs Adams') – Alessandra, Mohammed, and Antonio*
- *Their questions come easily.*
  - *They make good points about possible explanations for 'Mrs Adams''s behaviour.*
  - *They work well together – there's no tension ... indicates a close-knit class?*
  - *Alessandra seems particularly good at 'translating' her groups' 'slang' questions into 'proper' school questions.*
  - *Interesting paradox: despite their 'cooler-than-thou' exterior, the students seem to want to do well on their assignment (e.g., Antonio got right down to writing up the questions, making sure that it was dated, they were neatly written, etc.).*
    - o *Does this indicate a tension between who/what they feel they have to be (i.e., 'cool') and who/what they might really want to be (i.e., good students)?*
    - o *If so, how do they negotiate/resolve this?*

The 'Hot Seat'

'The Matron' – played by Jeremy
- *The questions asked are typical.*
- *His answers seem to be very 'off-the-top' of his head ... I guess that's the point of this exercise; they're also 'closed,' probably as a result of the 'closed' questions he's being asked.*
- *Doesn't seem to elaborate too much, needs a bit of prodding – i can almost see the wheels turning, as he tries to think of what to say*

'Mr Adams' – played by Nate
- *Key question: how much of his (and other students') answers are based on their own life experiences?*

- *The questions asked are a nice rebound off of Carlos's improv.*
- *What's with 'the guy thing,' 'being a man,' etc? Where is he getting that from?*
- *Noticeable contrast between what he says he'd do to Mary if he found out she was pregnant, and how he says he treats her now (e.g., Lets her do her own thing).*
  - *Seems he can't keep his character's story straight.*
- *Sexist!! (e.g., he didn't want his daughter 'spreading her legs' for some guy; his wife does 'wife' stuff like cooking and cleaning) – are those his own beliefs, or what he thinks 'Mr Adams' would believe?*
- *Interesting that he equates 'love' with a will to kill for that person.*
- *Contrast between his expectations of his wife and those for Mary, his daughter.*
  - *Ms S calls him on it – good.*
- *Students got lots from Carlin: could they see their own lives in his 'story'?*
  - *He has definite potential, if he's able to draw from human experiences and feelings like that.*
  - *He's another student whom I'd like to get to know better – I have a feeling that we all feel that way!*
- *Aside: Nate doesn't seem to take praise well ... I wonder why.*

'Mary' – played by Sam
- *Do his answers feed off those given in the preceding interviews? Probably ...*
- *He (and also Jeremy and Carlin) seems to be really trying to answer in the character's 'voice' ... They're really taking this exercise seriously.*
- *Key question: if you're a male student playing a female role, how difficult is it to 'think female'? What do you draw from?*
  - *What is Nate drawing from? He's definitely not playing a stereotypical 'girlie,' and he took the question about why he loves 'his' boyfriend in stride ... I wasn't expecting that ...*

Kathleen (White, female, first-generation Canadian, of Scottish descent, researcher) writes:

Preliminary thoughts
Arrived at the moment of 'Oh Canada' (sung by a Black female artist)

Teacher Ms S met me in foyer:
'I'm starting with the sharing of stories; it's risky given the life histories of

many of these kids, but I'm finding that the drama games are just not bonding these kids. And they don't share what they don't want others to know.'

Pause. 'I'm a little nervous about being observed by you in a research study because things that happen here are pretty complicated.'

(She's natural, so comfortable with them)

Brief meeting with principal
- *Happy about his decision to allow us to conduct research in his school because he's proposed a new grade ten drama course and it's good PR.*
- *Pleased with himself*

Preliminary documents
- *'What I need others to stop doing' – an excellent handout Ms S has given her students in her attempts to figure out how to make an inclusive community in this room.*
- *Dramatic Arts Grade Eleven Course Outline*

Room
Large windows, comfortable couch, boards, chairs, beautiful

Students
Brian enters 15 minutes early – Ms S: 'Brian, are you going to your first period mostly?' 'Yeah.'
'Good. Good to hear.'

Background
Stratford and Soulpepper – talk of upcoming visits from artists and fight choreographer. The program seems to make good use of the larger theatre community.

Resources
Excellent diverse collection of plays, Black artists, etc. on bookshelves. school has allocated a budget for drama – unusual and welcome news.

Class arrives   Grade Eleven 'Open'
Marvin as peer tutor
- *Ms S's ultimatum – lose a form, no replacements. I'm saving the trees.*
- *11:15 start but they arrive at 11:30.*

- *Bring our circle in closer.*
- *Student: 'Why do we have to write?' Familiar complaint.*

(Note: I need my laptop)

Ms S has been shaped by this environment. A really good teacher. I remember parts of myself in her.
Ms S: 'I'm so nervous with you here.' Two more times.

- *Body language of students says 'We don't care' but they're listening ...*

The stories of schools

They want to be paired up – have her do it.

Iver enters very late.
Ms S: 'And you're late today because ... '
Iver: 'Had to go over to Honest Ed's to show my social insurance card.'
Ms S: 'You gonna be working there?'
Iver: 'Yeah maybe. So is that acceptable?'
Ms S: 'Yeah. Because you're usually on time.'

Doing research gives story the weight it deserves.

My introduction of the research to the students follows.
I field one question: how long will you be here? I asked them how long they thought we should be here in order to really understand them. Lina said: more than 1 unit (curriculum, I assume). Another boy said over a long period of time.
They recap a play they've read and are aware of us. It's amazing how many people answer questions but are not heard.
In the recap, it's clear that it's uncool to be smart. They tease each other for answering.
Gender-cross casting is striking. The boys take on female roles without hesitation. This is normal here? Even when there are girls?
Ms S respects them and they know it. It's quite moving to witness this.
She wants me to come to drama club after school, which is different for the kids, different from the classroom routine.

Exit – Ms S in tears at door
I reflect on Ms S as a former teacher-education student of mine.

Kathleen: 'You are so comfortable in your skin now; it's a pleasure to watch.'
Ms S: [Earnestly] 'Thank you. Because you can't see it yourself. And I know I
have miles to go. Sometimes I think I don't know what the fuck I'm doing.'

A Room with Four Views

On 'Day One' a team of qualitative researchers stands on the threshhold of a classroom's door. They are strangers. They attend to and feel different things. Differently positioned eyes, different 'guilty readings' (Britzman 2000) of the dramas of people's lives, classroom life, high stakes, and everyday conversations. Schools are bursting to capacity with stories, different story-lines we choose to follow; my eye falls on one, another's ear attuned to a different one. This is qualitative ethnographic study.

A Note on Analysing Qualitative Data

Every reading modifies its object.

De Certeau, *The Practice of Everyday Life*, 169

Given the greater prevalence of technologically assisted forms of data coding and analysis in qualitative research, and the development of progressively more sophisticated qualitative analysis software, I would like to point to the limitations of such technology for post-positivist qualitative research given the challenges faced by my research team in the analysis of complex dialogues with youth and teachers about drama, creativity, school life, and education. After considerable thematic data coding (of individual and focus-group interviews, field notes, in-role student writing) and analysis from the first phase of field work – using N6 qualitative software – we found the process wanting in precisely the area where we were seeking a technological boost, namely, as a way of identifying themes across codes; that is to say, the coding of individual passages was made much easier through N6, but when it came to teasing out themes from the various codes, not to mention the difficulty in getting printouts that could be easily created and digested, we were wary of the ways in which N6 forced important coding decisions upon us. What we found was that N6 was effective for data management, but inadequate for the nuanced and complex work of data analysis. It gave us style, but not substance; it sacrificed the attention to, and containment of, complexity we were after.

From this initial work, we then attempted to cluster our different codes into thematic groups as a way of creating a contextual picture of our different observations. We were mindful of trying not to force the data into groups, but to get clarity around which themes seemed to be the strongest and which were outliers. We compiled a list from this data that comprised all the different coding groups, with some sub-groupings listed as well. It was at this point that a return to the original study objectives became necessary and a reread, in holistic terms, of the original transcripts, field notes, and sample writing. From this reread-ing came a list of six questions that I wanted us, as researchers, to ask of the data. These questions were not explicitly asked of the research participants, but were questions I wanted to ask of the data themselves. The questions were:

1 What does 'arts as good' mean in schools / for youth?
2 What policy-relevant practices are identifiable that support greater social cohesion in diverse classrooms?
3 What do aesthetic practices in schools have to say to the larger school culture with respect to their positive impact on the formation of youth identities and peer relations?
4 How, differently, might conflict be addressed in light of arts-based pedagogical choices?
5 What role does creativity have to play more generally in young people's encounters with curriculum?
6 How do students take actions differently in drama classes?

Using copies of the original documents for coding purposes, our team developed an analytical system we called the *Constant Comparison Grapho-Linear Imaging Matrix Coding Apparatus (CCGLIMCA)*. This is a rather complex name for a creative set of symbolic coding designs that were 'written into' the documents, in all instances where we felt any of the six pertinent questions were addressed. In other words, CCGLIMCA allowed us to do what we discovered N6 could not do, which was to give us a comprehensive and easily accessible way to identify data that seemed rich with regards to our lines of inquiry.

The interesting discovery in the development of our analysis system was that, for our purposes, N6 went about qualitative analysis the wrong way: rather than displaying all the codes in the data, it showed us all the data in the codes. That is, we were unable to create a printout that could show, at a glance, where the 'rich' data resided and how these data related to other emerging themes. It showed us, instead, all the data appearing under a given code, or all the codes used for a given bit of text, all of which was difficult to read and even harder to make sense of.

We needed CCGLIMCA to direct our attention to (a) how the codes were connected; (b) *which* students were discussing *which* themes; and (c) how our interpretation of the questions was related to our coding decisions. With our system we were also able to retain the original Microsoft Word formatting, which allowed for greater contextualizing because the interviews or the field notes were there in their entirety, the original text undisturbed, with all the coding taking place around the actual text. In effect, we returned to a more manual system that respected the sheer quantity and complexity of qualitative data and the surrounding contexts. What also became abundantly clear was that creativity would need to play a role in our own coding and analysis practices as researchers if we were committed to studying the creativity of drama classrooms.

Our approach with field notes was to share them, read them often, take note of the differences among our different accounts of classrooms events, and have rich discussions about why one's attention may have become piqued by one conversation and another's by a different one. Sometimes it was a simple case of where one sat in the room; other times it was a case of the amount of activity going on simultaneously. But our most interesting discussions as a team centred on the ways in which each of us developed different relationships with each site and on what issues we found most powerfully present when we were there.

Disenchanted Youth, Falling Test Scores, Rigorous Curriculum, and Other Prevailing Myths

Texts, facts, scores are devoured as credentials are inflated and value seeps out of the experience of education.

Grumet, 'Curriculum and the Art of Daily Life,' 86

Unlike the insights that young people express about what matters in learning, much of the literature in urban schooling pays inordinate attention to test scores. Recent policy initiatives in Canada and the United States have secured the supremacy of test scores in our evaluations of urban schools and their teachers, administrators, and students. Such policies as George W. Bush's *No Child Left Behind Act, Public Law 107-110* (or what the staff at Amor referred to as *No Teacher Left Standing*) link high-stakes testing with strict accountability measures. Lather, in her critique of what she sees as a 'governmental incursion into legislating the scientific method' (2004), argues that such incursions have produced a 'politics of science in the US accountability movement in public education' that is an unprecedented example of 'government as unilateral force.' Orfield (2002) summarizes what he argues are the two basic policy trends of the last fifty years: 'There have been two basic eras in US education policy since mid-century: a struggle for access and equity that dominated the period from 1960–1980 and a focus on competition and standards that prevailed in the 1980s and 1990s' (406).

While the US *No Child* policy might be the most notoriously named, similar policies and new testing practices in Canada, the United Kingdom, Australia, and most other Western countries have emerged from the very same neo-liberal discourses of accountability and global competition. Drawing a strong relationship between the rise in high-stakes testing and the decline in educational equality, Hursh (2005) explains:

> Proponents of high-stakes testing and accountability use the discourses connecting education with economic productivity, educational equity and assessment objectivity to gain dominance in the debate over education reform. These discourses are used to argue for and implement reforms in the structure and practices of schooling, including standardized testing with sanctions for teachers and students with low scores. Because the changes in the structure and practices fit together as a system – standardized tests require standards and enable accountability – resistance becomes difficult because each part is justified by the whole. (611)

Despite an unrelenting era of 'reform,' many scholars argue that the gap in educational achievement between rich and poor children is still widening. Anyon, in her important analyses of city schools in the United States (1997, 2005), has made the case that our strategies for educational policy reform have not adequately addressed other social policies that, taken together, would improve the lives, the life-chances, and the educational outcomes of inner-city children. In decades of educational reform, she argues, we have seen very little improvement. Despite this evidence, many neo-liberal educational reforms continue to exploit the discourses of democracy and social justice. In his examination of the 'machinery of social injustice,' political philosopher Brian Barry demonstrates that people's chances of rising or falling from their social location at birth in the social order have declined in the last twenty years to such a degree that some sociologists have begun to talk about 'social closure' (2005, 15). It also seems clear that in most countries attempts to address the historic alignment of class and educational achievement have failed. Achievement scores, while important, tell us very little about the quality of life and learning in a school. And as McNeil points out, 'sameness,' that is, standardization of all kinds, may be a symbolic proxy for equity, but it is not an investment in equity (2000, 198). It is obvious that our understanding of 'improvement' has been far too narrow over the last two decades and our unquestioning belief in the 'progress' of the global marketplace has been misplaced. Giroux (2003) paints a very grim picture indeed:

> Testing has become the code word for training educational leaders in the language of management, measurement, and efficiency. It has also become the new ideological weapon in developing standardized curricula that ignore cultural diversity by defining knowledge narrowly in terms of discrete skills and decontextualized bodies of information, ruthlessly expunging the language of ethics from the broader purpose of teaching and schooling. What knowledge is taught, under what conditions, for what purpose, and by whom has become less important than developing precise measuring instruments for tracking students and, increasingly, for disempowering and de-skilling teachers. (88)

The National Center for Educational Statistics (NCES 1990) has outlined specific predictive factors that lead to educational failure: belonging to a single-parent home, spending three or more hours at home alone each day, having an annual family income of less than $15,000, having parents or siblings who did not complete high school, having a limited proficiency with English, living in an urban area, and/or belonging to a racial/ethnic minority group. These 'predictive' factors (see also Paterson 1995; Swadener and Lubeck 1995) are familiar to any researcher who has spent time thinking about the challenges of urban schooling. However, Fasset and Warren (2005) have effectively critiqued such research on urban schooling, which has tended to focus on individual traits (race, class, gender, etc.) to the exclusion of other sociopolitical factors: 'Such studies are emblematic of the problem with the risk metaphor; an emphasis on diagnosis, at the expense of understanding, limits scholarly understanding of identity' (241). And as North American systems continue to be compared unfavourably in the popular press to the Japanese education system, as just one example, what seems obvious is that a system that was designed in the nineteenth century to educate about one-fifth of the population while channelling the rest into factories and farms takes as a basic assumption that only a small portion of children (White, middle-class) are worth educating or capable of higher-order thinking. The Japanese advantage, if there is one, is therefore not in test scores, but in a fundamental design that assumes that all children can and should achieve at a very high level.

I agree with Lather that an 'applied social science that can cope with the multiplicity of the social world' (2004, 768) is urgently needed. In my view, there is a serious crisis of imagination in the current climate of urban schooling, a scarcity of creative responses to complex problems. What is paradoxical about recent studies in the English-speaking world that have failed to demonstrate any sustained improvement in students' or schools' achievement rates is that creativity and the arts in general have been largely ignored. A stunning document completed by the Office for Standards in Education (OfSTED) in the United Kingdom in 2003 looked, in detail, at a sample of the lowest-attaining, in many areas of the curriculum, primary and secondary schools in England, which were achieving above national expectations for one or more arts subjects. Based on assumed polarities between the arts and sciences, it is safe to say that the arts are not normally seen as priorities in the long-term development of national educational systems; and yet OfSTED found that the arts had a significantly positive effect in many areas of social disadvantage and were especially important in regenerating local communities. This must also be seen within the context of the two most significant English national strategies introduced in primary schools over the last six years – the National Literacy Strategy (NLS) and the National Numeracy Strategy (NNS), which exemplify the high levels of central-government intervention that UK schools have experienced over the last decade and the 'blend of pressure and support' (Chapman and Harris 2004) that mark these initiatives attempting to drive up the standards at the lowest-attaining schools. These schools are primarily serving socio-economically disadvantaged communities, known as 'schools facing challenging circumstances' (SFCC). In Ontario we have recently adopted the English model with our new Literacy and Numeracy Secretariats at the Ministry of Education. OfSTED's own reports, and a series of evaluations by the University of Toronto, have expressed concern that the practical, investigative aspects of the non-core-foundations subjects were being neglected because of pressure to meet higher targets for standards in English and mathematics. However, in the majority of these 170 low-attaining schools the quality of work in the arts is assessed more favourably than that in English and mathematics.

In the 1000 lowest-attaining secondary schools in England (those with the least pupils gaining five or more A–C grades for the General Certificate Secondary Education in 2000), 30 per cent achieved above the national average of A–C results in at least one of the arts subjects. Among the 500 lowest-attaining secondary schools, 37 per cent achieved above the national average of A–C results for at least one of the arts subjects. This figure increased to 43 per cent in 2002.

In Ontario standardized tests are administered by the Education Quality Accountability Office, while US students write The Regents. The arts, as disciplines, are not a part of these national testing practices, so one cannot verify if the UK phenomenon is reproduced in North America. But if we are to believe the English numbers, to not pursue further why the lowest-achieving students and schools have results consistently higher than the national averages in arts subjects is akin to disregarding solutions that are staring us in the face. My lingering sense is that the numbers only really matter when they are understood within the context of individual schools, and not when schools are compared with one another or when results are wielded as a punitive measure. As the youth in our study articulate, the arts matter. And they matter because they strongly affect the quality of teaching and learning in a classroom and the general life of a school. The test scores in the arts matter because they tell us more about the quality of learning and the presence of creativity in any given context than do most other things. In primary schools they tell us whether teachers and children are integrating their learning and imaginatively trespassing into areas of interest; in secondary schools they tell us whether students are learning the values of working collaboratively, communicating across difference and through conflict, and engaging in original thinking.

A Word about Creativity

> No one ever told us we had to study our lives,
> make of our lives a study, as if learning natural history
> or music, that we should begin
> with the simple exercises first
> and slowly go on trying
> the hard ones, practicing till strength
> and accuracy became one with the daring
> to leap into transcendence, take the chance
> of breaking down in the wild arpeggio
> or faulting the full sentence of the fugue ...
>
> (Adrienne Rich, 1978)

Against this backdrop of high-stakes testing, it seems important, at this point, to address more explicitly the question of creativity in research, our use of it, young people's understanding of it, and its place in urban schools. Ideas about creativity, especially in the theatre, can be political. English playwright Edward Bond (in Nicholson 2003) argues that creativity comes from a need for justice, that it has, therefore, a fundamentally political imperative(Creativity in the drama classroom arises from complex social processes rather than from moments of individual genius] It is antithetical to the diagnostic forms of standardized testing and is compelled by deeper understanding of social processes. Even if we take the Romantic ideal that creativity is the result of inspiration from the muses, then it is not Plato's gods, but oneself / the other that is the muse in drama.

One of the more interesting aspects about any discussion of drama and creativity is the attention that must be paid to the group, the collective, the 'community.'In schools and beyond, drama is a collective experience; any notions of the introverted, solitary, creative genius are quickly dispensed with] Drama, then, invites different ideas about creativity – its pleasures, its uses, its dangers, its fundamental sense of the collective. Irish playwright Brian Friel (1999) captures this indispensable quality well:

> And a final nod to the axiom that theatre can be experienced only in community with other people. One can stand alone in an art gallery and gaze for three hours at an El Greco; or one can sit alone in one's living room and listen to Mahler. But one cannot sit by himself in the stalls and be moved by a dramatic performance – and for this reason: that the dramatist does not write for one man; he writes for an audience, a collection of people. His technique is the very opposite of the short-story writer's or the novelist's. They function privately, man to man, a personal conversation. Everything they write has the implicit preface, 'Come here till I whisper in your ear.' But the dramatist functions through the group, not a personal conversation but a public address. His technique is the technique of the preacher and the politician. Every time a curtain rises, a dramatist begins, 'Ladies and gentlemen ...' Of course his concern is to communicate with every individual in that audience, but he can do that only through the collective mind. If he cannot get the attention of that collective mind, hold it, persuade it, mesmerize it, manipulate it, he has lost everything. And this imposes strange restrictions on him because the collective mind is a peculiar mind. (18)

Because we worked in creative ways in our research, and often in dramatic and collaborative ways with the students, I wanted to develop some understanding of what students made of creativity, rather than assume that my own interest in it or privileging of it was shared. My instinct told me that using drama methodologically was not a simple question of changing methods, but involved an attempt to fundamentally change the thinking about the social givens in the classroom. The young people who spoke to the question of creativity in our interviews had at once both sophisticated and surprisingly pragmatic ideas about the role of creativity in their lives. To call on Rich (1978) above, they helped me to see that in the most basic sense their primary use of creativity was to 'study our lives, make of our lives a study.'

The students cited below are those who explicitly engaged with the idea of creativity when speaking with us; they are the ones who pointed us towards both philosophical and practical understandings of the concept. These early conversations with students helped us, as researchers, to shape some of our own questions about creativity. We were interested in assessing not whether the classrooms we were observing demonstrated creativity, but rather how students came to understand the concept, given their own interpretations of their classroom activities.

For Dion, creativity is too hard to 'show' and makes us too vulnerable:

Dion (Black, male, Jamaican-born grade eleven student at Middleview): Yeah, like most of the time I feel happy if I don't write about my life. Like the truth, you know what I'm saying? How I live. Because if I wrote about that, I'm telling you Sir, I would just start thinking, and what am I thinking? It's just not good; you know what I'm saying? So therefore I just leave that alone, you know what I'm saying?

Phil: You'd rather not go there, especially in class.

Dion: Yes, Sir, I could somewhere down there, but not too deep, because if I go too deep I'm just gonna get upset, trust me, so therefore, I just ... you know?

We wondered whether there was an environment or a kind of pedagogical/peer relationship that would allow Dion to 'go there'? Can certain environments more than others help students make creative responses to their lives and troubles? Does creativity have to look positive or can it be angry and difficult? What assumptions about how creativity looks do we, as teachers (and researchers), embed in our practices?

In some interviews, discussions about creativity and creative encounters with the curriculum in drama class sounded more like tests of endurance than the free flow of activity we sometimes associate with creative acts:

Eliza (Hispanic, female, grade eleven student at Middleview): Um ... well,
  Ms S [the drama teacher] has been supportive ... really, and ... well ...
  pretty much telling me ... that I should keep going.
Dominique: Uh-huh ...
Eliza: And ... well, I believe it.
Dominique: Okay ...
Eliza: And ... it pretty much helps me feel better about ... acting ... out things ...
Dominique: Okay ...
Eliza: ... with a bit more feeling than I usually would.

Lack of inhibition, with respect to students 'feeling creative,' was echoed in several of the school sites. The students themselves did not always equate this lack of inhibition with feelings of creativity, but how they spoke about it caused us to make this connection. Many students in all four sites pointed to feelings of creativity when they were afforded the space to stray from prescribed student behaviours. For example, Marly explains:

Marly (White, female, first-generation Canadian, of European descent, grade
  ten student at St Bernadette's): Because I like Drama and it's the only class
  where I can actually be myself and it's the only class where I can actually,
  um, you know, act all wacky without getting in trouble.

As is frequently the case, lack of inhibition was also coupled with notions of 'self-expression,' which many students associated with feeling 'creative.'

Hessa (White, female, second-generation Canadian, of European descent,
  grade eleven student at Middleview): Your mind expands when you
  express yourself.
Dominique: And do you think Drama helps you do that?
Hessa: Um ... yeah.
Dominique: How so?

Hessa: Well, maybe when you're acting ... you try to experiment with your-
self. Like how you project your voice, or improv your acting, and yeah,
receiving comments from everyone after the thing.

Sonya also alludes to a kind of self-expression:

Dominique: Do you think the writing that you do in Drama class is different
from other classes?
Sonya (Black, female, African American, grade twelve student at Amor):
Yeah, definitely.
Dominique: Why? Or, how?
Sonya: It's like, it's like just an open thing ... Like you just open yourself up,
and just let it all out. This is the one class you get to express yourself in.
Dominique: You don't get to express yourself in other classes?
Sonya: Yeah, but not as much.

Brianny, for instance, felt more creative when her whole body was
engaged:

Brianny (White, female, of European descent, grade ten student at St
Bernadette's): With the movement, I think it's good because it gives you a
different way ... a different opportunity to express yourself. Like when
you're moving around, you use your own individuality when you're doing
a movement.

Among the four schools, we saw a range of activities that might be
considered 'movement exercises,' from rudimentary warm-up activities and tableaux to involved physical depictions of scenes and emotional responses. But Brianny's explanation, like that of others, is concerned
with notions of 'individuality' and performances that break out of more
prescriptive ways of learning and being in school.
In the field of education, Ellsworth (1997) has begun an important
discussion about the body as teaching's 'other,' that is to say, that
knowledges of the body, desire, and emotion are most often pedagogically marginalized. I am also forcefully reminded here of Canadian arts
critic Kate Taylor, who recently claimed: 'In an age that is awash in
culture that is global rather than local, digital rather than analog and
broadcast rather than live, theatre's social importance and its excitement lies in its physical immediacy' (2005, R5). Misha, a young Serbian
man who had been in Canada only two years and had been struggling

with language issues, felt especially strongly about how his learning had been affected by the more physical nature of the drama class:

Misha: It – it's kinda different. First of all, like, when you come to the room, you kinda see, like ... there's no chair, there's no desk ... there's a floor ... You can even lie [down on the floor], you can even ... stand, you can even ... be, like, wherever you want. There's like, no, like ... Some classes, there's, like, actually ... you go to class, and you have to sit in the same place ..., like every day, every single day, in the same space. And, it's kinda boring (Phil: Mm-hmm). But, like, this place? It's kinda, you know ... And, like, you can talk, and you can kinda, more, like ... be, like ... energetic, right? Like ... Having, like, more energy than, like, in other classes. That's what I kinda feel like in Drama class.

Margo also addressed drama's pedagogy in her analysis:

Adam: Do you think working with imaginary worlds, like we did with the story drama, teaches you in different ways from other classes? If so, how? How is that different?
Margo (White, female, second-generation Canadian, of British descent, grade ten student at St Bernadette's): It's different because it's not like book and paper. This way, you can really express yourself in other ways. But, in other classes, you're kind of like ... sit, desk, homework, check, done, new homework, you know? But this way, it's more like a flowing kind of thing.
Adam: So in other classes you don't really feel you can build on stuff as much?
Margo: You do build, but not in the same way. Like, with Drama you can start a topic, and then you can flow into something else, and then you come back. With other classes, it's more like, here's the textbook, read the chapter, then you're done, then you start something new. There's not really any flowing.

Rakemena was particularly eloquent on this point:

Rakemena (Brown, female, Indian-born, grade ten student at St Berna- dette's): Um, I think in Drama we do imaginary things and I think that makes you think more creatively about life.
Phil: What do you mean by that?
Rakemena: Like the Willow Maiden [a story drama we did with them in the course of our research] makes you think okay what if I had been a tree, or

what if that was a real situation in our life, like in today's world, what if
trees were alive, what would happen? You think about it more, whereas in
computers and things, you're not actually doing imaginary things.
Phil: *Sounds like you think that's a good thing. What are some of the benefits*
of thinking imaginatively?
Rakemena: *Um, I think it makes you appreciate life more and it makes you*
think that it's good to think about different things.

There were a few students who had complaints about their drama
classes. But, in these instances, their dissatisfaction was with their teacher.
The students felt strongly that drama should be different from other
subjects, more open and creative; when it is not, they blame the teacher,
that is, they blame his/her rigidity or lack of emphasis on drama as
play and discovery. We heard, over three years, very few complaints
about the subject of drama. When students were not happy, the problem, in their view, resided with the teacher and not with the subject.

Good drama praxis, in our shared view, is the antedote to standardized tests. Most critics of Ontario's high-stakes grade ten literacy test,
which must be passed in order to graduate from high school, insist that
it forces teachers (and students) to follow a scripted curriculum. Drama,
as the students repeatedly described, should, and often does, operate
from another kind of logic. As we shall see in the following chapter, in
drama, meaning is analogous, personal, collective, metaphoric, improvised, and ambiguous, but rarely scripted. Both teachers and students
draw on previous experiences, cultural and embodied knowledge, and
raw instinct to navigate the curriculum and come to new or deeper
understandings.

3 SUBJECTIVITIES

The Social and the Artistic

But, to act, which is precisely the object of the theatre, is to change the world and in changing it, of necessity to change oneself. Fine. The bourgeoisie has changed the world profoundly, and now it no longer has any desire to change itself, above all from without. If it changes, it is in order to adapt itself, to keep what it has, and in this position, what it asks of the theatre is not to be disturbed by the idea of action.

Sartre, 'Beyond Bourgeois Theatre,' 52

Notwithstanding theoretical compatibilities with Sartre, I began this research persuaded, all the same, that drama in urban classrooms – in spite of the power of the status quo – opens up necessary imagined and real spaces for border-crossing and for imagining change and action, even in reactionary times. Our desire, then, was to observe where and when this important opening up happened, and in other cases, where and when and why it did not.

Can issues of power, aggression, safety, inclusion, and exclusion be productively addressed in high school drama classrooms, despite the institutional, pedagogical, and curricular constraints? My work in schools has proved, over and over again, that 'inclusion' and 'exclusion' are complex social processes that are negotiated and enacted moment-by-moment in classrooms. As the winds of the 'global education' movement gain considerable velocity, drama pedagogy, importantly, speaks to significant questions related to ideas of community and difference. It also, as theatre activist Augusto Boal (1979) would argue, critically disturbs the world of the bourgeoisie: 'The bourgeoisie already knows what the world is like, *their* world, and is able to present images of this complete, finished, world. On the other hand, the proletariat and the oppressed classes do not know yet what their world will be like; consequently their theater will be the rehearsal' (142).

⌐ Deborah Britzman (2001) is one theorist who often invokes the arts to think about pedagogical actions. Can 'imagining' the experiences of others help us better know ourselves in any way? She is asking whether, in aesthetic terms, we can somehow come to know ourselves through knowing the complexities of others: 'Is it ever the case that it takes one to know one? Are we unequipped to encounter anyone different from the imagined self? What does the writer draw upon to do such work as imagine different countries, different genders, different sexual orientations, and different histories?' (22). To know the other, then, becomes a question of both art and ethics.

The performances of adolescents/adolescence in the drama classrooms that we observed in our ethnographic research made explicit the dialogical relationship between the material subject (and her/his histories) and the imagined one. If we are raced, classed, gendered in particular ways, and entangled in certain configurations of power/powerlessness, how do we move beyond limiting conceptions of ourselves and others, if Sartre is to be believed when he posits that we are forever in the 'look of the other'? For we are both self- and other-constituted:

Phil (White, male, American-born, research assistant): Um, so something that came up in the focus group was this idea that Drama gives you freedom to express yourself. (Liza: Mm-hmm.) Do you agree with that based on your personal experience?

Liza (White, female, second-generation Canadian, of British descent, grade ten student at St Bernadette's): Yeah I do because you know as a lot of people have said, in other classes you're just told to write down your thoughts on a piece of paper and like some people can't do that, you know, because like I know I can't. Sometimes I can, but usually I kind of have to act them out. And that's how I think it is. I think you can just, you can show yourself a lot more from acting and being in a Drama class than you can by writing it down on a piece of paper. Like people get to know you, like they get to know how you're like by performance and stuff.

Phil: And why is that important to you?

Liza: It's important because a lot of people have this image of me which is not necessarily good, and by being in Drama and you know goofing off and having a good time you know making people laugh it gives them a new outlook. You're kind of like 'Hey maybe she's not this person we thought she was' you know?

Actor, writer, and academic Anna Deavere Smith (2001), when asked what motivates her to act, replies: 'On stage, I feel less bound by the notion that there is only one representation of myself in the world. Acting provides the possibility of metaphor and it is a way of taking the audience to another place' (132). We might take Liza's comments above in this light. There is always the possibility, in acting, of serious 'goofing off,' of 'goofing off' for real. Drama, at the very least, offers a flexible means of self-representation and this seems to be identified and especially valued by the youth we spoke with. When Deavere Smith is asked to expand on her definition of acting, she says, 'The actor is a vehicle of consciousness, projected through a fictional character, and the fiction displays great truth (ibid.).

Drama's pedagogy asks that the 'natural'(often stereotypical) images of 'self' and 'other' be given an element of the conspicuous. Practitioners often wonder what shape their pedagogy should take to promote the 'actorship' (Miedema and Wardekker 1999) needed for people to become the co-authors of their cultural narratives (cited in Bayliss and Dodwell 2002). On the street, youth tell us that there is little room for imaginative thinking or experimentation with one's 'identity.' The stakes are simply too high:

Ricky (Latino, gay, male grade twelve student at Redmount): Yeah, but, you know, people make their assumptions about everybody on first impressions, like, you know, Leroy, for example, I hear he gets, what, 99% average?

Leroy (Dominican, male, grade twelve student at Redmount): Yeah, I do good in school, yeah [laughs].

Ricky: But you look at him, you know, any teacher's going to look at him and say, 'Oh, he's wearing baggy clothes, oh, he's going to be a bad student, he's going to be trouble.'

Leroy: And then, I go up to them, and say, 'Hi, how're you doin?'

Ricky: Yeah, and then they get a little jumpy, you know?

Phil: Uh, huh.

Ricky: But I think that scene is everywhere. But, like, teachers do make their decisions on past experiences, which is good in a way but bad in a way because people have changed, and, you know, like me. I change my outfits

up. Like, one day, you know, I'll look like some preppy boy in Manhattan,
and the next day, I'm looking like I just came from – and it's funny because
the way I dress when I walk into a store, you know, with some preppy
clothes on, everybody's like, 'Oh, ok, he's cool,' and then I'll walk into that
store with my stuff on, and I'm getting looks all over the place like I'm
going to steal, you know?

If the space of the drama class is different, and the students say that it is, then there is one important question to ask: Can drama pedagogy do more than help the principles of inclusion along? Can it fundamentally reconstitute the negotiations among collaborators so as to create new modes of attending to and creating with others? If it can, we are one important step closer to discerning how a large and diverse high school, in Canada or the United States, or anywhere in the Western world, might minimize the schism between what schools purport to do for, and in the name of, students and students' disappointing and some- times damaging experiences of school.

⸢In our research we repeatedly asked: Can drama pedagogy make the critical, feminist tradition more 'practical,' 'lived,' and effective at the level of the everyday?⸥Just what does dramatic space open up? Does it ask from where we draw 'inspiration'? Can the influences of interpreta- tion be uncovered? And what analyses move alongside our 'impro- vised' creations? By bringing the embodied subjects into sharp relief, we not only ask where we are located but where we are imagining ourselves moving, in the fictional and the actual worlds. Drama peda- gogy offers a sense of trajectory, that is, identities/characters that can shift, change, take action, and move forward. This kind of flexibility and improvisation is increasingly less common in the school curricu- lum. Too much 'emancipatory' pedagogy implicitly claims to know the direction to liberation. And this, as we saw every day in schools, has not worked well for many students.

In his well-known play *Huis Clos* (*No Exit*), Sartre puts three charac- ters in hell and makes each of them the other's torturer. In Sartre's philosophical writings (1965) he fashioned the idea that 'hell is other people.' But Sartre did not simply believe that our relations with others are necessarily poisoned; this is, according to Sartre (1973), a misunder- standing of his work. He believed, instead, that other people are the most important means we have for knowing ourselves; we judge our- selves with the means other people have given us for judging ourselves. Sartre is arguing for a theatre of situations, not of characters, such that in our story-telling and our character construction we are responding to the situations at hand. It is, therefore, our actions in a given situation that create our character(s). Following this line of argument, one might also begin to ponder the kinds of situations of choice that could occur in classrooms: Under what conditions might I make my idea public? In which dialogues will I participate? How might I extend the artistic input of another? What positions of compromise allow me to collaborate? How does this situation / these people shape my performance? These questions point to the significance of the self–other relationship in theatre collaboration, in particular, and classroom relations in general. The use, therefore, of the concept of subject positions, from poststructuralist theory, is important to classroom research. The act of creating, then performing, a 'subject position,' or one's 'subjectivity,' points to the interactional negotiation of identity that Sartre is, himself, examining through theatrical metaphor.

It is also the case that drama education holds firmly onto the ideal that collective art can be imagined by differently positioned individuals within a group when they are involved in a collaborative process (see Booth 1994; Spry 1994; O'Neil 1995; Simons 1997; Winston 1998; Neelands 2004; Nicholson 2005; Ackroyd 2006). Most theatre practitioners tenaciously insist that, as Adrienne Rich (1993) says, an 'I' can become a 'we' without extinguishing others. This does not mean that drama always creates successful collaboration. Yet, in drama classrooms, pedagogy becomes a device that serves the art, and it is a social art form that benefits from divergent perspectives, as I will illustrate in the closer examination of the improvisation work and theatrical writing of the students presented in this chapter. Simply put, drama takes difference (and sometimes conflict) as its starting point rather than its challenge. In Niela's play that will be examined, for instance, conflict is central to her dramatic writing. But other students too speak eloquently about how their own writing and performing is engaged by the vastly different, and sometimes conflictual, perspectives that get included within the wide-angle lens of drama's pedagogy.

Returning to Sartre's premise for a moment, a theatre of situation, like improvisational drama, shifts emphasis away from fixed and predetermined meanings to the *context* in which meaning is produced. It is a precondition of emancipatory projects in drama pedagogy that change through art is possible. Paradoxically, however, the possibility of ever fully knowing *in our bodies* the material strategies of others, the limits of being, relating, and creating, in a social milieu such as a classroom, remains beyond drama's pedagogical grasp. That is why the emphasis on context and action becomes central.

It is important, at this point, to reiterate that the aim of our research was not to assess how effectively four very different drama practices held up the ideals of an emancipatory drama pedagogy. What we witnessed over three years with four different drama teachers would likely be representative of the wider field in the sense that we were privy to vastly different ideological and artistic emphases in drama practices. At Redmount, we often watched the largely Hispanic and African American students prepare Shakespeare monologues for state and national competitions held by organizations that promote the speaking of English, or we watched them prepare one-act plays they would perform for the community at an evening performance. At St Bernadette's we often watched students creating dramatic pieces around religious holidays like Christmas or religious interpretations of other holidays like Thanksgiving. They also worked from textbooks and were expected to learn the 'skills' and 'craft' of theatre production. At Amor, the teacher, who so clearly made it her mission to help create positive experiences of any kind for students who have had little success at school, often turned her curriculum over to the students as they developed improvisations that explored the notion of 'social cohesion' in literature and popular culture. Finally, at Middleview, the teacher was most attuned to the cultural ruptures between 'school life' and 'home life' experienced by her students, and thus developed a drama curriculum that would invite exploration of these disparate worlds.

Schools are places steeped in liberal humanist values. That is why notions of empathy, and 'walking' figuratively in another's shoes, are featured so prominently in most curricular constructions of drama education, no matter how different the particular practices might be. For instance, analyses of students' conversations go some way towards explaining what my research assistant Dominique has dubbed 'the unofficial multicultural doctrine' (Gallagher and Riviere 2004). As will be demonstrated, it becomes a very complex activity to discuss issues of race and racialization (which many students prefer to call 'background') when discourses of commonality and racial transcendence are ubiquitous. Students' relations are firmly located within the languages of multiculturalism. And yet there are clear moments, which will also be demonstrated, when race, for minoritized students in particular, becomes the most meaningful way to differentiate their world. This chapter will deconstruct four very different kinds of drama 'lessons.' But more than attempting to explain the curiosities of the drama curriculum, this chapter endeavours to unpack the stories of gender, race, and power relations that circulate among young people; these stories, in schools, effectively construct the category of 'adolescence' and often become the fodder for their creative work in drama. The first story, which takes the form of a well-crafted drama lesson, involves (officially) the study of movement activities, a Shakespearean text, improvisation, and whole-group discussion, but I use it here as a demonstration of a familiar set of dynamics we have watched play themselves out repeatedly in our urban sites. The second lesson speaks to the kinds of ethnographic artefacts that are particular to school-based research. Writing and engaging with others' writing is a common practice in drama classrooms. In this instance, the writing of students in one high school precipitated a certain crossing of borders for students of different social locations. This episode also clearly illustrates how the use of personification, analogy, and metaphor can become a form of resistance where youth culture vies for space in the canon of the official curriculum. The third lesson clearly demonstrates the limits of tolerance in liberal notions of education and asks what values related to sexuality and gender schools should reflect. It comes from a passionate classroom discussion, inspired to some degree from a travelling theatre company's play about HIV/AIDS; the episode undeniably unravels the homophobia brewing just beneath the surface of most high school classrooms and the tensions of religion in the 'secular' spaces of a public school. It also clearly demonstrates the reach of hetero-normativity in schools generally. In this instance, we encountered what cultural anthropologist Victor Turner would call a 'social drama.' Turner (1982) argues that social dramas occur when the equilibrium of norm-governed social interaction is upset. In our episode, deep conflict and anger lay just beneath the surface and resulted in a crisis of communication. The fourth lesson is an extended improvisation in which the whole class (including the researchers) entered into a fictional world together in order to investigate issues related to youth's concerns with a security-obsessed culture bent on minimizing 'risk.' In this lesson, 'we hold a mirror up,' in the familiar theatrical sense, to the various policing measures inflicted upon a fictional group of workers (the youth in role) in order to see how this kind of theatre pedagogy and analogous thinking might explore our sense of the imagination as *occupied space* in the current criminalizing of youth in and out of schools. These 'lessons' occurred at Middleview Tech in Toronto.

Social Dramas: Relations of Power, Gender, and Race

Works of art shimmer with self-consciousness. They are tentative, speculative, they create anxiety in the beholder. But they do not will communication, it is not a prima facie characteristic of their existence. That they do communicate something – almost certainly distortion – is an effect of their subjectivity encountering the subjectivity of the beholder.

Howard Barker, *Arguments for a Theatre*, 135

The ethnographic observation in year three of the project begins with a call to Ms S, the evening before, to confirm that Monday October 18, 2004, at 9 a.m. would still be a suitable time for our research team to arrive. The 'back-story' I get, however, is about a 'blow up' that happened in her classroom the Friday past. According to Ms S, two Black girls with 'a lot of power' in the classroom were taunting a fourteen-year-old White girl who, they had learned, was dating a twenty-year-old man. Another Black boy in the class stepped in to defend the White girl and Ms S, too, warned the students that it was inappropriate to talk about others' personal lives in the classroom in this way. There soon erupted a screaming match between the two Black girls and the Black boy, which ended with a deafening 'FUCK OFF' as the Black boy stormed out. What Ms S explained to me was that this boy, who was adopted by a White family (although she does not believe that the other students are aware of this), is read as 'White' by his peers, and his defence of the White girl was all the evidence needed to fuel what Ms S describes as a constant antagonism towards him. We were to arrive the Monday after this class. She didn't know whether Marvin would return, but wanted to warn us that there might be some 'debriefing' at the outset of the class. This was the context into which we were arriving.

Researchers always arrive mid-stream. Classrooms are forever in the middle of an on-going set of relationships. Although we were in our third year of research at the school at the time, and very familiar with it and with Ms S, this particular grade eleven class would be new to us. As we walk in, the students are amassed in a jumble of seats at the opposite side of the room. They are talking, listening to headphones. One male student, named Rally, is showing another female student his resumé. She teases him for including that he graduated from the 12th grade. About twenty minutes in, we have a class of nineteen students: six female, thirteen male, twelve Black, six White, one Asian. The first thing

Ms S tells them is that she will be in school tomorrow but not teaching their class, so they will have a supply teacher. Rally says, 'Are you sure you wanna do that Miss?' Ms S explains that we have guests today and that she is going to let them introduce themselves. She then says, 'This is Dr Kathleen Gallagher,' at which point a student calls out, 'You just said you were going to let *them* introduce themselves.' Laughter. Ms S agrees and I add, 'I can see that they don't let you get away with anything.'

When I tell them that Ms S used to be my student, Rally asks, 'Did you give her all F's and E's like she gave me?' Ms S explains that Rally has been a student of hers since Grade nine. Rally responds, 'Yeah, Grade 9 I had her for English first period and she failed me.' Ms S corrects, 'It wasn't first period.' Rally retorts, 'Oh okay, I just remember being very cold in that class.'

Rally is a tall, Black boy, braided hair, with a very expressive face. He rules this classroom with his wit and dominant persona. Today he is wearing the de rigueur baggy jeans, oversized shirt, hoodie, and the threads of an unstrung 'do rag' hang down in front. He has a cadre of two girls and a boy who act as his chorus, his audience, and his confidantes. Throughout the class he plays to them while staying in enough touch with Ms S that he doesn't get himself thrown out of class. Very nearly everything he does or says is for effect, to gain the attention of the class, but most importantly his friends.

Ms S's lesson is creative and well structured. She wants her students to make connections to the play *Macbeth*, which they will see at the Stratford Festival later in the year. She begins with a set of movement activities to warm the class up. For this, they need to stand in a circle. Ms S is continually asking Rally to stop talking and to join the circle. He complains that she is picking on him. Ms S tells him that she does this because he is a leader. He says, 'I'm not a leader, I'm a follower like all the other jackasses in this class.' Rally seems to want to be free to contribute whatever and whenever he wants without any accountability.

A White boy, Ely, turns to us and says in response to his classmates' antics, 'Somehow I don't think this will look good in the academic paper.' Ely is a withdrawn, stocky boy with a whine in his voice. He plays the role of dissident, often issuing cynical, wry, or critical comments about what is transpiring, usually with his head bowed and his stare fixed on the floor in front of him. We learn later that he has Asperger's syndrome.

Suffice it to say, the warm-up activity does not go very well. Ely says, making particular reference to the outside eyes in the classroom, 'We look like such idiots right now.' Moments later Ely walks by one of the research team on his way out of the room and says, 'You think this class is full of idiots, don't you?' Phil replies, 'No.' He says, 'Hmm. Well, you're wrong.' And with that he's out the door. Rodriguez (1998) might suggest that Ely's and Rally's engagement with us is pedagogical in the sense that they are attempting to educate adults about the malleability and contestedness of youth culture.

Ms S moves on to an interesting activity in which she asks smaller groupings of students to create tableaux (frozen pictures) spontaneously, as she calls out lines from Shakespeare's *Macbeth*. 'Screw your courage to the sticking post!' The students scramble to create something but there is palpable frustration in the room. Cries of 'That's not English!' 'Who talks like that!??' 'Nobody knows what they're doing!' But Ms S continues and before long I am reminded of how much students learn from their peers in a drama classroom. There seemed to be a few students each time who had some inkling about what the words meant. They quickly shared their interpretations with those around them and before long students were relying on one another to find the meaning.

Sitting in a circle again, Ms S asked the class what they knew about the position of women in medieval times. One boy yelled, 'They had to wear steel briefs, man.' 'Yes,' replied Ms S, 'some did have to wear chastity belts.' A White girl added, 'They just had to stay in a castle all day and wait to marry some rich guy.' A Black boy, Marcus, added, 'Yeah but that's just like gold-diggers now. They're women who marry for money not for love.' Ms S wants them to focus on the social prohibition against female achievement in feudal society, but the students are engrossed by popular culture references, prostitution, sex, anything to shift the movement away from the discussion at hand. 'But what would a woman who had ambition do in those times if she was limited by the social and cultural constraints of her day?' 'Be Zena and carry a sword or be Oprah and take power.' A Black girl finally finds the response Ms S is fishing for, 'Oh you mean like Nellie McLung?' 'Yes, tell us about Nellie McLung, Felicia.' 'Oh she was this stupid lady who wanted women to have the vote in Canada. Something dumb from grade ten History.' A White boy asks what a 'wench' is. 'That's what women are,' another boy replies. Ms S goes further, 'Now this ambition that Lady Macbeth had ... how can we understand that?' A Black boy replied that it's 'just like Adam and Eve, when Eve ate the apple and screwed

everything up for Adam, because all women are like that, they're ma-
nipulators.' Tenisha, a Black girl replies, 'Adam didn't have to eat it.
Just shows you how weak men are when they think they're so strong.'
Jerome replies, 'Yeah but if he didn't, he wouldn't get some of what he
wanted later that night.' Omnipresent understanding of men as preda-
tors, women as prey. Ms S suggests that such biblical stories often
portray women as evil. It is not clear at all whether the students made
the connection that it is a view we perpetuate rather than a reality; the
ensuing wilful misreadings are abundant. I am forcefully reminded of
how young women often demonstrate a strong investment in understanding how social organizations function because they have been,
historically, as Arnot (1982) has argued, positioned in the most disadvantaged places within them. The students continue to have some fun
with Lady Macbeth's line about 'unsex me.' But one Black boy understands this to mean Lady Macbeth's attempt to become a man: 'Ooh,
they did that in these times too? That's disgusting shit!' Ely, in response
to the tittering, says, 'It's not physical, stop the dirty stuff.'

There's a familiar divide at work in the seating arrangement: the
loud, funny, 'unruly' kids on one side; the quiet, shy, 'obedient' kids on
the other. Indeed, later when Ms S asks Rally politely to move to the
other side of the circle away from his cadre, he says, 'To the winners'
half?' Jerome, a Black male, hair pulled back in a bunch and one of
Rally's friends, says, 'Oh so I'm a loser then?' to which Ms S says, 'There
are no winners or losers.' Rally responds by launching into a monologue, 'Yes there are. The bums on Queen Street are losers. The losers
are on the street and the winners are successful in life ...' His classmates
encourage him with laughter. At one point in the frenetic, wide-ranging
discussion that refuses to be *Macbeth* or Ms S's carefully planned lesson,
Ely says, 'Nobody really loves anyone.' Rally retorts, 'Romeo and Juliet.'
Ely says that they would have fallen out of love if they had waited long
enough – 'Better they died when they did.' Ely is the voice of teen angst,
a smart young man whose world view is bleak. He appears to be an
'outsider' in this classroom. Ms S makes clear the discussion was intended to give us some insight into why Lady Macbeth is so intent on
getting her husband to ascend to the throne. Unfortunately, tropes
about women as gold-diggers, witches, and hookers overwhelmed what
was meant to be a feminist take on Shakespeare.

Ms S explains that they will now try an improvised scene between
Lady Macbeth and Macbeth, where they would all try to imagine how
Lady Macbeth might attempt to persuade him to find the ambition to

kill Duncan. Rally throws his hand up to volunteer to play Macbeth. A White girl, Tanya, offers to play Lady Macbeth. It is hard to know why Ms S chose Rally. The reasons are complex, but one thing is certain: she is working hard to make him responsible for his behaviour. As might have been predicted, however, Rally subverted the activity immediately, playing to his friends, and when Tanya – in role – said, 'I want this as much for you as for me, my love,' Rally responded with, 'I'm not really thinking about that right now, babe. I'm horny.' As Rally is doing his 'performance' and sexualizing every exchange between him and his co-improviser, another student laughs and says, 'He's like a kid in a candy store.' An astute observation it is; he's getting all the attention he craves, but like a 'sugar high' it's never enough.

After many such 'attempts' at the scene, and Ms S's patient intervention on several occasions, she thanks Rally and Tanya and tells them they can be seated. 'Why do you always cut me off, Miss? I'm always cut off' are Rally's parting words. Ely says to nobody in particular, 'It makes my head hurt.' Ely speaks his mind, although he also seems to have made a decision to be so clearly contemptuous of Drama and everyone in it that he is granted immunity. People just laugh him off, or disregard him entirely.

The physical work Ms S was attempting to do with this group was not successful because their performances *as students* were so overpowering that they could not, either physically or intellectually, enter into the possible dramatic interpretations or personas available.

Ms S asks them finally to read aloud a scene from *Macbeth*. There is not much enthusiasm in the room when she invites the class to take on roles. Averted eyes everywhere. Finally, she chooses three students, all three from Rally's group. At the end of the reading, Ms S asks what 'illness' in the play would attend ambition. A Black male student who is sitting on the window sill apart from the circle responds, 'They'll kill somebody to get what they want. Or they'll sex anyone.' This is Marlowe. Moments later, Marlow gets up and strides slowly through the middle of the circle to leave the room. He has asked to go to the bathroom. But in the centre of the circle, he stops, adjusts his pants, does a few dance steps, then walks out. It is commonplace for students here to 'perform' for each other, but this often displays disregard for the teacher and the work at hand. Another reading of this, however, might suggest that the interactive element of audience response in hip hop culture, 'the grammar of hip hop embodiment,' which celebrates 'the idiosyncratic, the offbeat, the polyvalent' (Gordon 2005, 379) is at play in the classroom.

And given the relative freedom that Ms S affords her students, the latter may in fact be the case. In this, and other instances, however, it works against her and makes it near impossible for students to remain focused on Ms S or her lesson.

We arrive at the end of class. Ms S asks each student to rearrange three desks and chairs. By the time we leave class, the lone Asian boy is quietly replacing all the desks and chairs himself. Never heard a word from him in the class; we wondered what sense he makes of it all.

Phil and I talk to Ms S after class, mindful of avoiding the appearance of being scandalized or thinking that the class was a disaster, and yet wanting to provide some input on how to untangle some knots. By year three, Ms S talks openly with us about her teaching choices and seems to welcome 'outside eyes.' I advise her to put in place some rules for conduct, in consultation with the students, so that she doesn't have to spend so much time reining them in. Phil kindly explains that he sees need for more structure and clearer consequences. We all agree that right now Ms S is working too hard for too little return. I suggested that I thought making the students party to negotiations over how they are going to work on this unit might decrease all the interruptions. Fine, Weis, and Powell's critical look at 'safe spaces' (1997) is pertinent. They point to the 'constructed negative' of the 'other' in schools and argue that democratic participation does not evolve spontaneously within multiracial groups of youth:

> If schools are to produce engaged, critical citizens who are willing to imagine and build multiracial and multiethnic communities, then we presume schools must take as their task the fostering of group life that ensures equal status, but within a context that takes community-building as its task. The process of sustaining a community must include a critical interrogation of difference as the rich substance of community life and an invitation for engagement that is relentlessly democratic, diverse, participatory, and always attentive to equity and parity. (252)

From the drama-practice perspective, one might also speculate that the students did not yet care enough about *Macbeth*, perhaps had little reason to care, that the 'hook,' as it is often described, had not succeeded in inviting and sustaining their interest. We knew Ms S would not give up, though. The next day, she would be back at it, labouring to make it matter.

As researchers we head off, back to the university, feeling almost guilty about the world we leave behind. It is a privilege and a challenge to watch a teacher work so hard. We are also now privy to the students' difficult and complex struggles with issues of power, privilege, race, class, and gender. In one lesson, we clearly observe how youth subculture becomes deeply entangled with discourses of race, gender, and (hetero)sexism.

From this description of one lesson, on a first day in a classroom, it was important to move forward with caution. As researchers, we needed to observe further the extent to which race and racism, sexism and homophobia play into and grow out of the relations between peers and between teacher and students, because we are interested in helping students and schools work more productively despite these ubiquitous high school dynamics. Part of a critical response is to first make visible some of the modes of behaviour and communication, and the levels of discourse, operating in the room. And, as Sleeter (2005) has argued in her study of how White teachers construct race, a structural analysis that views racism not as misperception, but as a structural arrangement among racial groups, is necessary. One of the ways we decide to proceed is first to set up clear guiding principles for relating to one another, and, then to turn to the creative work itself to capture the students' critical imagination.

Imaginative Trespassing and Ethnographic Artefacts

A private wisdom is being proclaimed from the rooftops. There is no contradiction in this. It is a contrived miracle – well, a trick of the trade. Because the public utterance must still retain that private intimacy where it has its origins. And even though the audience hears what it calls speeches, it hears too the author's private voice, that intimate language, that personal utterance. And that composite, that duet – the private and intimate set free into public canticle where both voices are distinctly audible – that is what makes the experience of theatre unique. And every time that happens the theatre fulfils itself again.

Brian Friel, *Essays, Diaries, Interviews*, 173–4

The performed and written 'documents' of this research took the form of acted performances, improvised role-playing, originally and professionally written playscripts, character writing-in-role, and solo and collaborative dramatic presentations. Doing research in a drama classroom is a dynamic activity. Culling data from the embodied interactions – the engagement with texts or 'scriptive acts,' as Trinh (1989) has coined it – and the acted performances of students is a very different enterprise from conventional qualitative participant observation modes or interview methods. Because we are talking about a kinaesthetic art form, we attend to the bodily situatedness and the social locations of participants and researchers within the fictions. Often, these 'fictional' locations are in dynamic dialogue with the 'realities' of their lives. And because we are talking about a kind of art/theatre project that relies heavily on the imaginary, we must attend to the monologic and dialogic creations and improvisations of the inventors of dramatic worlds. In short, the 'artefacts' piece of our methodological work represents a more direct inquiry into the medium of drama itself and exploits this enacted medium as a special window onto issues of power, identity, affiliation, conflict, and creativity in inner-city classrooms.

Angelina (grade eleven student at Middleview) on the 'scriptive acts' (Trinh 1989) of youth: 'Um ... basically ... just ... telling a story that might have happened to you, and feeling good about expressing, like ... sharing your thoughts and feelings and your memories with other people. And revealing, maybe, your past.'

Writing inspired through drama is a crucial source of 'data,' an important way to begin to understand how young people manipulate the medium and make tangible their dreams and imaginaries. Niela, an Ethiopian girl at Middleview Tech in the first year of the study, explained to Ms S that she was bored with school. As a result of this conversation, Ms S challenged her to write a play. A few weeks later, Niela submitted a full-length play to her teacher. Ms S decided to incorporate it into her unit on dramatic writing. After the class had spent some time reading professional plays that the teacher hoped they might 'connect with,' she decided that the whole class should, together, read Niela's play. According to Neelands and Goode (1990), one of the most important purposes of metaphor in theatre is to invite comparison between what is being symbolically represented and the real area of experience that is referred to. With Niela's permission, they proceeded to take parts and read her story. It was not, according to Niela, very far removed from her 'real' life. Although the play has the face of realism, it, too, is a constructed reality. The play begins this way:

Bleeding between the lines
by Niela H

Scene One
Yazmine (she is narrating the story): 'To be or not to be that is the question:
which once a great writer William Shakespeare wrote. What did he meant by
that? I'm the age of 17 and an only child of divorced Black African parents. I
had a lot of time on my hands so I wrote poetry, lyrics and stories. Oh I forgot
to introduce myself. My name is Yazmine Ahmad, I know it's not an African
name but my parents wanted to be different. I always wanted to be a singer,
writer, model, or fashion designer but things can hold you back like being in a
grave six foot under with no way out. You're probably asking how did that
happen to a 17 year old that doesn't do anything but write. I have no answer to
that but if you live in the hood, you don't have a problem the problem have you.

The play, curiously, had three endings, in the following order:

Scene Fifteen
(A week later. At Liyah's birthday party)

Yazmine: Is everyone love it?
People: Yeah.
Yazmine: Good.

(She walks over to the bar and hugs Liyah.)

Yazmine: Happy birthday girl.
Liyah: Thanx girl.
Yazmine: No prob. Now let's have fun.

(She grabs Tamia and Liyah to the dance floor. Yazmine's mom come to
Liyah and hugs her. Suddenly Andre and his boys walks in the club.)

Yazmine: Who told him about the party?
Tamia: I don't know.

(He comes behind Yasmine and kisses her at the back of her neck.)

Yazmine: What do you want?

Andre: You.
Yazmine: It's over.

(Dwayne and his boys surround Andre and his boys.)

Dwayne: I think you should leave her alone.
Andre: Why? So you can fuck with her.
Dwayne: You think you're bad nigga?
Andre: I'm the hardest nigga up in here.
Dwayne: Yeah, you really think you the hardest nigga?

(They start pushing each other and Yazmine goes to break it up. Then Yazmine spot one of Andre's friends pull out a gun. She pulls Dwayne out of the way. Unlucky, the bullet that was meant for him got her in her back.)

Dwayne: No.
Yazmine: It's ok.

(Yazmine's mother push away the crowd to find out that her only child was shot.)

Yazmine: I love you.
Mother: Yazmine ... No!!! Why my baby?
Yazmine: Well yeah that my story and as you can see life isn't always fair. That's just the way it is.
The end

Ending Two
(Dwayne and his boys surround Andre and his boys.)

Dwayne: I think you should leave her alone.
Andre: Why? So you can fuck with her.
Dwayne: You think you're bad nigga?
Andre: I'm the hardest nigga up in here.
Dwayne: Yeah, you really think you the hardest nigga?

(They start pushing each other and Yazmine goes to break it up. Then Yazmine spot one of Andre's friends pull out a gun. She then grabs the gun from him and shoots his friend.)

Dwayne: No Yazmine put the gun down.
Yazmine: No they almost killed you.

(Then suddenly Andre shoots Dwayne.)

Yazmine: No ... Dwayne no.

(Dwayne falls to the floor and she runs to him.)

Yazmine: Dwayne talk to me.
Dwayne: I love you ... you was all I had.
Yazmine: Please don't go.

(He did answer ... she cries turns to Andre.)

Yazmine: This is for everything you did to me.
Andre: What are you going to do.
Yazmine: Shoot you ... I hope this hurt cuz I know I am.
Mother: Yazmine ... No

(The screams of fear fills the air as he drops to the floor. Everyone runs out of the club and the police runs in and arrest her.)

Yazmine: Well yeah that's my story and as you can see life isn't always fair. That's just the way it is.
The End

Ending Three
(Dwayne and his boys surround Andre and his boys.)

Dwayne: I think you should leave her alone.
Andre: Why? So you can fuck with her.
Dwayne: You think you're bad nigga?
Andre: I'm the hardest nigga up in here.
Dwayne: Yeah, you really think you the hardest nigga?

(They start pushing each other and Yazmine goes to break it up. Then Yazmine spot one of Andre's friends pull out a gun. She pulls Dwayne out of the way. Unlucky, the bullet that was meant for him got her in her back.)

Dwayne: No.
Yazmine: It's ok.

(Yazmine's mother push away the crowd to find out that her only child was shot.)

Yazmine: I love you.
Mother: Yazmine ... No!!! Why my baby?

(Everything pause and lights are off in a few moments Yazmine is on stage now with spotlight on her.)

Yazmine: STOP ... did you notice that every Black story end up like this ... It's not like it don't happen a lot but the point is that is shouldn't even happen ... Can someone give me a remote control ...

(Someone walk on stage and gives her a controller.)

Yazmine: Thanks. Now I'm rewinding all this and go back to a place where I felt peace, where I felt safe and where I can make a change ... So let's rewind ...

(Everything rewind and now Yazmine is a little girl. She was sitting with her mom and dad.)

Mother: So what did you talk about in school today? (The mother is fixing Yazmine's hair.)
Yazmine: Well we was talking about what we want to be when we grow up.
Father: So what do you want to be?
Yazmine: I don't know but I know I want to be alive.
The End

From my previous study of drama in classrooms, I have learned that the 'Other' in drama class is an important part of self-understanding. In researching the social, several important studies argue that the construction of a 'Self' is very clearly articulated through the fixing of an 'Other' (see Razack 2004; Weis 2003; Kimmel 1994; Fine 1994; Hall 1991; Giroux 2005). Drama, by definition, is a social art, not a solitary experience. People make theatre for others to see, or in the case of classroom drama, it is often the self-spectatorship that makes for the important 'audience' experience. In drama, as in life, we are self- and other-constituted. Because the shared reading of Niela's play seemed to be a significant experience in the classroom, I asked some questions about the experience in our first focus group (a mixed-sex group in this instance, although we conducted single-sex focus groups as well), partly wanting to understand one young woman's impact on her peers and partly wanting to follow up on my earlier research in drama (Gallagher 2000) that situates learning in the interactions between players, in both their 'real' and 'acted' behaviours and performances:

Kathleen: So, here's my first question: what was it like for you, reading Niela's play ... as a class?

Nate (Male, Latin, heterosexual, Portuguese, atheist, working class, difficult, misunderstood, spontaneous, straight up): It was ... it was different, because it came from a student, not like ... not like ... some guy that writes plays all the time.

Kathleen: Ahh ... right, right.

Nate: Yeah, so ... It was, like, interesting to see, like ... to like read some – like, a rookie play.

Kathleen: Right. And did it have an effect on what you ended up eventually writing yourself?

Nate: Well ... yeah. Because ... I ended up writing something ... something that actually happened. And that's, like ... It just – it just ... made me write something more real than, like, what I would have wrote.

Kathleen: Ah, okay. More based in your life?

Nate: Yeah.

Andre (Male, African Canadian, heterosexual, English, a little Patwa [Jamaican], Christian; phrase: If you want it you'd better work): Like, me, I knew Niela for long, and ... to see that she could write something like that, is just, like ... a eye-op – it's just a, a eye-opener to me, because, like ... that was a good play. And I, like ... it's like ... it's like, what ... we're going through, like, a lot these days. So, it's like ... I – I'd be ready to perform that play any day.

Kathleen: Hmmm ...

Andre: Yeah.

Kathleen: That's neat.

Angelina (I am female, I was born in Halifax Nova Scotia. But I'm Hungarian. I speak Hungarian, French, English, and a little bit of Spanish. I'm in Grade 11. I do not work at the time. I like to latin dance and just basically dance to any music. I also like sport, almost every sport.): I have something to say. Um, I think Niela's play gave us a lot of advice ... on how to *treat life, and ... like ... how to live our lives differently. She, like ... it's advice. Like, not to get pregnant, or not to have ... not to go into ... drugs, or ... stuff like that.*

Kathleen: *Do you mean it had lessons in it for you, in some way?*

Angelina: *Yeah.*

...

Kathleen: *What was the experience like of writing your own play? I understand you've done that most recently ...*

Angelina: *Express our feelings [rising intonation]. And, um ... basically ... just ... telling a story that might have happened to you, and feeling good about expressing, like ... sharing your thoughts, and feelings and your memories with other people.*

Kathleen: *Hmm. So, that was a –*

Angelina [interrupting]: *And revealing, maybe, your past.*

Kathleen: *Does that happen more in Drama than in other classes, do you think?*

Angelina: *Yeah.*

Kathleen: *Are you describing something like personal sharing? [Murmurs of agreement from the group] Why is that ... do you think?*

Angelina: *'Cause ...*

[Several people start to talk at once.]

Angelina: *Because ... other subjects are based on –*

Alessandra (White, female, second-generation Canadian, of British descent) [interrupting]: *In Drama we get to do more plays about ... ourselves, and stuff like that, and work with other people.*

Angelina: *Drama's basically expressing your feelings, and ...*

Alessandra: *Yeah.*

Angelina: *... showing what you have beneath ... everything ...*

Nate: *Yeah, you don't really have a chance to do that in other classes. Except for, maybe, English, like ... during certain ... certain times.*

Kathleen: *Novel study? Or –*

Nate: *Yeah.*

Andre: *Drama ... Anywhere ... there's Drama, you just ... open up to the real you. Like, you don't gotta ... hide. Just, yeah. Just, open your mind, just express yourself.*

Alessandra: *Like, act it out. Not like ... you don't write reports, or anything. You just act. Like, you ...*

Kathleen: Okay, so tell me this ... I'm going to pick up on something you're
all – you all seem to be saying: how come it – does it ever make you feel
very exposed to your peers? Because we all know it can be ... stressful,
to be ... in – in high school. So if you are expressing all of that personal
stuff, and it's the 'truth' about you, how do you feel safe ... in Drama?
Andre: It's just ... Me, it's just take it or leave it. Like ... when I'm in a Drama
class, it's just ... I'm just gonna be me. That's it. That's just it. I just ... I
just lash out, and I don't care.
Kathleen: Right.
Andre: I just like it. That's all.
Kathleen: Andre, is it different in other classes?
[Nate starts to say something.]
Alessandra: Other classes, I'm still myself, but ... I open up way more in ...
Drama situations.
Kathleen: Huh.
Nate: And, you're basically allowed to [be open], because, like ... it's Drama,
and you're, like, you're acting out, and if you make a mistake on acting, or
if you have – and, you gotta, like ... you gotta show yourself anyway. So,
it's not like you're ... it's not like you can be embarrassed. If you did that in
the street, or something like that, it'd be a whole different story.
Kathleen: Right.
Angelina: And, you're not the only one [rising intonation]. So, everyone else
is co-operating, and ... and acting out ... And, maybe they're acting like
themselves, or maybe not. But, you still – you still don't feel alone [rising
intonation].

There is no question that the 'group' feeling, however that is differently
understood, is significant. Nicholson (2002) put forward an important
idea about trust in the drama education field. Here, trust is viewed as a
performative act, wherein the emphasis shifts to participants' demonstrations of their trustworthiness and towards problem-centred resolutions. The group renegotiates, at every instant, what trust looks and
feels like as they collectively explore their similar and different feelings
and cultural beliefs. This would be a multicentric approach that situates
'difference' as central to, not a diversion from, the possibility of collaboration. Students also stress the importance of accomplishing something,
or succeeding at something despite being young. Nate, in a later interview session with Adam, helped us to also understand the individual
stakes of 'success' within the group:

Adam (White, male, first-generation Canadian, of Polish descent): What do you think might prevent you from being actively involved in drama class?
Nate: Um [seven second pause], well nothing now, cuz, I'm just interested in uh, just, I guess, it's just like a whole new opportunity. I had other opportunities, but I blew them, and now, to me this is like, this could be probably like my only chance to actually get something going.
Adam: How do you mean you blew them?
Nate: Just, over stupidness, like [seven second pause], you know, just regular kid stuff, just skipping off, and all that time, the time back then, and, I blew, I blew getting into English and stuff, becoming an English teacher. I blew chemistry. So, yeah, I got this last opportunity, I guess. [Nate's voice has gotten really quiet by the time he finishes.]
Adam: What made this one different?
Nate: It's actually fun. I like writing English, so, and then after, and watching your writing getting done with actions, it's a whole, uh, whole different story.
Adam: How does that make it different?
Nate: It just, it brings life to your words.

The students in the class took a great deal from the experience of sharing the writing and imaginaries of a peer. Niela's story is a deeply gendered and racialized story. It is written as a memory play, and throughout she explained that it speaks of her own experience as a Black, female, only daughter of a divorced parent. These were obviously very significant identity markers for Niela and it is also what her peers most clearly heard and responded to in her play. One can never be sure to what extent life seeps into dramatic writing, what liberties are taken, what imaginative trespassing has taken place, in the journeys into one's own or another's life.

Anna Deavere Smith (2001), well known for her play *Twilight: Los Angeles 1992*, based on the L.A. riots, says, 'I create plays in which I play many different characters. I tell a story with many differing viewpoints and build a picture of a large community, using only me (133). When I asked Niela if she would consider talking to us about her experience of writing the play and having her peers read it, she wrote a very long note that she gave to me the next day. It began:

As I entered drama I thought I would only enter the class for the credit but I came out with a new experience and a way in knowing myself more. I like the surroundings, the vibe, the support that drama gave. For people like me that don't find that often in school, it has been real helpful. Drama has been my escape from the real world and the more I've involved myself into it, I find my peace in mind through drama. I always thought I wasn't really shy until I've really got into drama but when I started, I seen myself shy more often. Some of the reason for that is because I am scared of reading out loud and when I do, I stutter or trip over my words and I hate hearing myself sounding dumb ...

Following the class reading of Niela's play, Ms S asked the students to begin their own piece of dramatic writing. They were to start their own monologue (a shorter piece of dramatic writing) from the simple prompt 'I remember ...'

Andre: I remember growing up how everyone was tight with each other. Everyone would chill. Everyone would go to the parks, to the pool. Now you look around from those days and there's only about three or four people still keeping it real. Girls I grew up with are pregnant Niggas. I chilled with boys who are dead and people who I used to look up to are long gone. All I can do is laugh and just keep my head up. I feel like a fool. I can't believe I'm in this car with my tightest boys about to go into this bank and jack it up ... 'Alright we're here. Everyone spread out and grab a different teller,' one of my boys say. Now we're in the bank dress in Black from head to toe. 'GIMME THE MUTHFUNKIN MONEY BITCH' is what I heard. This is going too fast for me. I freeze, look around. I'm the only one left. What was I thinking? I feel like such a fool. The only thing left to think is will I rat on my boys or do ten years either way.

Mohammed: I remember when a kid walking in streed of Afghanistan. Looking all these things around, thinking that I will grow up and do something for my heart ... knowing nothing except that I almost got killed by a bom. I remember bin laden meeting me. That's just a joke. I remember the things that happens to me and my family. I remember those people that gived their life [to] me.

After some sharing among peers of their written dramatic work and the reading of Judith Thompson's monologue 'Pink' – about a ten-year-old White South African girl talking to her dead Black nurse in her open coffin, shot in a march – a very heated discussion ensued about racism. Many different opinions were expressed. The vast majority in this class are students of colour, with a minority of White students. The tension was apparent in the room right from the start, but there were also strong attempts to argue for 'colour-blindness,' an insistence that there are 'bad people in every race.' The most vocal in the class were urging what appeared to be a notion of equal discrimination for all races, that 'bad people' are bad whatever their race. There was very little understanding of systems of racism and, unsurprisingly, most students cited personal experiences as the grounds upon which to present their 'un-racist' or 'understandably racist' attitudes. In drama classes, the material often leads to these kinds of open discussions on issues of interest. Most drama teachers would recognize this description of a passionate, vehement debate following a drama activity.

The following day, Ms S had her students reflect in writing on the previous day's discussion with the following prompts: What did you agree with / not agree with? Why? What are your thoughts today? What would you like to add to our discussion? In drama processes, there is the possibility of both reflecting within the drama and reflecting upon it, usually some time after the experience. Andre's reflection, included here, elucidates the strategies and 'attitudes' many Black students speak of in such candid discussions:

Yesterday in class most of the things that came up were racism. Racism towards Blacks, Whites, Asians, Afghanis, Pakistanis etc. ... how things were then and how they are now. Things that I said were the difference between a Nigger and Black person. I don't know if the world thinks all Blacks are Niggers, but there's a difference in my view and a lot of other people's. A nigger can be any ignorant person whether Black, White, Asian. Most of the time a nigger is Black but a Black person is just like any other humble person on the street. Things I heard other people say in class were things like when an average Black male gets murdered, the news doesn't really give any background on him compared to a White person or a celebrity. I agree with that statement fully because I see it happen all the time. What I wanted to add to the discussion was even though all of the apartheid and racism that went on before, and still is going on, people of colour especially blacks have come a long way. I haven't really suffered any direct racism in my life but I can tell because of the way I dress and look that people think lower of me. I've noticed that when I first came to the school last year that a certain teacher didn't even get to know me before he started insulting me. Of course I didn't take that abuse, I had a few words to say about him to his face before I dropped his class. On the street, people will eye me, and I've been stopped by cops countless times for minding my own business. Sometimes all you can do is laugh at stuff like that.

Andre's analysis corresponds to that of other Black youth who pitch 'ghetto' performances of self against notions of 'acting White.' In her case study of a California Partnership Academy, Staiger (2005) cites youth who explained the difference between 'nigga,' which they said was an insider term, and 'nigger,' which they said was a racist slur. Andre, above, is offering 'nigger' as a degradation that is befitting any 'ignorant person' of any race. As with many studies of minoritized youth, the power of the racial boundaries of identity is palpable.

As researchers, we are left asking what strategic or coping mechanisms are being invented and refined by youth in order to survive the essentializing and destabilizing forces at play in complex urban classrooms. This research, then, became greatly interested in looking at drama's capacity to break open the limited and limiting discursive and aesthetic practices and prescriptions of school life. How are such issues of cultural hegemony and power both absorbed and confronted by youth? We saw clear evidence that drama provokes passionate debate, but can it do more than 'explore' these issues? Foucault (1984), considering a 'disciplinary society,' posits that the disciplines are techniques for assuming the ordering of human multiplicities, that the disciplines *oppose* the instrinsic, adverse force of multiplicity. In *Discipline and Punish* (1977), he further argues that with the advent of disciplinary mechanisms in the period of the Enlightenment, '[a] "political anatomy," which was also a mechanics of power, was being born; it defined how one may have hold over other bodies, not only so that they may do what one wishes, but so that they may operate as one wishes, with the techniques, the speed and efficiency that one determines. Thus discipline produces subjected and practised bodies, "docile" bodies' (138).

But what of drama that crosses disciplinary boundaries, drama that breaks out of timetabled activities and thrives on the productive tensions of multiplicity, or what Foucault might have, later, described as the behaviours of productive citizens? What does imagination count for? Does drama, by nature, stand for something different in the highly disciplined and regimented routines of 'school'? This last question was provoked by two formidable experiences in one of our research sites. These two experiences, recounted in the following two sections, serve to demonstrate the kinds of exclusions, the force of cultural hegemony, the challenges to safety experienced by youth, and the issues of institutional and peer surveillance and control that we found pervaded urban schools.

The Gay Other Not among Us: Sexuality and Its Guises

Theatre draws apart. It draws the audience away from its beliefs. It draws the social from the individual. It draws the individual from himself. At the exit doors, the audience finds it hard to sew its life together again. Some of this audience secretly hopes it cannot be drawn together again.

Barker, *Arguments for a Theatre*, 127

It was the day following an HIV/AIDS theatre presentation by a travelling company that Ms S, at Middleview, tried to carefully balance her commitment to running a classroom that did not patronize young people *and* to protecting a volatile space that was fast filling with hateful commentary about homosexuality. As was her style, Ms S was deeply interested in what her students thought of the performance. The play, itself, did not address homosexuality in any way; it followed the stories of two straight couples who had contracted HIV. What is presented here comes from the compilation of four copious sets of notes, of four researchers, who aimed to follow verbatim the vehement discussion from start to finish. It is 6 December 2002.

Dramatis Personae
Ms S: Teacher, White, female, Jewish, Canadian-born
Dion: Black male, Jamaican-born
Shahbib: Brown male, Iraqi-born
Perry: White male, Canadian-born, of Estonian descent
Natalie: Black female, Caribbean-born
Niela: Black female, Ethiopian-born
Janus: White male, first-generation Canadian, of Greek descent
Craig: White male, first-generation Canadian, of Spanish and Scottish
*   descent*
JP: White male, ethnicity unknown
Nate: White male, first-generation Canadian, of Portuguese descent
Lenna: White female, first-generation Canadian, of Portuguese descent
Rosaria: White female, first-generation Canadian, of Italian descent
Kathleen: White female, first generation Canadian, of Scottish descent,
*   researcher*
Dominique: Black female, first-generation Canadian, of Caribbean descent,
*   research assistant*
Phil: White male, American-born, research assistant
Brent: White male, Canadian-born, ethnicity unknown

Paula: Black female, Canadian-born
*Adam: White male, first-generation Canadian, of Polish descent, research
assistant*
Viviana: White female, first-generation Canadian, of Portuguese descent

Ms S: What did everybody think about the show yesterday?
Dion: Was one of the actors gay? It's screwed up in the head to be gay.
*Shahbib: Look at all the pretty girls in the world, and you're going to fall in
love with someone named Bill?*
*Perry: With all the stuff that's happening in the world, why do people care
about gays so much?*
Natalie: Gays carry disease. That's why people care.
*Ms S: Natalie, is that what you got from the show, that gays carry disease?
Before we go on with this discussion, I am going to ask you to think before
you speak. If what you are saying is homophobic or full of hate, I am going
to ask you not to say it. Homophobia is just like racism; it's hating some-
body because they are a member of a group.*
Dion: People choose to be gay. It's not normal.
*Shahbib: It's a disease – it is not natural. My religion says to punish gays –
there have to be 2 or 3 witnesses, then you can kill them if you find them
together twice.*
Niela: What about a girl and girl being together?
Janus: Why do gays have to show off that they're gay?
*Shahbib: Every book, religious, that is, says it's wrong. I don't hate them;
I hate what they are doing.*
*Craig: Let's think about it democratically. Just like during Black History
Month we respected that and learned about that.*
*JP: Being gay is the result of having too much female hormone. What if
somebody with Turret's Syndrome swore at you, would you punch them
out?*
*Perry: No gay person has ever robbed me, punched me, beat me up. Has a gay
person ever beat you up?*
*Natalie: If kids see homosexuality on television, like two men with a baby or
something, that would be really bad for them. But I say just be what you
want to be, if you are homosexual, just be that way.*
*Nate: I have no problem with gay people. I agree with Natalie, though, I do
have a problem with two gay people raising a kid. It might make them be
gay when they don't want to.*
*Ms S: Kids are exposed to many things, as I am sure many of you in this
classroom are aware, but that does not mean that they will grow up to*

become what they see. As long as parents love their child, it is a very great gift, no matter who the parents are. But this idea that children will become what they are exposed to is just baloney. If that were the case, gay people wouldn't become gay, because they are always being exposed to hetero-sexual culture.

Shahbib: Is God not true then?

Lenna: Pre-marital sex is a sin too and you have pre-marital sex.

Shahbib: Yeah, but that is not as bad as homosexuality. Being gay is much worse.

Rosaria: I think if a gay couple raises a child it might mess up that child since it will be difficult for them to go to school and see how different they are. Guy and guy and girl and girl is weird.

Kathleen: Raise your hand if you have ever heard of divorced parents. [Many hands in the air]

Ms S: There are all kinds of families – not just one type of family that is right.

Dominique: You say that it is tough for children who have gay parents, but think about children who have bi-racial parents. It is just as tough for them because some people think that is wrong, so are you saying we shouldn't have bi-racial couples?

Shahbib: But it's not the same thing, it is not natural, it's not right.

Ms S: Shahbib, that is what the KKK says about people of different races being married.

Shahbib: So if I have sex with a dog in the privacy of my own home, is that right? Since I am not doing it in public, you can't criticize me can you?

Phil: First of all, the dog cannot give its consent to having sex with you, so if you are equating homosexual sex with rape, you are wrong. Secondly, you mentioned that every religious book on Earth says that it is wrong to be homosexual. But if you check, you will find that every religious book also says that it is wrong to judge another person. We are taught to respect and love each other; otherwise we get hate and hate leads to killing.

Ms S: Shahbib, we have talked about this before. I understand how practicing your religion can make you feel vulnerable. There are many times where I feel vulnerable practicing my religion because people might want to kill me for my beliefs.

Shahbib: What if you were in a religious state and they said it was wrong to be gay. Would you criticize that?

Ms S: It would depend on whether I was of that religion or not. But, yes, many people criticize their religion. I have many criticisms of my religion but I still consider myself a part of it.

Craig: What's funny to me is that America is a male-dominated world. You never see anything about lesbians though. Guys are scared of gays because *they are worried that they might become gay. [This prompts much laughter and cross-talk.]*

Janus: *I'm okay with my sexuality. I know that I think she's hot [indicating Niela]. I work with guys who are gay. When I first started working with them, I didn't like them. But then when I got to know them and I didn't know they were gay, I liked them. Then what am I supposed to do when I find out they are gay, turn my back on them?*

Nate: *Gay sex is wrong because it doesn't create life.*

Ms S: *Plenty of heterosexuals have sex without having children; they do it because it feels good. By that criterion, you would be discrediting heterosexual relationships as well.*

Brent: *I'm no religion, so this may be easier for me. It's all lies – I follow my own rules. Being gay is not for me, but what's the difference between me liking women and other men liking men? Do whatever makes you happy? Think about witch hunting – how many innocent people lost their lives? And all they were doing was using herbs as medicine, and that's okay now. Religion is just used as something to hide behind.*

Janus: *Dion, you are not okay with yourself.*

Dion: *Why do you say that?*

Janus: *When you find out a friend of yours is gay, you're going to punch him out? Then he is not really your friend; you don't really like him for who he is.*

Niela: *You can't judge gay people – they are human.*

Rosaria: *How can you be so hateful when you don't even know a thing about it?*

Dion: *When you learn something as a kid you will not forget it for the rest of your life.*

Craig: *Think of humans as animals, because we are all animals. Think about dogs having sex, they enjoy it don't they? And we all know that if you go to the zoo you will see monkeys masturbating.*

Kathleen: *Craig has brought up a really good point. In high schools we never talk about sex as pleasurable, so we all hypocritically pretend that that's not why we like it.*

Craig: *Let me ask you this: where's the male G-spot?*

Niela: *I was taught to reject gays – everybody, my parents, my friends, my religion, taught me to hate gays, but I don't. You have to realize that if you don't accept them it is because you are close-minded.*

Shahbib: *I agree, but in this case it is okay to be close-minded.*

Kathleen: *That's just what Hitler said about the Jews. 'I'm a Christian but in this case it is okay to kill.'*

Dion: *Yeah, well, what does that matter? Hitler's dead.*

Phil: Hah! He's alive and well.

Janus: Where, I don't see him?

Paula: In people's minds.

Natalie: If you were gay, you wouldn't think it was wrong. I have gay friends; that doesn't make me gay.

Janus: You say being gay is wrong, but so is pre-marital sex.

Shahbib: I agree. But being gay is worse.

Kathleen: It would help not to attack people; attack their ideas if you must, but let's avoid attacking people directly.

Rosaria: People are scared and defensive. They're scared of what they will find out.

Shahbib: I have read a little bit of the Bible, but I don't know everything it says in there. But in the Qur'an – I am not going to bring it in because I don't care what you think – it says that if you meet someone who's gay you should try to change them. And if that doesn't work, and you have 2 or 3 witnesses who see two people actually having sex you can punish them. And you can even kill them – and I have no problem with that.

Craig: If extra-terrestrials came to Earth what would you think?

Vivianna: They're trying to take over the Earth?

Craig: Right, you jump to that conclusion because people don't know how to handle the unexpected.

Nate: Shahbib, how does it make you feel when people like you are targeted as terrorists?

Shahbib: I don't like it, but I also don't mind it. It depends. There are 300,000 Muslims in Toronto. When a man who was going to one of the mosques was found to be gay, he was thrown out of every mosque. Every single Muslim agreed that he should be thrown out of the Nation of Islam.

Rosaria: What if a group said we should throw heterosexuals into the sea? [She was picking up on Dion saying that gays should be thrown in the sea.]

Dion: They couldn't – I'd like to see them try. We are too strong. Let them try.

Natalie: I'm going to ask a question: if gays ganged up on heterosexuals, how would you feel?

Dion and Shahbib: Don't worry about it. It's not going to happen.

Perry: People following religion, I have noticed that they only follow the rules they want, and forget about the rest.

Niela: Let's just end this conversation; we're not going to change their minds (gesturing to Dion and Shahbib). This isn't new to me, I have talked to them before about this, and they aren't going to change their minds.

Ms S: I don't think we should think about this as only educating two people. We are all learning by being involved in this discussion. It's an important discussion to have, along with talking about racism and sexism.

Dion: Why does she always bring racism into it?

Ms S: This is a conversation about divisions within societies. And I know it is hard to sit here and listen to it.

Perry: I don't hold it against them for how they feel. I feel the way I do, and they feel the way they do. But it is better to talk than to fight.

[At this point Dion stands up and leaves the classroom without explanation.]

Rosaria: You can feel what you want, but it has to be grounded in reasons. You can't just say what you think without having some reason for it.

Shahbib: Miss, what does the Torah say about gays?

Ms S: I don't know exactly, but I do know that it says that if a man masturbates he should be stoned. I'm Reformed, I practise, but I am not observant. I have lots of problems with the teachings of my religion.

Kathleen: I have taught in high school for ten years, and in university, and have observed a lot of classes and I have to say that this is one of the most engaged debates I have ever witnessed. You are lucky to have Ms S as a teacher. Other teachers might have shut this discussion down in a minute. Even though it is difficult, it is also important to expose these conflicting views if we want to move ahead and be responsible for a more just society.

Ms S: I'm going to cry – I'm sorry, I feel very emotional. I love this class a lot ('We love you, Miss!' they respond). I want you to know that I respect what people say and that doesn't change what I think of you. We always have very intelligent discussions in here. I hope we can be more open in the future to having our views challenged if they exclude or marginalize others.

Perry: American History X is a great movie about just this stuff.

Ms S: It's fitting we have this discussion on December 6th Does anybody know why?

Shahbib: Canada's first massacre. Fourteen women in Montreal.

Ms S: Right. And why did he kill them?

Niela: Just for being women.

Ms S: Right.[6]

---

6 This verbatim scene, and three others not included here, became the basis of a staged ethnographic play that Philip Lortie and I performed at various academic conferences.

These kinds of heated debates are characteristic of many drama classrooms. In this instance, the work of a travelling theatre company had provoked the classroom debate. And in this charged discussion, constructions of masculinity, femininity, sexuality, gender, race, and religious belief were batted about the room at lightning speed. To be sure, homophobia, in this classroom episode, was central to the ongoing constitution of heterosexual masculinities (see Nayak and Kehily 1996). Kimmel's definition of masculinity, and examination of its social construction and interactions with race and sexuality (1994), helps us understand more about the ways in which homophobic attitudes get rationalized, normalized, and even justified in many school contexts. Kimmel writes:

> I view masculinity as a constantly changing collection of meanings that we construct through our relationship with ourselves, with each other, and with our world. Manhood is neither static nor timeless; it is historical. Manhood is not the manifestation of an inner essence; it is socially constructed. Manhood does not bubble up to consciousness from our biological makeup; it is created in culture. Manhood means different things at different times to different people. We come to know what it means to be a man in our culture by setting our definitions in opposition to a set of 'others' – racial minorities, sexual minorities, and, above all, women. (120)

For Kimmel, the development of masculinity is a 'homosocial' experience. 'Man' is self-made and based on homosocial competition. Masculinity must be proved and proved again, for women, for other men, and for individual men themselves. Kimmel's hegemonic masculinity within the dominant culture is the masculinity that defines White, middleclass, early-middle-aged, heterosexual men. Citing Brannon and David (1976), Kimmel suggests that this dominant masculinity relentlessly repudiates the feminine. He argues: '[W]hatever the variations by race, class, ethnicity, or sexual orientation, being a man means "not being like women."' 'This notion of anti-femininity,' he offers, 'lies at the heart of contemporary and historical conceptions of manhood, so that masculinity is defined more by what one is not rather than who one is' (126). What is particularly key to Kimmel's argument is that the perfor-

---

We hope to perform the theatre piece further at high schools. The entire play and its subsequent analysis has been published as K. Gallagher (2006) 'Sexual Fundamentalism and Performances of Masculinity: An Ethnographic Scene Study,' *International Journal of Gay and Lesbian Issues in Education* 4(1) (2006).

mance of masculinity is basically *for other men*. In insisting that masculinity is a homosocial enactment (whose overriding emotion is fear), he argues that men are constantly under the scrutiny of other men. 'We test ourselves, perform heroic feats, take enormous risks, all because we want other men to grant us our manhood' (129). Kimmel proposes further that homophobia is a cause of sexism, heterosexism, and racism – a compelling argument given the dynamics on this day at Middleview. Shlasko (2005), too, persuasively suggests that '[r]acism, sexism, and homophobia together seek to regulate people's sexuality in specific ways that make meaning not only for sexuality but also for gender and race' (125).

Our teacher at Amor in Manhattan, Carm, is very conscious of anti-homophobia policies in her school and seems to feel some responsibility for implementing such progressive policies in her own practice as a drama teacher. What is also clear from her description of her context is how homophobia works effectively with sexism and racism, and that the best efforts at 'inclusion' do not, in any fundamental way, challenge the power relations in her diverse classroom. For males, being 'included,' first in an artistic and then in a social sense, means being swept up in a complex web of oppressive relations of gender and sexuality. In short, it means being able to perform the right kind of (hyper)masculinity:

Carm (White, female, American-born, of Italian descent, teacher): Right, because what happens is that, um, it [acting a role that is different from who you are] opens up the dialogue.
Kathleen: Right.
Carm: We're a school that has zero tolerance for, for (Kathleen: Homophobia) ... homophobia, yeah. We're not allowed, we have a verbal abuse policy, so you're not allowed to call anybody 'fag,' you know. You're not allowed to call anybody, you know, 'dyke' ... And, um, so ... it, it just fits into who we are, about, you know, learning to get along. And, what happens is that, like, in the show, um, they [the students] wanted to put in a scene about what the hallway feels like at the 10-minute break, because the show is about school tone (Kathleen: Right), because we're having issues with school tone. So, this hallway scene is our most ... macho ... you know, 'gangsta,' you know, 'guys,' and it's a gauntlet. It's a gauntlet for the women, and it's a gauntlet for our gay men. And they don't like the way it feels. And, in this scene, one of the gay students, they included him in it, they're like, 'Salvador, you be in this scene, you be in this scene.' And, he's uncomfortable ... Like, you could see that he doesn't overdo it. But, he's in the scene. So, it's including him in, in a world where he ... normally,

outside of this room, he isn't included (Kathleen: Mm-hmm ...). And, in
this room, the guys asked him to be a part of that scene (Kathleen: Right
...). Now, my other gay student's not as out as Salvador. He's very ... he's a
lot more sophisticated in his way. And he just felt like [paraphrasing her
student] 'No, I don't think I could pull that off. I'm not kind of like ... I'm
not very "ghetto," so I don't think I could pull that off.' Whereas Salvador
does put on the whole, kind of like ... [imitates Salvador's demeanour], you
know, like that kind of thing. So, he can pull off being ... you know ...
ghetto-ish ... But, he's gay and he's out. He's very out (Kathleen: Uh-uh
...). And the kids are like, 'No, you be in this scene, you be in this scene.'
Not like, 'Oh, he can't be in this scene 'cause he's gay.' No, he's an actor
(Kathleen: Right ...) and he's gonna play this role (Kathleen: Right ...).
And so, that made him feel ... 'Oh, okay, I'll be in this scene.' Where would
you see that happening in a high school setting except in a drama class,
where people are able to do ... you know? He would not be chosen in this
group, to hang out with this group (Kathleen: Mm-hmm ...) outside of this
room.

Naturally, as researchers, we have great concerns about what Salvador
is being 'included' in, what 'proper' sexist and homophobic version of
masculinity he is able to don for the sake of the drama. We weren't
privy to any subsequent classroom discussions that attempted to
deconstruct these so-called normal and familiar social roles. The performance the teacher speaks of was aiming to conscientize the rest of the
school regarding issues of discomfort and exclusion that many students
feel in the hallways. As is always our worry with drama, we found
ourselves again concerned with the ways in which oppression is replicated – dramatically – in order to 'expose' it. In these instances, critical
analysis is often absent and students are left to accept the simplistic
message that homophobia and sexism are 'bad.' This, in turn, reproduces the erroneous assumption that prejudice is in people's heads and
the psychological view that changing the prejudices or misperceptions
people hold will change institutions.

  The heated scene at Middleview, presented above in its entirety,
provides an astonishing picture of the passion and fear with which
young people react to issues concerning sexuality. Policies of inclusion
or verbal abuse will, we fear, do little to address the complexity of
beliefs and assumptions about homosexuality, or the 'heteroprivilegist'
(Crowhurst 2002) judgments displayed in that discussion. Butler (1997)
might call this an instance of 'excitable speech,' a kind of hate speech

that has a performative force, that constitutes both the listener and the speaker through its illocutionary or 'shame-enacting' moment.

A critical element of homophobia, according to Pronger (1999), is the fear of the erotic violation of gender: the fear of the exposure of the tenuousness of gender and the fear of the disruption of power relations. The students' insistence that gay men have too many female hormones or that two men with a child is profoundly 'unnatural' would suggest that an erotic violation of gender, and not simply an irrational fear of homosexuality, is at the centre of the students' expression of homophobia. These fears also confirm their belief in a dichotomous sex-gender system: that there are only two sexes and that gay men (and lesbians) can only be explained on a female–male continuum. Butler (1993) argues, too, that an emphasis on the social construction of 'gender' leaves unchallenged the biological determinism of 'sex.' '[T]oo many female hormones,' therefore, or any such challenge to biology can only lead to notions of abnormal gender. Paechter (2006), in her study of constructions of masculinity and femininity in schools, offers that schools 'constantly collapse gender, which could be read as being about masculine or feminine behaviour and preferences, into sex, that is, bodies by treating children according to those [bodies] ascribed to them as sexed beings' (130).

Students' general discomfort with sexuality is affirmed by our teacher, Carm, at Amor school in Manhattan. As a drama teacher, she makes attempts to address this issue, and, in doing so, illustrates clearly Pronger's theorizing of the fear of the erotic violation of gender:

Kathleen: How do you break the barriers down ... between students?
Carm: Well, we do a lot of – we start off with a lot of name games, because, I want them to not walk in here and say 'She,' or 'He' ... get rid of that. It's got to be their name. And so, we do a lot of name games. But, I do it in a way that it's also a lot of body work, so they have to touch each other. And, then, I actually do some physical work with them, like, where they have to, you know, make contact. Um, you weren't here last week, but, sometimes I just have them come together and just hold each other's hands for ten seconds. And, I – I'm like, 'This is an acting technique.' But, it's really just to centre them, and for them to make physical contact. And, I won't tell them when I'm doing it, so if they're standing next to a guy, they have to hold the [hand]. That's a huge ... I mean, that's gigantic. High school? I mean, two teenage boys holding hands with each other for ten seconds? And they'll do this for a while and then break apart, and I'm like, 'Okay,

we have to start all over again.' Thomas [one of the students] will yell at somebody, 'Hold his hand! What's the deal?' So, you know, I'm like, 'What's gonna happen? Do you think that that's, like, something magic that, now, from this point on; you're gonna turn into a woman, because you're touching ...?' And so, I – by, day 4 or 5, they're doing trust work with one another and, um ... And, I do a lot of physical body work that's as goofy as possible. You know, like, doing silly – I make up silly dances, and I tell them, like, it's, you know, I'm gonna teach them a dance, and they're gonna be, like, insane, where they have to do really crazy manoeuvres, and I put on all different styles of music, and I tell them to try to fit that dance into the style of music. And, of course –

Kathleen: *So, this is the inhibition breaking?*

Carm: *Yeah. And of course, it will not fit. And, they're trying to make these steps fit, because I'll pick, like, um, an Indian piece of music, and the dance is very 1–2, 1–2 ... Indian music is not like that. And, they're trying to fit it in. And, so just the – the laughter, trying to make this dance work within that music, I just see it – just, it melts. The barriers just ... melt away.*

Kathleen: *I'd like to pick up on something you said, because the last time I was here, we talked about how this could be a space that might be more tolerant and open to people who – or students who ... don't fit the classic moulds (Carm: Mm-hmm ...). And, if two boys are afraid to hold hands ... would you have any students whose sexuality is not ... heterosexual, and so, holding hands with the same sex wouldn't be a distasteful thing to do? (Carm: Mm-hmm ...) How do you ... how do you incorporate that, or make your exercise an inclusive ... kind of activity?*

Carm: *Well, what ... What happens is that we make fun of it, actually. I was, like, 'You know, it sounds like we need to have a little bit of role-playing on what – how we develop our sexuality.' I said, 'So, if I said "one-two-three" right now, and I pointed to you with my magic finger, and made you ... and told you what sexuality you had to be, would that work?' [Mimicking her students]: 'Nooo ...' [Carm again]: I said, 'Oh, so how did you choose what sexuality you were going to be?' And they'll say, 'I don't know, it was just a feeling.' I'm like, 'Exactly. So, by me asking you right now, to make connections, to make contact, to hold somebody's hand, well, you're learning how to trust. And, am I changing – will I be able to change your sexuality?' [Students]: 'Of course not.' [Carm]: 'Well, then let's let go of any notions of that. So, my gay students who are holding women's hands right now are not going to be turning, you know, heterosexual, and my – my straight students are not going be turning gay. It's just a matter of making connections.'*

In Carm's explanation above, it is interesting that she is imagining that the homosexual students in her classes are boys, not girls. Our students at the Toronto girls' school, in a focus group discussion, had some disagreement about how 'safe' it was to be a lesbian in their school. What seemed clear, however, is that the school effectively silences any discussion about homosexuality, so that the sense of safety is dependent upon covert relations between young women. This is not simply because we are in a Catholic school. James Butler's research in non-denominational schools (1996) also explains the connection between masculinities and sexuality but also the apparent absence of lesbian identities in schools:

Kathleen: I'd like to ask a question that, um, is ... really comes from my sense that society is becoming more tolerant, rather than less tolerant. So, I'm wondering if you know whether there are any girls in the school who might be lesbians, who feel ostracized by ... the attitudes, especially in a Catholic school.

[A few seconds' pause]

Mara (Portuguese Canadian, second-generation, female, grade eleven student at St Bernadette's): I don't think they're ... feeling ostracized.
Kathleen: You don't think so? How come?
Mara: 'Cause, they're so –
Fanny (White, female, third-generation Canadian, of British descent): Open with it.
Mara: I wouldn't say open with it (Fanny: They are, though), Because they're not doing anything together, to show it ... (F: Umm ...) [some murmurs of disagreement from Fanny and Teimi] ... unless you've seen it [Fanny and Teimi begin to laugh]. Okay, whatever. So maybe – [she's cut off by all the laughter and cross-talk] ...
Kathleen: Right. (Mara: But, they don't care) And so the school doesn't – What does the school do about that?
Mara: Nothing. They haven't heard anything.
Fanny: Or, they don't know –
Kathleen: Is there a feeling that –
Fanny: [interrupting]: Yeah, exactly. They don't know about ... those kind of ...
Mara: Yeah.
Adrianna (White, first-generation Italian Canadian, female, grade ten student): Only the students know ...

It was further revealing that after the heated debate at Middleview, several of the female students in the class hovered around the class-room door after the bell, complaining to one another that they hadn't been given an opportunity to express their views. Two of the most vocal girls in this conversation were Muslim. Living their intersectionality, their gendered-racist oppression, they were obviously disturbed by their (double) 'silencing' on both issues of gender and faith. Instruc-tive here is Calliste and Dei's conceptual frames for working with the concepts of race and gender as categories of difference (2000). They suggest that anti-racist feminism raises questions about how to support 'difference' without simply reiterating an objectifying framework, and argue that 'difference' could be taken up more subjectively by paying attention to multiple, shifting, alternative socio-political and cultural positions beyond conventional categories such as gender and race (12). There is clearly a great need to theorize qualitative research that moves beyond the single-dimensionality and competing subjectivities of hu-man life.

Aware, too, of the politics of representation, and of the essentialism that obtains in the description of such scenarios, we researchers became particularly conscious of the dangers of this kind of essentialism in the classroom, of how pervasive and consequential it is when students of colour are positioned in empirical research in ways that 'reveal' them as standing in for their race/culture/religion, a move seldom made in the case of whiteness. Dion, one of the most vocal participants in the homo-sexuality discussion, a Jamaican-born, Seventh-Day Adventist, stormed out of the room towards the end of the discussion. Much later, in an interview, Phil asks Dion what might be going on on those days in class when he doesn't feel like participating:

Phil: Okay. So what might prevent you from being actively involved? So on those days when you think, 'Ahh, I don't want to do this'?
Dion: Um, sometimes the discussion. Depends what the discussion's about. Like for instance, I don't like the discussion about um for instance gay, I don't like to hear about them, you know? If they're going to discuss that, I want to be out of the class. That's just me, I can't change.
Phil: So yeah, we had that big talk about uh homophobia, homosexuality, and you were a big participant in that discussion. Uh, but then you did leave.
Dion: Yeah I did leave.
Phil: In your opinion, is there any good reason to have that kind of talk? Do you think there can be anything positive that comes from that?
Dion: Sir, that's just the way I grew up still like, you know. Back in my

country, that's how I see they react and it's hard to change because you know
like Friday I turned 19 and grew like that when I was one and I start under-
standing, you know what I'm saying? So it's hard to like you know, I'm just
going to stay with that decision, you know what I'm saying?
Phil: So, you don't think that will ever change about you?
Dion: Sir, I don't think so, straight.

Throughout the interview, Phil tries to understand whether it is that Dion feels that others in the class would think he was gay if he played a gay role or whether it is something else. In their conversation, he persists with trying to understand why Dion has demonstrably strong feelings about this topic. Finally, with a quiet eloquence, Dion explains very clearly:

Dion: Yes sir, it's something else. Basically, I don't care what people think,
  you know? That's just plant inside of me, Sir, I can't get rid of it, you know
  what I'm saying? Like, it's just in me you know, how I see people back
  home deal with the situation, the whole situation, gay situation, just in me,
  Sir, just in me. It's like it's plant, like, you know something that grew up
  inside of me like from a little plant, you know what I'm saying? Into a big
  tree, you know what I'm saying?

Two weeks after the classroom discussion, Dion was expelled from Middleview for brandishing a metal pipe.

The Middleview classroom discussion provides evidence of how sexuality, religion, and other identity categories and affiliations are being positioned against one another as a matter of course in high schools. Even as researchers, our bodies were made manifest, our subjective experiences drawn in, and our ethical responsibility challenged. It was clear, in subsequent discussions, that each of us felt culpable, disappointed in ourselves that we hadn't intervened more. We were struggling with some futile notion of 'objectivity,' and with our position as researchers in the classroom. Adam, in his researcher reflection, writes:

And I felt compromised. I had passed as straight. I have no doubt about that,
not after today. I kept looking for the little glances, the subtle body language,
kept listening for the murmured comments or stifled giggles, yet there were
none of those – I had successfully 'passed.' Part of me thinks that's great – my
identity hasn't compromised the research dynamic – and yet a huge part of me
rails against that. Does Phil wonder about whether being a man compromises

our research? Do Dom and Kathleen worry about what being women means for what they will hear or witness? Does Dom worry her blackness will change that? Do Phil, Kathleen, and I worry about the many ways our whiteness affects, or indeed limits, what we will witness, or even be able to see or hear? ... And I know one other thing – I would choose it, I would choose to be gay. I wouldn't have chosen it back then, when I still felt embraced by parents, culture, church, God, and felt blissfully unaware of the extreme conditional nature of that embrace. But knowing what I know now – knowing that being gay made me grapple with all these complex questions of oppression, power, difference, gender, sexuality, compassion, justice – knowing that struggle made me the caring, strong, proud, AWARE person that I am today – knowing all that, I would choose it again and again, and a thousand times over.

In my own reflection written a few hours after the episode, I can now hear how much more conflicted I felt than I was prepared to reveal to the students.

December 6, 2002. (The day, by horrible coincidence, that the Toronto District School Board layed off all social workers and attendance counsellors in schools.)
This day has been horrific in many respects. I was part of a 76-minute class on reasoned, justified, hatred of gays. For this session, gay had to be other. Gay had to be outside 'our' space. Gay was banished. So where did we go? I retreated into the chalk brush, the important task of delivering it to the person who was speaking, blaming, hating, imploring, defending. So much defending. Adam started journalling. Dom kept her head down. Phil wrote and spoke, wrote and spoke, wrote and spoke. I wanted to help Ms S keep order. I needed to help Ms S. I was trying to keep people protected in the room, even those whose views were abhorrent to me. Otherwise there is no hope for change. I could feel my heart pounding. I moved around the circle of chairs, hoping that my mere presence could assuage the fear in the room, calm the shaking hands of kids who dared to speak against homophobia ... Every time Rina spoke her hands shook. And pierced-up Rina is strong and confident ... What did I do when I taught? How did I not break down every second? After class, we instinctively brought the five chairs together, emotionally drained; each in our own turmoil but collectively carrying the burden of witnessing. Ms S shares that she has been afraid to tell us that she is going to leave teaching. She can't do it anymore. She can't exist in automatic pilot, as an authoritarian, or as the complacent teacher she sees all around her. It's not the school, she insists, it's the profession. 'Yes there are great and powerful mo-

ments, but you give so much and you get so little.' Over time, she is depleted. I fall in with my feelings of ethical compromise. Can I not do more with this research? We get to leave and she doesn't. On an ordinary day she has sushi with us for 20 minutes after class and then takes the rest of it with her on the run. She has more kids, classes, issues to take up. I feel guilt about this. I can't do more. I can't save her and I know wanting to is not right. She tells us she has to get out. My research assistants are kind and supportive and in their own hells. Phil is affirmed in his disdain for the institution. He vents and he should. Sensitive men like him need to name it, other masculinities that is. Adam is invited to speak by Phil. I have been giving Adam space to be silent, worried that he is not interested in speaking, trusting that he would speak if he needed to. He speaks. 'Do I out myself and risk it becoming all about me?' 'Do I out myself and forever change the role I am playing in this research, in this site, with these kids?' I remind him that it was not a safe space. 'I was scared actually.' I know he was. We all were; some more than others ... We talk a good long time the five of us. We hug in that way that anyone outside this moment would read as mushy or uncontrolled. We do it anyway. There was some comfort in this, this touching. So we do. Leaving Ms S behind as we always do, we move off, push off, pack it all back in, head back to the university. What is the ethical framework for conducting research in conditions drastically different from my own working and living conditions? I invite the RAs to write. Forget the research, just get it out. We may want to share it later. Get the notes out from the conversation but take space today to get your own thoughts out. Talk to people you love. Dom says she's going home. Phil says he's going to the computer lab to compose while it's fresh and he's on fire. He says he also wants to investigate alternative readings of the Qur'an. I drive Adam back to our office and he writes for 2 hours in his little notebook. I bring him a glass of red wine.

Being a party to this classroom discussion made it ever more challenging to conceptualize difference in abstract ways; bodies are present and always marked. Such episodes demand that we carefully rethink the linkages we draw between and among gender, sexuality, culture, experience, and race for ourselves as researchers and teachers.

The episode also clearly cautions us about representations of Islam in the West. Rizvi (2005) describes the 'intense struggle within Islam between those who view Islam in terms of an "authenticity" and those who regard syncreticity as essential to the development of a modern view of an Islam committed to democracy and justice' (176). In their study of identity experience among progressive gay Muslims in North

America, Minwalla, Rosser, Feldman, and Varga (2005), for instance, found that Muslim identity is three-dimensional – religious, ethno-cultural, and colour-based – when integrated with a gay identity: 'As a religious identity, gay Muslim's relationship to *Allah* (God) and a rein-terpretation of the Qur'an and traditional condemnation of homosexu-ality appears necessary' (113). Some of the views presented as 'Muslim' by Shahbib that day were later challenged in casual conversation by two Muslim girls in the class who had not spoken during the discus-sion. Several students alluded to that informal conversation in later interviews. This is what Branch (1996) might describe as lessons (in identity) learned from the competing curriculum. It is certainly a lesson again in the power of the informal curriculum and how much youth listen to and learn from each other. It is also a lesson in how calcified identities can become when they turn into the battleground for ideo-logical positions. In one interview, Peter was clearly trying to challenge such fixity of identity and reintroduce the complex social world that was left behind in the heat of debate that day in the classroom:

Phil: *Do you think talking like that changes anything?*
Peter (White, male, second-generation Canadian, of eastern European de-scent, grade twelve Middleview student): *What, openly like that?*
Phil: *Mm-hmm.*
Peter: *Yeah. More gets passed around, more information passes through and then people will get the chance to look at sides. Because a lot of people take this side without looking at the other side, right. I mean a lot of people look at the Middle East as a terrorist haven which I think is bull, because you don't look at what those people go through, you know, those people were practically starving so we can run our cars and have our big buildings like corporations, like Wal-Marts here. They're starving because of that, be-cause we pay them 50 cents an hour, even in China and stuff too. People don't think about that kind of thing right?*

Most certainly, the world of multiplicity destabilized the established school curriculum on that day. But what do such accounts tell us about how school knowledge and classroom pedagogy is organized?

Teachers, including Ms S herself, revisit their teaching actions regu-larly, and on this particular day Ms S was attempting to balance her desire for better understanding of those students most demonstrative about their homophobia with working hard to reclaim a 'just' and 'safe' classroom environment for all her students. If confronted by such a discussion again, she might make different choices. But what I most admired about Ms S's facilitation was her efforts to keep the doors to social justice open by pointing to the ways in which our (school) communities have been historically, and continue to be, cultivated through processes of exclusion and injustice. Ngo (2003) argues that the next generation of school-based initiatives on Lesbian/Gay/Bisexual/ Transgendered (LGBT) issues must focus on 'systemic change principles that address the larger interrelated nature of systems of injustice and oppression' (111). Further, Ms S's 'exercising of authority' (Rizvi 2005) was performed in ways that were ever conscious of the greater subjection to discrimination that is the experience of some of her students. As Kumashiro argues (2001), early LGBT movements tended to universalize gender and sexuality and not pay enough attention to how racism complicates heterosexism and gender oppression. Masculinity is, in our episode, demonstrably inflected with race, class, and sexuality.

Ms S is well aware of how some students, particularly minoritized ones, are currently constituted and how they might be reconstituted in public pedagogies. Even though postmodernism has effectively critiqued 'experience' as the unrepudiated grounds for knowledge, precisely because experience and perception are always mediated discursively, we still have before us, in classrooms each day, the material realities of students' lives that are unknowable to us in any real sense. In these instances, most teachers take their students' word for it. What they say they experience is the basis for what they know about the world.

Ms S never lost sight of her own position of relative power in the discussion and, therefore, her responsibility to her students. Nor did she allow heterosexuality to go unnoticed. She consistently brought heterosexuality into the discussion so that students might begin to question what it means to be straight, and not simply what it means to be gay. Like Sedgwick (1990), she considered sexuality an issue of continuing and defining importance in the lives of people across the spectrum of sexualities. While not specifically doing a 'queer pedagogy' (see Shlasko 2005), she did critique heteronormativity and condemn its violences while opposing, in several instances, the boundedness of identity. She accomplished her difficult work on this day by helping the youth in her charge to be heard and to hear things that invited them to think through the complexities of their own sexual, gendered, racialized, and religious identities and affiliations. And she remained steadfastly committed to them, even in the moments where their ideas seemed both unsophisticated and deeply offensive. One might say that she engaged with ignorance as a form of knowledge (see Luhman 1998 and Britzman 1998), and this, in teaching, is a courageous thing to do.

Dark Dramas: The Occupied Imagination

Any reaction to stimulus may be causally explained; but the creative act, which is the absolute antithesis of mere reaction, will forever elude the human understanding.

Carl Jung, 'On the Relation of Analytic Psychology to Poetic Art,' 23

During the course of our research, we frequently used drama as a research method. Drama educators think in this way; they privilege doing over talking. Just as researchers cannot ever know to what extent a respondent's stated reasons are consistent with or indeed explain her behaviour, theatre practitioners become wary of too much talk, having learned from bitter experience that an idea that sounds brilliant may not be reproducible on stage. Discussion (such as the homophobia episode reported above) and enacting (such as the improvised drama examined in this section) are, unavoidably, different forms of communication, each with their own rules, contexts, and expectations. As researchers we wanted to uncouple the notions of analytical distance and truth, to really engage with the students, to perform with them and follow the many different routes they might take to their truth claims. This forced us also to carefully think through what might get lost in the translation between our field study of theatrical enactments and our written analyses. We were troubled over how to construct meaning in our analyses that would remain faithful to the spirit of all that cannot be written, spoken, or removed from its context. In short, we conducted participatory research with the students in this study because we understood one of the primary tenets of drama itself as a research methodology to be that the fictional, active, and even unconscious world of the drama elicits understandings and utterances that would otherwise be inaccessible. Like Wilshire (1982), I accept that we should allow the possibility that art can tell us more about who we are and the cultural contexts in which we live:

[S]o theatre, philosophically understood, is the theory of acting and identity – or what we must suppose about persons if we would understand how it is possible for them to be convincingly projected and enacted on the stage. In sum: to recreate the world in a 'world' of theatrical imagination makes us aware of conditions of the world's being and meaningfulness that had before lain in the obscurity of the 'taken for granted.' (91)

The 'world as a stage' metaphor has little to do with masks and magic and much more to do with the dialectical interplay of life and art. And this is why the notion of 'performatives' (Austin 1962; Butler, Osborne, and Segal 1994) from postmodern theory has resonance. To put it most simply, drama brings people together in concerted action and, thereby, people bring worlds into being. In this way, drama performs an act rather than simply makes a statement. And the 'suspension of belief,' rather than 'disbelief,' in drama worlds has the possibility of renewing our perception, challenging our assumptions, and making the familiar strange. Philosopher Herbert Marcuse fittingly asserts that art is the practice of freedom and that our best protection against conformity lies in the expression of the 'uncolonized imagination' (Becker 1994, xx).

Doing drama with youth in the contexts of their schools told us something about the local organization of consciousness, but the unconscious manoeuvres, too, in drama pervade the discursive and social realm. This was obvious in discussions with students when they could not always rationally explain choices that they made in the context of the fictional. Redman (2005) describes this as an inner world of unconscious fantasy: 'From this perspective, then, the social is always saturuated with (indeed, at least in par, made and remade from) unconscious fantasy, just as the terrain of the unconscious is always saturated with (and, in part, made and remade from) the social' (535). Ricky, a Latino, gay, grade twelve student at Redmount, explained the metaphorical and subconscious work of drama in the following way:

I read a story where there's this guy, you know, who has a rough time at work, and every day before he comes home, there's a tree in front of his house that he touches, to leave all his anger with that tree, and all the frustration of his job on that tree. And he walks into the house and everything is left on that tree. And in the morning, when he's leaving for work, he touches it again to get it all back, so he can take it back to work because he has to deal with his problems. And I think that's what doing scenes and doing shows is for us, what we gotta put on the show, and then once the show is done, all that anger is left there, and we're able to move on.

What this also means is that our analyses cannot simply reduce the event of drama and youth into issues, ideas, or arguments because, stories, histories, and metaphors matter equally.

Denzin (1997) claims that ethnodrama is 'the single most powerful way for ethnography to recover yet interrogate the meanings of lived experience' (94). We wanted as much as possible to place our research act within that alternative setting to capture the process of students' theory-building as they moved from what they represented as their beliefs to what they could represent 'on stage.'

This approach to research might go some way towards realizing the desire, articulated by many school-based researchers, to give more authority to student voices in student research (see Fine and Weis 2003; Weis and Fine 2000; Yon 2000; Lesko 2001; and Thomson 2002). Unlike the more traditional methods of qualitative research, creating with the students an analogous theatre world would open up, we hoped, the possibility for critical engagement among students themselves; this world would make possible the generation of theory through spontaneous talk, critical watching, and engaged action. Students are always living by and challenging theories; our drama work with them provided a context in which their theories could be articulated, tested, and reformulated.

In an effort to 'give voice' to young people in many empirical studies, the 'data' – young people's words – are often summoned in a kind of 'show and tell' or reality test for those ideas or 'discoveries' we might well already hold as truths. Empirical research must hold itself to the rigorous intellectual inquiry so important to the theorizing of the everyday, to the conceptual or philosophical as well as the phenomenal realm. Too often, this 'reality syndrome' of empirical classroom-based research is devoid of the imagination and theoretical probing necessary to produce new knowledge in the field. Often enough, the words themselves, the citations culled to illustrate 'findings,' do not, alone, articulate the profound new ideas one would hope to bring to light. Too often they are left to stand in for what it is we already know. 'Keeping it real,' in other words, often anchors researchers to only those things that can be or were spoken in the given context. I desperately wanted to resist this reductive form of reporting. Instead, I hoped that recounting an exploration of ideas through drama would make theoretically and contextually rich the experiences we had with the youth in our study. I hoped to let their words not simply 'illustrate' but also interact with the complexities of the research, the philosophical dimensions of our inquiry, and our own theoretical constructions as researchers.

In discussions and interviews with students, we were beginning to see emerge a theme from our data that I termed 'Identity-Representation-Surveillance':

'First of all, I wouldn't have a jail. All I would ask the students [if I were the principal] is how they would like to see the school run.' (Carter, grade twelve, Redmount School)

'I think the locked bathrooms, the I.D. swipes and the sweep rules are totally unfair.' (Damien, grade eleven, Redmount School)

'It feels like we're a bunch of robots.' (Adeline, grade twelve, Middleview Tech)

This would be the theme we would use to initiate a drama with the students. Philip and I devised an extended improvisation activity that we hoped would allow students to imaginatively enter into a created world that would ask them to both improvise and reflect upon their understandings of, and responses to, this prevalent theme of their concerns about how they are represented and watched. Henry (2000) persuasively argues that '[t]he structures of qualitative research and of dramas take innovative forms in which means and ends, thought and action, intertwine in an unpremeditated, improvisational fashion. Both involve ways of knowing which people use in their everyday lives: existential knowledge' (51).

In short, on this particular day, in the second year of the study, we decided to move the research inside the art frame. Shifting into role as two uncaring bureaucrats conducting an employee review, we moved inside the questions; we went from asking 'How does it make you feel when ...?' and 'What would you do if ...?' to the matter itself. The students were thereby faced with choices not just about how to react, but also about who they were enacting. The fictional world was asking them to be attentive to the 'aesthetics of self and questions of self-stylization' (Michael Peters, cited in Besley 2003) and the multiple and shifting dimensions and relations of power. In this meta-context, they were, in effect, 'living out the drama of the post,' as Best and Kellner (2003) describe it, an era which has produced 'novel social conditions for today's youth who are engaging innovative and challenging cultural forms, [within] a dramatically worsening economic and political situation, and [an] ever more complex and unpredictable life' (80).

It occurred to me, only in hindsight, that this methodological shift was resonant with what Dorothy Smith (1999) sets up as an alternative to 'established sociology.' In this alternative, she does not treat experience as knowledge but as a place to begin inquiry, where the aim of the inquiry is not to explain people's behaviour but to explain to people the social – or society – as it enters into and shapes their lives and activities (96). Her alternative is built upon a social theory of knowledge, which 'begins in a world of activity, the doings of actual people' (98).

What we did with the students is artificial, to be sure. We created a 'fictional' world/workplace of fictional people in order to build theory together with youth, or as Foucault has suggested, to theorize in order to explain our experiences when we notice 'something cracked, dully jarring, or disfunctioning in things.' But is this theatre-making world any more 'artificial' than a researcher's reconstruction of the 'actual one' for the reader? *Theoria* (to 'look at,' 'contemplate'), the form of knowledge that is called theory comes from the same root as does the word theatre ('a place for viewing'). New theories, I would suggest, become imaginable in the moment of dramatic improvisation, the moment when our latent, embodied, and experiential knowledge is called on, when our 'actions' become the fodder for the creative responses of others, and when the quality of our communication depends on our ability to take others in. What had been emerging in our conversations with youth we aimed to re-present through the verisimilitude of a created world. What this methodological move afforded us was a shared point of reference, across a range of very diverse lived experiences, to examine precisely how the social, the political, the ideological are entering and shaping our lives and activities.

'Interviewing,' within a sustained improvisation, this analogous world allows the researcher to consider carefully what 'listening to' might mean. For youth, story and storytelling become an especially powerful means of communicating. If narrative knowledge is embodied in storytelling (Lyotard 1984), the better question to ask, perhaps, is how, as researchers, do we enter into young people's fictions and retellings? We found one way to do that through the remove of the fictional, the convention of creating an alternate world, which allowed us, ultimately, to co-construct knowledge with the youth.

There were about twenty-five students in the class on this day. The entire episode was recorded on video. We asked the group if they were prepared to go into role with us, to give us all another chance to work through some of the themes and issues we had been discussing with them in interviews and through the course of the research. They seemed quite keen to work with us in this novel way. We reiterated that we would all be in role together, that Phil and I would be 'employers,' the bureaucrats, here for their six-month review. We also suggested that we would have time to 'unpack' our fictional world together after the drama. Upon re-entering the room, we proceeded to call some 'employees' up, while others were asked to wait in line. In role, I played the Processor, arbitrarily calling students up to be 'fingerprinted' and verified in my laptop computer. I then sent them on to Phil, the Interviewer:

Interviewer (White, male, American-born): What department are you in?

Kayla (Black, female, Caribbean-born) [Straining to hear over the noise]: Excuse me?

Interviewer: What department are you in?

Kayla: I don't know ... I just started, nobody told me anything.

Interviewer: Hah! [To Processor, loudly] She doesn't know what department she's in! [Laughs. The rest of class is momentarily quieted, then begins to react to Interviewer's display of contempt.]

Processor (White, female, Canadian-born) [To everyone waiting in line for interview]: We're assuming everyone knows what department they're in. [To individual employee] Do you know what department you're in?

Interviewer: You don't know what department you're in. Where do you go everyday? [Pause] This is a six-month review, you have been coming to work for six months and you don't know what department you're in?

Kayla: It's not my fault.

Interviewer: What do you mean it's not your fault?

Kayla: Because I am an employee, the employer is supposed to send me there.

Interviewer: Kayla Ford ... now I have to look through the alphabetical list. [Pause, looking for her name on list] Okay you're in Gardening, just for future reference, you're in Gardening. You know all those flowers and stuff? That's what you do.

Interviewer [Looking over Manager's report]: Okay, well this is fairly consistent ... You are giving your manager Monique quite a bit of resistance. She says that you also, several times after work, have been seen loitering around the building.

Kayla [Very serious, surprised]: Loitering around? That's funny. Every time I'm here I am working. [10 second pause] If I am not shown respect, I will not give respect.

Interviewer: Okay, well that attitude is going to be problematic in a place like this. The customer comes first. If you expect the customers to hold your hand and bat their eyelashes at you ...

Unsurprisingly, the heat of the moment swept us into ambiguous territory where our fabricated setting held real-world implications.

During the one hour of in-role work, students at the back of the room were engaging with each other while we fingerprinted and interviewed others at the front. The whole experience had a feeling of uncertainty both in terms of the improvisation and for us as researchers. It felt risky throughout, both dramatically and methodologically. While interviewing Alessandra, Phil barked out to the rest of the group:

Interviewer: If you don't have any identification, I don't know what you want
  us to do. I don't know you. You could be anyone. You need picture I.D.
  Could that be any clearer?
Sabicca (Black, female, first-generation Canadian, of Caribbean descent)
  [Calling from the sidelines where I'd seated her]: I have a question. So I
  don't have I.D. So what am I doing here? Can I leave?
Processor: No, you have to wait.
Sabicca: I have to sit here?

[I do not reply but five minutes later I call Sabicca up to 'fingerprint' her.]

Sabicca: So what's all this for?

[Processor does not reply but directs her again to the side of the room to sit
  and wait.]

[Three minutes later]

Sabicca [calling out]: Are we getting paid for this? 'Cause if not, I'm going
  back to work!
Processor: Well you may not have work to go back to.

The final moment of our extended role play was signalled by Sabicca. Tired and frustrated at having waited in line the entire time without ever being processed or interviewed, she could no longer tolerate the injustice. She bellows out her objections, attracting the attention of everyone in the room, and is eventually backed by a semi-circle of employees as she leads the charge against the Processor and Interviewer.

Sabicca [Loud and angry]: It's not our fault that you do not know how to run
  your company, Sir! We have been standing here for two and a half hours!

Interviewer: If you don't have identification tomorrow, you won't be seen. We
  spent a lot of time today dealing with people who did not have proper I.D.
Ms S (White, female, Canadian-born): Will we get our identification back?
Interviewer: We do have some I.D. that we have reason to believe is false
  identification, so if you need that I.D. back, come back at 9:00 a.m. tomor-
  row.
Huge outcry. The Processor and Interviewer pack up to leave. They inform
everyone that they are now going to take lunch, so the employees can either
wait here, or leave and come back in 90 minutes. They exit the room and the
drama ends.

To the very last, our intent as Processor and Interviewer was to treat
the employees with a disinterested discourtesy while forcing them to
succumb to the privations of a badly executed security and employment review. In doing so we anticipated that we could shape events in
such a way that it would be nearly impossible for the students to
participate, at whatever level, without making sense of (a) why they
were here in the first place, (b) their reaction to what was happening,
and (c) the implications (both personal and social) of going through
such an experience. It was obvious to the students, I believed, that our
fictional world of the 'employee review' was analogous to their depictions of the practices of bureaucracy and surveillance in their schools.
They also understood that we were asking them to think critically about
the many complaints they had previously made to us in interviews and
in general classroom discussions about these dehumanizing processes
of schooling. In retrospect, our dramatic goals neatly corresponded
with our goals as researchers inquiring into the knowledge that students produce in drama classrooms in urban schools, an equivalence
that, in our view, strengthened the argument for moving our research
inside the art experience itself.

Our encounter with the fictional gave our subsequent interviews with
students a quality and depth I imagine would be difficult to reproduce
without having experienced, together, such a shared context; without
having, however briefly, transformed our space. As bell hooks (1992)
beautifully captures the idea: 'Spaces can be real or imagined. Spaces
can tell stories and unfold histories. Spaces can be interrupted, appropriated, and transformed through artistic and literary practices' (153).

The students' bodily reactions, even from those who did not speak
throughout the entire role-playing event, conveyed a sophisticated understanding of the terms of our engagement. The following debriefing
exchange stands out for us as an example of how fluid the boundaries

are between the social performance in the classroom and the performance within the drama. At this moment, we ask the students what
was going on in the various corners of the room, while our interviewing
process was happening at the front. There were, after all, twenty-five
people in the room, in role for close to one hour, and Philip and I could
only deal with one, or at most two, at a time:

*Sabicca: I wanted to know what happened to him [Andre, who was being
interviewed by us]. I wanted to know what did he say to you.*

*Philip: Yeah, you were the one who was like, 'Now wait, there were three
people, three people have been let through.' Like you were keeping track of
everything that was happening.*

Sabicca: That's exactly what I do, I always keep track.

Philip: Your whole thing was you were looking for justice.

Sabicca: Yes I was. There wasn't any though.

Philip: You were saying this is unfair.

*Sabicca: It **was** unfair. It was completely unfair. Because one guy didn't have
I.D., and he got in before people with I.D. got in, and he got accepted for a
job. And I was like, 'What the Hell?!' And I was like I have been sitting
here for how long? And then Charlie went before me, I was the only one
without I.D. that didn't go. And then that came at the end, and then you
guys gave me a hassle. You said I have to go to Human Resources. I was
like 'Oh what the Hell, Human Resources, where? I've been here for so
long, they'll put me on hold again? No, I want the answer right now!'*

[Noisy reaction from several students ...]

*Andre [Smiling mischievously. To Sabicca]: Coming unprepared, and always
wanting to get in front, like, shut up.*

*Sabicca: Get in front?! See that's the attitude I'm talking about. [General
laughter] I didn't say I couldn't wait. I would wait! But the fact that
people were going before me and I came before them and they didn't have
I.D. either ... that was unfair. So shut the hell up! [Everyone laughs.]*

A fascinating shift occurs during Sabicca's recounting: she becomes
upset all over again at the memory of being relegated to the back of the
line and seems to enter back into that context (as suggested by a shift
from past to present tense). Andre responds in kind by chastising her
character for coming unprepared and expecting equitable treatment.
This banter is reminiscent of their 'characters'' talk during the drama.

Despite the obvious levity, this is a picture of students engaged in their learning. They are exploring the basis for claims of privilege, justice, the influence of perception on reality, and the meaning-making of individuals and the collective. And although this dialogue involves one-upmanship of a certain familiar adolescent kind, it is on its most basic level a collaboration, a dance between two selves and their performances. As Susan Sontag (2001) strikingly portrays the relationship: 'Art is seduction, not rape. A work of art proposes a type of experience designed to manifest the quality of imperiousness. But art cannot seduce without the complicity of the experiencing subject' (22).

In one session with this group, following our in-role work together, we invited the students to interview each other, in pairs, with any questions they might like to ask one another about drama, about school, about whatever topics they find of interest. There followed a particularly poignant and memorable exchange between two female students, included here in its entirety. In this exchange the role of 'researchers' is adopted by the students as they point us, once again in their questions, towards the sense of space and open pedagogy that they believe accounts for the 'difference' they feel in drama class:

Loralei (Black, female, new immigrant, born in former Congo, moved from South Africa to Belgium, then to Canada) to Sabicca (Black, female, first-generation Canadian, of Caribbean descent): What is it about drama class that gives students their self-esteem?

Sabicca: ... Self-esteem, wow ... You know what it is? I think this class builds character and character kind of, you know, I took this class, first, to, uh, kind of build my character. I took on the play, just to build my character, right? (Doug laughs and mutters, 'upgrading?' to her. Sabicca turns towards Doug, nods, and continues.) Yeah, you know? Just to upgrade myself, but then I started liking the play and enjoying it you see ... I got a whole new, I got to a whole different level of self-esteem after doing the play, so ... I don't know what it is ... you know? I don't know ... it's something that's unexplainable. It's kind of like faith [pronounces it as 'fate']: you know it's there but you can't see it. I don't know what it is. I can't explain it. It's just there and you know it.

Loralei: Wow.

Sabicca: Ok Loralei, when students walk out of this class, why is it that it's a different story when you walk out of here? When you walk out through those doors right there, why is it different? Why do things change? Can you explain that to me?

Loralei: Um, I have to keep my focus here, but it's really hard, um ...

Sabicca: Yeah, try to keep your focus, focus on the question.

Loralei: Ok. Um, I think that ... it's a different story because it truly is a different world out ... It's a different world out there even though it's the same exact building, you know, there's other classes, but, it really is, like, a different world out there. Everything is, like ... In other classes, especially compared to drama, everything is pre-organized, like, the teacher has a lesson plan for you; you have to do this; you have to do that; yeah, they know, you know, to copy notes from the board, whatever, but, like, in drama, when you come in, like, even the teacher might not know what she's going to do [Teacher and everyone laughs], you know what I mean? No offence or anything to you, Miss! [laughs, others too]. I think it really helps that, you know, like here you're really able to be like, in the spur-of-the-moment, you know? You're able to make spontaneous decisions as opposed to other classes, where it's organized, you do it, it's given to you, you know? It's kind of like the cafeteria menu. You go to the cafeteria, like, that's all the food that there is, if you don't like anything, you don't have a choice, that's what they're going to serve, you know what I mean? So ...

Sabicca: You feel restricted.

Loralei: Exactly, right. It's very restrictive, so that's why I like drama. It's actually a freer environment, so, that's what makes it different when you walk out those doors.

Sabicca: Ok, so, a freer environment.

Loralei: Yes.

Sanjeet (South Asian, first-generation female): Can I add to that?

Sabicca: Ok, go ahead.

Sanjeet: I don't think it's necessarily that drama teachers don't plan, I just think it's that they're more open than other teachers to ...

Loralei [interrupting]: That's what I was saying, that it's a freer environment.

Doug: Not all the time.

Loralei: No.

Sabicca [addressed to all her classmates]: Can we stay focused here? This is my interview. Oh yeah, this is the Sabicca show now, forget Oprah! [laughs].

[Students start shouting: 'Sa-bi-cca!, Sa-bi-cca! Sa-bi-cca! as talk-show audiences do when they're welcoming their host.]

Sabicca [laughs]: See? That's the freeness I'm talking about! And now, can I get some quiet please? What is it about drama class that gives students their self-esteem?

Loralei: Ok. Gives students their self-esteem ... I'm not a cocky person but I am confident. There's a lot of people who get the two mixed up.

Sabicca: Right.

Andre [interrupting]: Thank-you, thank-you, I appreciate it!

Loralei: Just because you've got confidence doesn't mean that you're cocky, you know what I mean? And, um, for me, already ... I don't know where I get it from, I really don't, but like, um, ok.

[Bell rings.]

Ms S: Please stay five minutes extra.

Loralei (resuming): What also helps build other people's self-esteem in drama class is when they, cause, like, when you're a teenager, it's really hard to trust other people, especially adults, and especially people with authority because they also take advantage of you, so, and it's just as hard to trust your peers as it is to trust those people. So drama class, I find, because this is, like, my 2nd year – I took it in grade 11 and this is grade 12 – um, I notice that, like, it's really important to trust your peers, and once you can do that, I think that you're much more prone to have confidence, because people are egging you on, they're supporting you, do you know what I mean? So, it helps you build your confidence. It helps you to build your self-esteem and confidence in that way, and because you have to perform, you have to be in that situation, it helps you because once you're up there, you know, it's your time, it's your show, it's your time to shine, do you know what I mean? And you don't get a lot of opportunities to do that, so I think that helps you to build your self-esteem.

Sabicca: Thank-you, have a good day [said in the manner of a talk-show hostess ending the show. Doug leads the same 'Sa-bi-cca!' chant as before].

4 URBAN OBSESSIONS

Pedagogies of Conflict

Theatre might be viewed as a de-civilizing experience, a series of permissions to transgress, an act of indiscipline or a mutiny whose forms are inverted reflections of conventional morality or moral speculations given entitlement of expression by virtue of the physical and emotional barriers separating it from the world.

Barker, *Arguments for a Theatre*, 110

Since I began formal research into drama in high school over ten years ago, I have struggled to articulate how these classrooms, in the hands of wise teachers, hold out the promise that conflict might be better understood. Too much time in schools is spent on how to 'manage' conflict and on punitive modes of address; tomes have been written on the subject of 'bullying.' Governments, the world over, continue to spend millions on 'comprehensive anti-bullying plans.' My own view is that there is much to be gained from a creative exploration of conflict, the very kind that routinely interrupts the functioning of most high school classrooms. We arrived at Middleview, in year one of the study, on the heels of a school-wide 'bullying intervention.' The administration was attempting to address the 'growing problem' at the school. To this end, they devised a survey that was to be completed by every student in the school. Its purpose, they explained, was to find out how prevalent the problem of bullying was, who the bullies were, and what kind of bullying the students were experiencing or witnessing at Middleview. The survey promised that the teachers and administrative team would

use the data from the survey to create an Anti-Bullying Plan. By the end
of our third year at Middleview, there had been no follow-up from the
survey exercise.

Middleview School Survey on Bullying

*This survey is anonymous. No one will ever know that you have given this
   information.*
Please <u>print</u> your answers.

1. What kind of bullying have you <u>witnessed</u> at Middleview?
*Physical bullying (e.g., hitting, punching, kicking, slapping, pushing,
   shoving, pinching)*
*Verbal bullying (e.g., name calling, put downs, racial slurs, threats, intimi-
   dation, spreading rumours)*
Electronic bullying (e.g., ICQ threats and/or harassment)

2. What kind of bullying have you <u>experienced</u> at Middleview?
*Physical bullying (e.g., hitting, punching, kicking, slapping, pushing,
   shoving, pinching)*
*Verbal bullying (e.g., name calling, put downs, racial slurs, threats,
   intimidation, spreading rumours)*
Electronic bullying (e.g., ICQ threats and/or harassment)
*Perhaps you have never been a victim of bullying. However, it is likely that you
know who the bullies are at Middleview. Perhaps you are the good friend of a
bully? Who are the bullies at Middleview?*
*Your ideas are important to us. How can we (students, staff, parents) stop
bullying at Middleview?*

*THIS SURVEY IS CONFIDENTIAL. DO NOT DISCUSS YOUR RE-
SPONSES WITH ANYONE. PLACE YOUR COMPLETED SURVEY IN
THE ENVELOPE PROVIDED. THANK YOU.*

Teachers and students alike were greatly troubled by this survey. To
many, it seemed an overt plea to have students 'rat each other out,' and
this, according to many students, was entirely the wrong way to go
about it. Ms S was troubled by her required participation in this exercise. She, too, thought it was fraught with problems. In an interview
session, Ms S was clear about the careful steps she takes in order to
ensure an inclusive and safe environment in her classroom: 'Drama's

not an automatically ... you know, safe and respectful and community space. You have to really work hard to achieve that, both as a teacher and as a class.'

At Redmount, Amor, and St Bernadette's, students and teachers frequently insisted that there were 'no diversity issues.' We took this to mean that the social processes inscribed with power centred Anglo, White culture and celebrated sameness. Our conversations with youth are echoed by Raby's study (2004) of adolescent girls living in or near the Toronto area, which found that these adolescents denied and downplayed racism in their schools, narrowly defined racism as individualized rather than institutional, and conceptualized racism in a way that privileged whiteness. At Middleview, however, where diversity seemed to thrive in the drama classroom, the goals for 'community' did not appear to as readily include the familiar liberal multicultural attempts to smooth out differences and find commonalities. Commonalities may indeed have been discovered, but not through artificial, normalizing, or hegemonic means. At Middleview particularly, drama class was about understanding human relations and challenging assumptions, and sometimes this meant that differences could not be reconciled:

Dion (Black, male, Jamaican-born, grade twelve Middleview student): Yeah. I said that's not how my country, that's not how we do it in my country. They say, that's not how we do it in our country, so therefore you can change sometime but you can't change someone opinion. That's the way they grew up, you know? If they do that in Nigeria that's the way they are going to stay; I do that in Jamaica that's the way I'm going to stay.

Phil (White, male, American-born, research assistant): So how do you, if you have those perspectives when you're working in the Drama class, how does that influence the work? How does that affect the kind of work you can do together?

Dion: Sir, I think it could affect a lot because everybody don't agree on one situation, everybody's like, 'Yo, I agree about this, I agree about that, so you know?' We obviously can't make it right, you know what I'm saying, Sir? So therefore in order to do your work properly and, you know, work things out everybody have to come to one agreement.

Phil: And how do you do that?

Dwayne: Sir I don't know, you know. That's the truth, but. My opinion Sir is standing still. (They both laugh.)

In countless interviews, students offered sophisticated understandings of conflict and its place in their lives in schools. Despite poorly conceived school plans to contain or control conflict, despite visits from 'bullying experts' and the police, it was the students who shed most light on the complexities of social cohesion and their understanding of how conflict operates in the drama classroom:

Sanjeet (South Asian, first-generation Canadian, female, grade twelve Middleview student): The drama classroom plays a huge role. Again, if it was drama but we all sat in straight rows and desks, we wouldn't interact as much, but, um, it's very open. And maybe it's a reflection of what the class does to you inside. It opens you up, just like the open space, um, yeah ... And it's conducive to, um, discussions, like when we sit around in a circle, you see everybody and you can make eye contact and, you know, people are nodding their heads so you know when you say something, they agree with you. Whereas if someone behind you agrees, you have no idea.

Kathleen (White, female, first-generation Canadian, of Scottish descent, researcher): So, I'm going to ask you, in that space, you can see people nodding and agreeing with you, but you can also see, possibly, people disagreeing with you, or because you're also open, and people are more, ... as you said, more 'outgoing' than in other contexts, that can also cause people to come into conflict or disagreement with each other. Has that been your observation, and if you see that, how do you think that plays out in the drama class?

Sanjeet: Uh ... Disagreement is good. There are definitely disagreements in the drama classroom ... Um, how does it play out? It never gets serious. Partly because you make friends – or at least acquaintances – with everyone, so you're conscious about your impact on the rest of the classroom. It's just not possible to, uh, not to like someone in the drama classroom setting; you're likely to work with them, or be paired up with them at some point, so it's very, very conducive to making, uh, resolutions for your problems, because, if you don't, it's going to be problematic not only for you but for the rest of the classroom. And maybe because of that, the rest of the class has a bearing on how soon you become friends with the other person. (pause). And disagreements are important.

Kathleen: Why?

Sanjeet: Why? It depends on the topic, but, um, just – it has an impact on how dimensional you are as a person. And, again, speaking society-wise, um, it's important to be educated about how other people feel, so that when you make decisions you know how much they impact others.

Yet, there was also a contradiction that presented itself over and over in discussions with students in all four schools on the issue of conflict. Students we interviewed – particularly in New York, where conversations turned towards the question of conflict – often vehemently argued that there was a tacit pact to 'leave problems outside.' The irony we felt as observers of these various drama classrooms was that conflicts between people and about ideas were regularly vented. To my eye, conflict was seldom banished from these sites. Instead, there seemed to be many opportunities to work through complex problems artistically. Calvin's analysis of the dynamics of the drama classroom helped to elucidate this observation for us:

Calvin (White, male, first-generation Canadian, of European descent, grade twelve Middleview student): I like to get my private side outside. Because a lot of people have a lot to say and I find that some people could share stories together and put them together and just really analyse both their stories and say, 'Wow, you've done this in your life, this is what I've done. I give you suggestions for if this happens to you.' So you really learn from other people and other experiences. And that's the way I was taught in life, is that you listen to other people and you learn from their mistakes, or their gain and what happened to get their gain. When we're in class and we're talking about certain things like this, we listen to the way people think and listen to opinions, you really get to know, get a better look on life because you're always stuck to your own opinions so you really can't make up another opinion if you're narrow-minded. But if you hear other opinions it really makes you double think, it's like, 'Is this right?' kind of thing, 'cause like 'This is what they think and this has been good for them, could I do this too?' And that's what I think about bringing out your personal life and stuff. It really gets you to, you really get to know the other people and know where they come from and be able to really know the way they think and the way they are and why they are the way they are.

Was it because of the pedagogical impetus in drama classrooms to open up conversations and make present diverse world views that the youth felt that the role of conflict in their lives, often as a healthy mode to differentiate themselves from others, was not undermined? It is hard to say with any certainty, but from our observations it was clear that, pedagogically, drama did not shut down conflict but aimed to channel it in the direction of the creative work.

In our Toronto girls' school, the students talked about how 'catty' girls are, how they 'fight over the stupidest things,' how gossip functions in their school, and how this kind of emotional violence is often 'more dangerous than the physical stuff.' Driscoll (2002) beautifully articulates the paradox of girlhood in the following conception: 'Girls figure both the pleasures and threats of technologized cultural progress and the promise and failure of the modern' (303). And once again, when I probed, in a girls' focus-group discussion at St Bernadette's, about how conflict erupts in drama classrooms, the following exchange confirmed what students in the other three schools repeatedly expressed about drama's particular pedagogies:

Maraiha (White, female, first-generation Canadian, of Portuguese descent):
  It's funny, 'cause it's only in the Drama class that I feel that way.
  (Kathleen: Yeah?) [sounds of agreement from the other girls]. It's only in
  the Drama class ... I have no idea.
Kathleen: Why? Why is that?
Faye (White, female, second-generation Canadian, of British descent): It's
  because we get to interact with each other. In other classes (Maraiha: Yeah,
  I guess it's something like that), you're sitting here, and someone's sitting
  there. How are you [to] interact –
Ruby (Filipino, female, first-generation Canadian) [interrupting]: Yeah, and
  the teacher doesn't, like, like you talking to anybody (Faye: Yeah), kind of
  thing? (Faye: Yeah, like, even the people around you ...) Like, you have to
  stay quiet in the class and do your work, and ...
Faye: Even the people around you, you're not, like, gonna be that close with
  them, right? (Ruby: Yeah)
Kathleen: So, let me push that further, because, it's human nature to have
  conflict, right? So, if you're allowed to interact more, the potential is that
  you're allowed to know each other more and maybe become a community.
  It's also possible that you can get at each other more. Would you say that's
  true?
Arla (White, female, first-generation Canadian, of Portuguese descent)
  [hesitantly]: It is ... 'cause, like, any opportunity to have somebody argue
  with somebody, is a given. And, if you hear rumours, or if you don't like a
  certain person by just the way they look, which happens on an everyday
  basis, then arguments will occur. But if you come into something with an
  open mind ...

Kathleen: What about arguing about the thing you're working on in Drama? When it's about the work, and you have a conflict? How does that get resolved?
Faye [quietly]: Compromise.
Kathleen: Compromise.
Arla: You kind of gotta cut down the middle, and divide things, and mesh them.
Maraiha: We haven't argued about it yet. [laughter and comments from the group about how it's too soon in the semester for arguments to occur]
Faye: It's mostly, you know, someone gives an idea, and someone had a different idea and, like ... you (Maraiha: You combine them) mesh the two ideas (Maraiha: Exactly). And then, it just makes it better, usually, like, you know ... You have the different perspectives of different ideas, and bring them together. It just makes it, like ... a whole new dynamic (Kathleen: Mm-hmm).

The Classroom as a 'Location of Possibility'

So many teachers are like that, even if you don't make a first impression, there are so many teachers that *categorize* you, and, after a certain amount of time, you *do* start to believe it, so it's *really* hard to find that confidence to be, like, 'No. I'm not like how they think I am,' and overcome that. I really wish a lot of teachers would not think like that because that's what they *do*, and a lot of them do it *subconsciously* and it's just something they need to *break*, to break that cycle.

Loralei, grade twelve student at Middleview

I came to Middleview one day, in the second year of our study, with a newspaper article from a major Toronto daily published that same day. I read aloud the story of a suburban school's 'one-day anti-discrimination event.' As part of African History Awareness Month (marked annually in February in Canada), this suburban high school meted out inequity after inequity based purely on the colour of a randomly assigned ribbon worn by every student. The green ribbons stood for 'disadvantage'; these students sat in the back of classrooms, were never called on, could only use certain washrooms in the day, were not permitted to eat in the cafeteria. The purple ribbon signified privilege. When I explained this exercise to the class, Sabicca earnestly asked, 'So do the Black kids have to have a green ribbon too?' – a simple question that points so clearly to the redundancy, in her mind, of a symbolic marker for those students already so clearly 'marked' with disadvantage in the school. The point of the reported activity was to dramatize the kinds of discrimination that Blacks have suffered in supposedly tolerant societies. This school activity, however, is emblematic of the kinds of educational approaches and 'cultural training' that typically de-historicize and de-contextualize the history of Black people, a project accomplished through the psychologizing and individualizing of history. Such 'awareness or intercultural training' ignores the history of colonization and assumes that knowledge and behaviour skills are enough to alter social relations and raise consciousness (see Warren and Adler 1977; Bhawuk 1990; Seelye 1996; and Samovar and Porter 2001). At Middleview, however, the story set off a lively debate about the problems and politics of commemorating African History Month in a mostly White suburban school as opposed to a diverse, urban one, such as theirs.

While trying to imagine how such an exercise would play out in their diverse, urban school, the students offered insights into how little can be taken for granted when speaking of, or seeking to build, school community. Loralei believed that, were Middleview to attempt this exercise as part of its African History Awareness program, it would fail completely:

Loralei (Black, female, born in the former Congo, moved from South Africa to Belgium, then to Canada, grade twelve): They did it in a predominantly Caucasian school. And they got the reaction they wanted, basically. I think if they did it here – because I don't know how people in Whitby live, they're just like us I guess, but it's a very different environment. But here, it's urban, there's a lot of different cultures and different people and I think if they did that here, they'd have a lot more controversy and a lot more anger maybe and people taking it the wrong way. 'Oh look what we did over here,' but if they did it here, it would not have given the results they wanted, so they went for the easy way.

As a founding member of an African Students' Association at the school, Loralei spoke from experience: recently, they had had great difficulty in reaching an agreement as to what should be done to mark their history, since people either wanted to remember, move on from, or avoid altogether the topic of slavery in the African experience. The various opinions of students on these matters carry significant weight if Gordon (2005) is right when he argues that Black youth have become the repre-

sentative and authoritative voice of Black communities in general because of a particular valorization – in his view problematic – of adolescence through popular culture and the media. In our attempts to debunk
our own racialized and gendered myths about youth, Lesko's critique
(2001) of the construct of 'adolescent development' in the literature is
helpful. She argues that our 'developmental demand' pulls us towards
certain 'characteristics,' a tendency she sees as driven by an imperative
for individual improvement and 'higher' achievements, which, in turn,
recreates norms of whiteness and masculinity. Lesko sees the discussions about evolutionary roots of adolescence as imposing a strong
interest in *the future* over the present or the past (191). What *we* may
then call 'commonsense' developmental notions of youth, with our
foundational theories of adolescent development, *youth* may indeed
experience as binding stereotypical social roles. Countering this in our
research required an epistemological shift.

It is clear that one of the greatest dangers in staging these African
Heritage celebrations is the reification of racial inequity that inevitably
results from attributing African history to Africans while often exoner-
ating contemporary Western society based on a presumed enlightenment. In our conversations I found myself repeating that it is not simply
Blacks who need to remember or learn about African History; Whites,
too, need to examine how their lives are shaped by the horrors of
subjugation and oppression that many of our ancestors visited upon the
African continent and by our continued participation, often through
disengagement, in the on-going colonization of African people. Loralei
bemoaned the fact that White students and faculty were reluctant to
help the African Heritage club plan their activities, and that when they
did help out they faced disparaging comments from others. She was
also troubled by the number of people who complained about the very
idea of an Afro-Heritage club:

Loralei: OK. I'm not naming any names but even some members of the
faculty were saying, 'Why can't we have an Asian club?' Who's stopping
you?? Get your ass up and do it! That's why we started our club ... And
we didn't exclude anyone because you don't necessarily have to be Black to
be in our club ... (Sabicca: Exactly!) So I don't know what we're doing
wrong.

A telling feature of most classroom discussions of racism is the temptation to find a conclusion that places those present outside the stream

of history. Rich and Cargile (2004) conclude that nothing short of what they call 'White Identity Transformation' is needed in order to build a real multicultural community, and that such a transformation is, in fact, facilitated by conflict. If these 'transformations' occur, they argue, such grand narratives as meritocracy, for instance, are challenged. Tatum (1997) argues, however, that for many White students, meaningful discussions regarding race are difficult because they 'struggle with embarrassment about the topic, the social awkwardness that can result if the "wrong" words are used ... [and] the painful possibility of being perceived as a racist' (xvi). Instead of looking back on a dreadful legacy and finding ourselves horrified and ashamed, we White people often move to dispel our unease by defining ourselves as exceptional, as somehow more enlightened than our predecessors, and therefore not implicated in what appears to be none of our doing.

I spent some time in the classroom that day talking about collective consciousness and the responsibility I feel for a shared collective history. Andre, a Black male student, agreed with Loralei that nobody should care about the skin colour of someone willing to help the African Heritage club. Similarly, he continued, why should anyone care if a White person owns a Black television station or magazine? Perfectly in keeping with the discussion's emerging liberal themes of colour blindness and equality, Andre's comments failed to account for the broader context of continuing racial inequality, effectively positioning racism as an artefact of American history, rather than a current social reality. The ubiquity of multicultural discourses may offer one possible reading of this exchange; another reading might suggest that the opinions expressed by some of the Black students were strategic. If, according to Comer and Hayes (1991, cited in Williams 2003), our schools ignore the sociocultural characteristics of Black students and, on a structural level, prove inhospitable to Black culture, perhaps Andre's comments can be construed as evidence of how Black students 'must adjust to the dominant culture that is reproduced in schools, which is that of White middle-class Canadians. Total assimilation into the dominant culture, and no representation of African culture causes cultural oblivion' (Williams 2003). In other words, we discovered, as Fishman and McCarthy (2005) did in their classroom research, that historical frameworks for students' stories and personal experiences are necessary for productive talk about race. This turn in the conversation may also be one example of what is now often termed 'the new racism,' which seems to effectively evade notions of race, racial injustice, equity, and democracy.

While Phil, a White, male, research assistant, is pointing out that a successful media venture may not simply represent a White executive's business acumen but may also be attributed to a racial inequity that is the living legacy of fifteen generations of slavery (three more than the twelve generations of Blacks in the United States who have lived 'free'), Sabicca, a Black female student, suddenly asks about the reparation payments – forty acres and a mule – that were never made. As just one representative of millions of descendants of slaves, she suggests that she is owed something more than the 'freedom' to earn a wage.

In response to Sabicca's genuine dismay over the United States government's failure to offer reparation payments, Phil offered a pragmatic explanation: the cost of the crime perpetrated so dwarfs any conceivable method of compensation that none can be offered. Phil was well aware that his reply failed to address the greater issue of just how improbable it would be for the American people and their representatives to expose what is at the roots of the mythic 'Land of Opportunity.' Loralei promptly replied by recounting her disgust at President George W. Bush's refusal to apologize for slavery, or, at least, to publicly admit the crucial role it played in ensuring the survival of the fledgling nation:

Loralei: 'I will not apologize.' Yeah, he said it at a press conference recently or
    something. You 'freed' them, yeah, but even when they were 'free' it didn't
    change the fact that they're Black. And it matters. It even still matters
    now. They built that county on slaves, you know what I'm saying?
Sabicca (Black, female, first-generation Canadian, of Caribbean descent):
    Yeah. So did England so the Queen could steal African gold and diamonds.
Kayla (Black, female, first-generation Canadian, of Caribbean descent): Why
    does Bush have to apologize for slavery? What did he do? Was he a part
    of it?
Alessandra (White, female, second-generation Canadian, of British descent):
    White people feel ashamed so they'd rather not think about it at all.

I was reminded, in this instance, of Nakagawa's exploration (1987) of the sociopolitical stakes in the 'breaking of silence' around another of history's most shameful racist events, the internment of Japanese in North America during the Second World War:

Why must you reopen old wounds? We reopen those wounds precisely
    because they have never healed, and they must never be permitted to

heal – for healing is only in one sense a covering over (hence, a closure); healing is also, importantly, revelatory and enuciative ... And if the wound is anesthetized and the scar forgotten or cosmetically concealed, does not the healing moment likewise recede? (29–30)

As might have been expected, Loralei's comments touched off a debate concerning the metaphysical quandary of where to place the dividing line between past and present; of how to assess the impact of history on our present relations. Students were divided over President Bush's, or any living person's, obligation to atone for something s/he did not do, but from which s/he either directly or indirectly benefits. Amidst the heat generated by increasingly adamant statements as to the seat of the president's authority and his responsibility, we interrupted the discussion to suggest that rather than just talking about these matters, we could think it through another way: by making dramatically present some aspect of the current conflict. The move to a drama structure was intended to both capitalize on and complicate the students' adamant opinions by placing them within an *embodied*, theatrical context. Dialogue, in theatre, is more than mere dialogue, for it is also the action of the play; that is, the action is made manifest through words. Our sense, at the time, was that we might find a way, through making our problem physical and dialogic, to challenge the grand narratives of individualism and personal responsibility that are typically summoned to represent some form of 'objective truth.' Rich and Cargile (2004) maintain that these monologic and pervasive stories 'minimize the gains stolen from African-Americans and other people of colour for over 400 years and provide a view of the US as a fair country where racism no longer flourishes' (354).

In keeping with our improvisation work, which explored issues of security and surveillance in the fictional context of a workplace review, we were seeking again the opportunity to examine, critically *and* dramatically, what happens when differing world views, as embodied within a fictional setting, are held to mutual account in improvised encounters. In dramatic terms, this discussion formed the pretext for a scene we were now 'getting on its feet.' Similarly, as researchers, we were also now ready to test our assumptions, or to move from fact-gathering to theory-building. We wanted, as much as possible, to place our research act within that alternate setting to capture the process of students' theory-building as they moved from what they represented as their beliefs and their opinions to what they could negotiate with each other, through the distancing mechanism of 'the stage.' Pedagogically speaking, the productive power of conflict would direct us.

At this point, I was most interested in exploring the related concepts of racism and privilege, and so we began with Augusto Boal's dramatic, pedagogical activity (1992), which aims to stimulate imaginative thought about conflict through inanimate objects. We asked the students to arrange chairs in such a way that one chair would be clearly more powerful than all the others. After trying several different iterations, we eventually agreed that the configuration in which one chair stood upright in front of 'bowing' chairs – a group tipped forward to resemble kneeling figures – made it most obvious which chair had the power. We would incorporate this layout into our subsequent scene by requiring all entrants to bow to the president before being permitted to speak. Phil, offering to begin the forum theatre exercise, asks for a volunteer to play the 'president.' Andre responds:

Janeen (White, female, visiting student teacher) [Walks up, lines up all four chairs in one horizontal line facing down, as if bowing in front of the 'powerful one.' A few impressed 'ooooh' sounds.]

Ari (Bi-racial [Jamaican and French Canadian] female, first-generation Canadian): They're bowing down!

Phil (White, male, American-born, research assistant): Yeah. Wow. OK, alright. Just because of time, we're going to pick the one that's bowing. I think what we're going to do, to replicate this in the scene is, the person that's powerful, every person that comes to see him/her has to bow at their feet, before they can speak. The powerful person just simply won't listen to you if you do not bow. Do we have a volunteer to be the power person? [Andre leaps up and sits in the powerful chair. Phil and students laugh.] OK, Andre. Your mission is very clear. You don't feel guilty about any-thing. You have nothing to apologize for. You are, let's say you were freely elected ... uh, you're basically George Bush. [Phil enters, stands, then bows, facing Andre, who is sitting in the 'powerful' chair]: It's been documented that you've many years profited from our labour so how can you look at me, and say that it's 'over'? When you look at any city street you see the effects, the effect that slavery has had. [long pause]

Andre (Male, African Canadian, heterosexual, English, a little Patwa [Jamai-can], Christian): How can I look at you? I understand that slavery has been ... [pause] Yeah, well with 4 million people I don't see how me apolo-gizing will make them feel hot [i.e., better].

Phil: Well, we're saying that it will. It will allow us to, at least, begin some discussion about where we go from here. Without that, all it looks like is we have a hostile, White administration.

Andre: What do you plan to do after I say 'sorry'?

Phil: Well we can begin conversations, we can begin workshops with the government to maybe begin some programs around acknowledging the role of slavery in ...

Andre [interrupting]: Let's pretend I said sorry and let's start.

Phil: We can't move forward without an apology. There won't be any grassroots movement without you to acknowledge what happened.

Andre: Well I'm very sorry but ... apologies are ... unnecessary. If you start, I can help you with whatever you want but apologies are out of the question.

Phil: Well, I don't know if you can afford politically to say that.

[End of period bell rings.]

Andre: I'm here. I'll continue to be here. Anyone who disagrees with me, off with their heads [He chuckles. Some laughter from the class].

Phil: OK, well thank you, Mr President, for meeting with me.

Ari: Shit, the bell! I wanted to play you, Phil.

And as things go in the daily realities of classrooms, the end of the period bell sounded just as we might have begun to improvise a scene between the president and a representative of a Black coalition making her case for reparations for the descendents of slaves. We wanted to create a scene in which someone who directly or indirectly benefited from exploitation of a group would meet with a representative of that group seeking a public apology and reparations. What we came to realize in physicalizing our discussion about power and improvising the beginning of a scene between the two characters – an unrepentant president and a human-rights advocate – is that drama is a potent research modality for those particularly interested in negotiating embodied meaning with research participants. Nicholson (2005) argues that the aesthetic in drama, that is, the engagement of the senses and the potential for somatic learning, creates a particular discourse on the body (57). Making drama, then, is an effective tool for embodied exploration, but it is also, therefore, a potentially risky one. At every turn, the sensitive drama teacher is attempting to 'protect' the participants within the drama so that the critical reflection within and beyond the drama will be productive for those engaged in the work.

With more time we would have borrowed from Boal's 'forum the-atre,' wherein all 'spect-actors' can contribute to the unfolding action. However briefly on this day, this was nonetheless a moment that made tangible for me bell hooks's notion (1994) that the classroom can be a 'location of possibility.' Unlike the contrivance at the (largely White) suburban high school to mark Black History Month, we avoided re-inscribing the generalizations and stereotypes such events invoke. In our view, the didacticism of the 'discrimination event' and the fixing of identities in ahistorical contexts altogether lacked the power of the arts, and drama in particular, to address specificity and examine relations of power. These kinds of discrimination days, instead, reinforce the self/other binary and minimize the opportunity to create a dialogic commu-nity; students are destined to 'play out' inscribed roles, against a back-drop of inert history, but are seldom asked to consider their own relationship to privilege in the present moment.

In her provocative introduction to her study (2002) of schools and schooling for children and youth in a 'disadvantaged' area of Australia, Thomson speaks of the 'virtual schoolbag' that different children bring with them that differentially equips them for the work of learning. She argues convincingly that educational and social disadvantage are inex-tricably linked in children's lives and that their *embodied* and *experiential* knowledge – my extrapolation – offer them greater or lesser degrees of access to cultural and human capital with which to begin their learning. Our research activity attempted to bring alive these differences and demonstrations of power. It also invited participants to co-create, al-lowing multiple voices to weigh in with their own knowledge and experience. And this, in turn, allows for the fluidity of meaning that the students seem to insist upon while helping them to see – in their own terms and through their own theory-building – that context affects everything. We wanted our research to push against the simple di-chotomies so often presented by youth who, in moments of conflict or disagreement, are often compelled (like most of us) to strategically revert to the stereotypical positions they can most easily reproduce. Here was our opportunity to let 'embodied knowing' and the experi-ential knowledge of others affect the way we come to know the world, our collective histories, and ourselves. As Gilman (1985) points out, 'the internalized representations of reality mirror the fantasies of the individual, but are always shaped by the individual's place in the stream of history.'

Alternative Literacies and the Sociology of Aesthetics

Philip: I would like to ask two questions that are related: When do you feel
smart in class and when do you feel stupid? And that can be any class, not
just Drama.
Charlie (Male, first-generation Canadian, gay, East-Asian descent, grade
twelve student at Middleview): Okay, when do I feel smart? Um, it's
usually when a teacher, we're discussing a topic and I add something to the
topic that I feel strongly about, that the teacher understands where I'm
coming from and she agrees with me. That's when I guess I feel really
smart. Um, in terms of, oh when I feel really dumb, I guess it goes along
the lines of the same thing. If I try to add in something to a discussion and
it ends up being ignored, or the teacher's like 'Uh, well you know that may
be true, but blah blah blah,' that's when I feel dumb, because I think when-
ever I do try to add in to a discussion I try to think of something that I feel,
that I have something important to say and when it ends up being thrown
back in my face, not intentionally or anything, that's when I start to feel
dumb.

In a post-study conversation with Ms S, she explained to me that she
felt, as a teacher, that she was 'going against nature' with her students;
that schooling was 'wrong for them, wrong for their bodies.' As Hattam
and Smyth (2001) found in studying the phenomenon of 'dropping out,'
students' marginalization can be as troubling for teachers and schools
as it is for students. Schools, it is true, have tremendous difficulty
understanding the alternative literacies of youth. Sometimes they attempt to domesticate these literacies, through mostly well-meaning
multicultural events, but at other times youth popular culture and
alternative literacies so charge the space socio-politically that they are
effectively shut down by the cultural imperialism of classrooms. In
response, historically marginalized youth often develop sophisticated
ways of cultural participation that are, all too often, not acknowledged
or legitimated by schools (MacLeod 1987; Willis 1981).

Grossberg (1994) puts forward an interesting set of pedagogical
models, one of which best expresses the complexity of culture and the
difficult task for teachers of reading that complexity. This 'pedagogy of
articulation and risk' is one that 'neither starts with nor works within a
set of texts but, rather, deals with the formations of the popular, the
cartographies of taste, stability, and mobility within which students are

located' (18). In our experience, drama is ideally suited to this kind of pedagogy. The extent to which any given teacher creatively harnesses or fearfully contains that 'articulation and risk,' however, varies tremendously.

A growing body of research (see Morrell and Duncan-Andrade 2003; Finn 1999; Valenzuela 1999) challenges the popular idea that urban youth, and particularly students of colour, are academically disengaged. Studying forms of resistance, for example, Gordon (2005) argues that 'the orthography of hip hop stands as a refusal to seek recognition in a system of rules in relation to which black, brown, and beige youth have been politically and pedagogically constructed as illiterate' (379). Ms S has a very keen sense of just how much schools, and not students, are missing the mark on the question of literacy:

Ms S (White, Jewish, female, second-generation Canadian, teacher): Oh, I don't know ... my English – I felt like my English class was a disaster this semester. I did not know how to ... I mean ... I have to ... find a new way in. There's a different set of challenges here at this school, but ... I couldn't, I really felt like I didn't do a good job in my English course this year.

Kathleen (White, female, first-generation Canadian, Scottish descent, researcher): Tell us about the different set of challenges with this school.

Ms S: Well, the literacy, right, that's a big one.

Dominique (Black, female, first-generation Canadian, of Caribbean descent, research assistant): The lack thereof, or ... ?

Ms S: Well, just ... So many different ... no ... not lack thereof. There are students with a high level of literacy, a high level of literacy in, in certain things, but not necessarily in analyzing literature (Kathleen: Right; Dominique: Okay). I mean it's what that whole curriculum demands, right? I mean ... there are kids who know ... they could tell you every single part of a car, and they could tell you exactly how to fix it. And there are students here who've memorized 3000 lyrics, but haven't passed the literacy test, you know? It's what ... which kind of literacy is privileged, it really disadvantages ... And, you know, the whole literacy test has also ... really made a lot of students hate English literature.

Ms S is intuitively articulating what many studies of literacy are coming to understand more clearly. As Godley (2003) argues, '[L]iteracy learning, as a form of interpersonal communication, is not only an academic endeavor but also a negotiation of social identities and thus a social practice that can delimit or offer new possibilities for students' self images and life choices' (273). The problem of literacy is compounded by the almost open hostility between the theory and practice literatures. While the practice-focused research tends to isolate the practices and procedures of teaching and learning (what and how boys and girls read, for instance), the theoretically oriented research is concerned with philosophical or sociological understandings of educational contexts (see Weaver-Hightower 2003; Skelton 2001). I would suggest that drama pedagogy holds a middle ground in this debate, bringing theory and practice together in atypical ways.

Current assessments of literacy are particularly challenging for students for whom English is a second, third, or sometimes fourth language. These minority language students are multi-literate, but nonetheless struggle with an increasingly powerful conservative force in school literacy programs. Despite many advances in our understanding of second-language acquisition, and much research that situates the 'literacy problem' within school programs rather than with students (see Gee 2004; Morrell and Duncan-Andrade 2003; Cummins 2001; Mahiri 1998; Lee 1993), the deficit model still dominates many literacy approaches with urban and minority language children. In Ontario, 22 per cent of the grade ten student population comes from non-English-speaking home backgrounds; in urban centres the proportion is much greater (approximately 50 per cent in the Greater Toronto Area). The most recent (2004) provincial testing data show that 50 per cent of those designated as English as a Second Language (ESL) students failed the grade ten literacy test.

Jin explained his early experiences of linguistic discrimination (see Rampton 1995; Lippi-Green 1997) in a Canadian school in this way:

Jin (Chinese-born, male, grade eleven student at Middleview): Because first when I came to Canada I didn't know English, not one word. Um, I think people did stereotype me but I don't think I got it because I don't know what they say. I can feel it from the way they act, from the way they look at me. I feel like they stereotype me for being this foreign kid who's annoying.
Isabelle (Bi-racial [Korean and French Canadian], female, research assistant): And how many years ago did you come here?
Jin: Uh, I came here when I was ten years old. And I'm 19 now, so that's 8 or 9 years.
Isabelle: And how does it feel now? In terms of stereotypes?
Jin: Uh, I don't think anyone stereotypes me anymore because I'm no different from now, because they say something I can understand and I say some-

thing and they can understand. So I don't think nobody stereotypes me anymore.

Bransford et al. (2000) speak to the importance of students' engaging prior understandings in the learning process, integrating factual knowledge with conceptual frameworks, and taking active control of the learning process. Clearly, home and cultural knowledges, skills, and beliefs significantly influence how youth 'read' their environment and how they organize and interpret their observations. Drama creates an especially rich context that is wide open to students' interpretations. The fuller an entry into a shared fictional world a student might make, the richer and deeper the private meaning-making will be.

When we recall the in-role work we did with the students when they were asked to enter into the fictional world of an 'employee review,' Jin was one of those students who did not make it up for an interview, but he nonetheless had built a surprisingly rich context for himself that fed into the post-drama writing we asked the students to do:

Isabelle: Can I take you back to that episode? Remember when we did that drama and Kathleen and Phil were with that company and you were being interviewed and so on and you were asked to write a letter in role to Betty, the director of personnel? How was that writing exercise for you? What did that make you feel like, how did that feel?

Jin: Uh, I didn't feel much because I wasn't very interactive with the whole program. I wasn't interviewed, I wasn't talked to, I was just leave in the corner, nobody noticed me. So at the end I just wrote a letter to Betty that I don't even work here, I just got dragged in.

Phil (White, male, American-born, research assistant): I remember that. You wrote that you were just walking on the street and somebody said, 'Come on in.'

Jin: Because I was in a suit and I was carrying a briefcase and somebody just mistaked me for I worked in the company and they got big news so they just dragged me in. So they presumed that I worked there but I don't. I was just walking by. I don't even have a job, so I just write about their stereotype of me.

Phil: Okay, but I have a question about that though.

Jin: Yeah.

Phil: With that Drama, I mean, I guess what I would want to know is, you didn't get called on but did you, as you were sitting there watching, did it feel like you were watching a Drama, watching a real situation, or were

*you kind of looking around going, 'Oh well, they're not talking to me so I
guess I'll just wait here until it's over.'*
Jin: *Oh yeah, I feel I was in the moment; I feel like everybody around me had a
purpose, they were doing something, they were getting serious, they were
competing, they were talking loud and they were very into their issues.
Somebody just got fired, somebody got raised and I really feel like they did
get raised or they did get fired. They're mad or they're happy; I just feel like
this guy in this place. I'm just curious about what's happening, figuring
out what's up.*
Phil: *Okay so you made that decision in the drama to be somebody who didn't
even work there and then wrote about that?*
Jin: *Yeah.*

What is so interesting about this is that in the absence of an engagement
with us in the drama, Jin built up a context for himself, engaged in a
kind of 'peripheral participation' (Andersen 2004) in the fictional world
and created a clear justification for his participation. How often, I
mused, is this peripheral participation the only kind experienced by
minority-language speakers in the classroom? Here, however, the drama
created a context for critical literacy and not simply a surface-level
processing of a text or activity. Jin was reading all the social practices
that contexualized and gave meaning to the unfolding story. This context, invented by Jin himself, then became central to his written expression; there was, in fact, a reason to write. Jin is assessing how language
intersects with power in the context of the drama and how his actions
are both enabled and constrained by the social givens of that context.
He finishes by explaining to us:

*Before I took drama, last year is the first time I ever took drama, and before
that I had little confidence. I don't dare to talk to anybody else in my class
and because I don't know, I might have this trauma, I have to start over and
nobody can talk to me and I can't talk to anybody. So I guess I have a little
shadow there. But ever since I start taking drama I build my confidence and
people were kind to me and I guess I open up and accept more people. I guess
it helped me a lot to understand that high school isn't this big jungle that you
go in and you just make sure you come out in the end and that's it.*

Clearly Jin is pleased with the confidence he has come to feel, which he
attributes to the drama class. This could be read as a claim for drama's
'transformational' power, but what is more interesting about Jin's re-

sponse, I think, is that he clearly has a new narrative, a new way to imagine himself as he walks through the halls and the students gathered in those halls. Drama did not do this; rather, its mediated, suspended quality made possible situations in which Jin's own capacity for self-representation (or self-deceit) was reflected back to him by his peers and teachers. That is, the drama room became the staging area for a host of explicit demonstrations of the elasticity and negotiated nature of social relations and of identity, a place to disprove theories and debunk myths and stereotypes. It is the quality of interaction in the improvised moment of creation between actors – a sociology of aesthetics, as I have come to understand it – that fosters a form of communication and, by extension, self-representation not typical of the regimented social roles allocated to high school students.

Charlie also remarked on the racial stereotyping that is prevalent in school. For him too, drama class was, to some extent, a reprieve from its ubiquity:

Charlie: I think in Drama class you hear a lot more about um individuals in terms of like their opinions, their views, their outlook on life. And, I think that kind of changes your perspective in terms of if you have these kind of stereotypical ideas of certain people it does kind of open your mind, and I think it allows you to interact with certain people that you don't get to outside of Drama class.

Phil: Have you felt that through your participation in Drama maybe stereotypical notions about you ... have you ever felt that people's attitudes have changed about you?

Charlie: Um, I personally don't exactly know. But I think maybe to a certain degree in terms of interaction. Because I don't know, like, when I was first in the class, I felt like 'Oh I am the only Asian individual there.' It kind of made me feel like a minority and that I was being singled out, and being looked at like 'There's an Asian guy,' but afterwards, when you work in your groups and with partners that kind of diminishes in your mind because you are working together to focus on Drama. And then that kind of breaks, I guess, the stereotypical views of how people see you and how you see them. It kind of works together.

Misha, a new immigrant from Serbia, clearly describes his learning experience in drama, the relationships of time, of space, the active imagining, and the social interaction that enrich his conceptual and language-acquisition processes. In his analysis, the social constructivist and socio-linguistic views of literacy are working in tandem:

Phil: So, has drama changed anything about your experience of school?
Misha (White, male, Serbian, new immigrant, grade eleven Middleview
  student): I don't know. It makes me more open. Makes me more talk. It
  makes me ... I learn more English.
Phil: Why do you think that is?
Misha: Because we talk, we, we ... you know ...
Dominique: You don't talk in other classes?
Misha: Yeah, I talk in other classes, but in Math class, teacher talk, and I –
  after, I doing my homework ... in my Fashion class, I'm ... sewing, and I
  might talk, but ... I talk, I talk, like, in different way. I talk [like] 'Eh,
  what's going on? What's happening?' You know? 'How you doing?' Those
  words. I'm repeating them every day. But, the words which I'm hearing
  here in Drama class is ... they're different. You know? I'm hearing different
  words, I'm hearing different experience, I'm hearing, you know, different
  things.

Performances and Strategies of Gender, Culture, and Style

Drama is just another way ... Drama's just like uh, uh (12-second pause) I
guess Drama's like another way of how life is. I don't know how to say it.
I think Drama's how life is.

                              Maniqua, grade eleven student at Middleview

There is no question that, in all four schools, the processes and practices
of the drama classroom created a different kind of school experience.
The difference I am speaking of here has mainly to do with the ways in
which drama can create an analogous context in which there is always
the possibility of both identification with and distance from the drama.
This is a process I have termed the sociology of aesthetics, that is, an
aesthetic experience that resides in the connection between what a
person already knows (of herself and her community), feels, and desires and what a new experience might offer. Drama makes explicit the
social context, in that one person's aesthetic response is intimately tied
to the performances and responses of the group.

   In drama, we attempt – collectively – to frame our lives through art as
we come to know the world and our sensuous responses to it. As the
teacher places the dramatic frame around learning, something entirely
forgettable for students is shaped into something worth considering. A
deliberate or explicit probing, or what Radford (2000) might call creative thought, invites co-creators to 'play at the boundaries of sense'
(53). Bruner (1986) speaks about the creative act as bringing about a

'shock of recognition,' or what Radford describes as something speaking to something 'within us.' The other principle at work, seemingly at odds with these ideas, is the notion of distance or alienation from an event, in effect a dis-identification. Here I am suggesting that the dramatic 'frame' serves to *distance* the players from the subject in such a way as to ultimately *engage* them aesthetically, or offer multiple ways into a story, which may in some ways be 'too close to home.' I am interested in this idea of the *aesthetic experience* for the ways in which it helps to cultivate sociological questions about representation and the nature of cognitive and embodied dramatic engagement. Key to my view of dramatic engagement is the notion of a provoked imagination.

Let me offer an observation of drama practice at Middleview that may illustrate this point further. We arrived there one day, when the grade eleven students were in the middle of an extended improvisation of the story of a pregnant teen who was living in a group home. At that moment the teacher was asking for a volunteer to go into role as the girl and be 'hot-seated.' This is an improvisational structure in drama that invites a student to be interrogated in-role as a character within the unfolding drama. Dramatic time stands still while teacher and students alike ask questions of the 'character' in order to develop further the context, narrative, and character(s) of the improvised story. A large, confident, White, male student volunteered to 'play' the pregnant fifteen-year old girl. The class screamed with excitement when the teacher allowed him to take the 'hot-seat' in the middle of the room. Rather than make the comedic portrayal we were all expecting, the young man who took on the role listened carefully to the questions and responded with a profound, and unexplainable, recognition/identification that had clearly been unforeseen by all present. Several weeks later, I asked the group of students in a focus-group discussion how they remembered that day in class:

Kathleen: Remember when we first came into your classroom, and ... you guys were doing role-playing? And people went up and sat in the chair, and you were performing different roles from a drama that you were doing, that you did before we came, about a pregnant girl in a home, or something like that? Remember that?

'Yeah' from the group.

Kathleen: Remember Jake played ... the pregnant girl?

Nate (Male, Latin, heterosexual, Portuguese, atheist, working class, difficult, misunderstood, spontaneous, straight up): Yeah.

*Kathleen: Okay ... [some snickers from the group] My memory is ... that he
was really good. That his improvised performance was a really good ... a
really effective interpretation. And, he's this big guy, and he's playing a
pregnant girl. But, nobody laughed. That's my memory. Why was that?
Why did people take that seriously, if that is actually what was going on?
[Everyone in the group begins speaking at once]
Allissa (White, female, Latina): Because he was ... acting good.
Andre: That was ... like, a ... Emmy-winning performance right there.
Kathleen: He – he what?
Andre: That just slapped everyone in the face. That performance ... That was
like, a ... Oscar-winning performance right there. Like ... he just did it. I
was, like 'Whoa.'
Alissa: Yeah, he was right ... into the role.
Alissa and Venus (White, female, first-generation Canadian, of Portuguese
descent): He took it seriously.
Nate: Yeah, certain people just –
Venus [interrupting]: And also, it's not ... being ... uh ... a young girl that's
pregnant is nothing to ... laugh at. Because ... people probably ... like,
thought of it seriously, and ... didn't – they didn't think it funny. They
didn't think it was funny. So, like ... everyone took it seriously.
Kathleen: What were you going to say, Nate?
Nate: Certain people just take initiative like that. They know how ... they ...
like ... It kind of shows ... it kind of shows to some girls that, like ... guys do
know how to, like ... they know how to take certain things serious.*

What is interesting about this unpacking of their drama world is not
only that we, as audience, were surprised by Jake's ability to 'recognize,' or possibly identify with, something about the plight of the young
woman and authentically depict it in his embodiment of the role, but
that the drama structure had given him enough 'distance' from whatever his own private moment of recognition was in order to publicly
'perform' the artistic moment. By contrast, if we recall earlier interviews with Dion, who would not play a gay role – nor did he feel school
was a safe place in which to write about his own life – we might also
suggest that Jake enjoyed enough cultural capital in his classroom to
risk his social position in order to experiment with a dramatic position.

What is further notable about this classroom episode is that for Nate,
the last student to speak, this was a moment of aesthetic representation
that 'spoke to him.' It was a moment in which a new kind of masculinity was permitted into the normally heavily rule-governed space of

acceptable performances of masculinity, in terms of both the fictions students undertake and the so-called real social performances of masculinity: 'It kind of shows ... it kind of shows to some girls that, like ... guys do know how to, like ... they know how to take certain things serious.' At the very least, this moment was important for Nate because it was a performance of masculinity that was 'real' for him; a different masculinity was imagined in that space, a new imaginary provoked, and it resonated with Nate in an important way. Hence my term the 'sociology of aesthetics,' a concept germane to my understanding of the drama classroom: one person's aesthetic engagement is, more often than not, intimately tied to another's in the collective enterprise that is improvised drama.

I am persuaded that these moments of rupture in drama work have something fundamentally to do with the notion of performance, or at least with how the performance of artistic and social roles remains productively incomplete and in perpetual conversation. Unlike, for instance, traditional notions of gender as a stable, albeit socially inscribed, *fact*, gender performance alludes to a reiterative (Butler 1990, 2004) and incomplete *fiction*, with profound moments of discovery, resonance, and truth. In earlier feminist studies, many have argued that the feminine is always 'on show,' while hegemonic definitions of masculinity have also reinforced an oppressive and fixed masculinity that forecloses the interruptions possible in notions of performance. Connell's theoretical connection of masculinity to Gramscian notions of hegemony (1995) illustrates well how multiple versions of masculinity, in societies, are in a constant struggle for dominance. In drama, however, there is always possible a complexity and multiplicity of gender expressions. Contrary to essentialized or normative views of gender, the idea of gender expression or gender performance can be constructed as a form of diversity.

A group of boys in a single-sex focus group at Redmount was particularly effusive on the question of what is afforded through an alternative space, a space where stable meanings are regularly toyed with. What particularly struck me about this boys' focus group were the counter-hegemonic gender expressions revealed and the many contradictions about traditional masculinity that had been awakened for these young men, evidence of an ongoing process of self-redefinition; the metaphoric and analogous world of drama had planted the seeds for other possible masculinities. Identity, for them, is indeed a 'struggle and a process' (Hall 1990):

Philip: How does being in this theatre institute ... even if you're not going to become an actor, you know, and the chances, are, as you know, very slim ... Well, you always have to think that way, but you also have to have a back-up plan. So if you don't become actors, I'm just going to assume that you don't become actors, don't even go into theatre, what has being in the theatre institute given you? Upon graduation, how will it benefit you in the future?

Steven (Bi-racial [Black and White], male, grade twelve student at Redmount): For me, I think, for me, theatre has made, it's made like a big impact, cause, when I first came to school, when I was a freshman, and I was a quiet kid, and you would never see me talking, talking to anybody, I was just walking my way, but then when I got to the theatre institute, it was like, they pushed you, to just at least talk, throw your ideas out, even if it was, like, the craziest idea, just throw it out there. And then, they'd be like, 'Oh, OK,' and then they'll listen to you, and then, that was the strangest thing. But being in the theatre institute, it's like, it makes you, it engages you with other people, it like, they make you, like, how can I say it, it's like, it's like, it's easier to communicate with somebody else that you don't even know. It's like, when Leroy, like, I met him, like, in the sophomore year, I didn't know him, and, like, I had different views about him, but once, like, we started acting together, you could see his personality clearly. And I know Ricky since Junior High, and we acted together, like, you see people clearly, by acting. It engages you more, it gets you to communicate more, and it just follows on.

Ricky (Latino, gay, male, grade twelve student): I think it also left us with a second family that, we know, we're all here for each other. If we ever need to talk about something, 'cause, I know, like, there are other institutes in here, like the pre-med, teaching, right, if you walked into their classroom, you probably don't see a lot of chemistry that we have, and they've been together also for 4 years. But because acting needs us to be, you know, talkative and friendly with each other, you know, it helped us to grow. The first thing you do when you walk into the theatre class, you say, 'Hi, my name is Ricky,' and you tell them about yourself. And there's been time when shy people have been, like, 'Oh, I don't want to go up,' you know, and then we'll be like, 'We'll get back to you, and like, after 2 or 3 people go, it'll be your turn again, and you're going to have to go.' And it helped us open up, and, like, me, personally, I feel like I have a second family to look to, you know?

Leroy (Dominican, male, grade twelve student): Yeah, ah, man, when I came to this school, ah man, I came from New Jersey, I had all my family, my friends over there. When I came here, I was like, 'Ah man, all alone, in New York.' And this high school, I'm a nobody, and you know, I joined the theatre institute, and it made me feel very welcome, very close circle, you know, and it started building up a lot of my confidence, you know, and, I feel like I was able to do anything from that little bit of confidence, you know, walk around the hallways. I know a lot of people now, you know. I got to go out to do sports in the school and everything, you know, and theatre it just gives you, I don't know, it makes me feel like a person, you know, like, I have a lot of confidence now. When I look at people, I always look at them in the eye, shake their hand, make myself very presentable, and I feel like my true character and personality just comes out, speaking to them, and I hope people when they see me, like, they think I'm a relatively good person, just by looking at me, like the way I carry myself, proud, I hold my head up, 'Hi, how you doin?', being polite, and that's incredible.

Joseph (African-American, male, grade eleven): Um, definitely growth. You, by coming to this institute, you grow. Acting ... there's a lot of learning experiences, you know, you, um, you see yourself in different places, it's like an adventure, you go away, you become other people and go to other places, and then, you do whatever you want to, and, I mean, definitely, definitely, you, together, this family is really, really big, and, um, um, I moved around a lot, you know, and coming here, I have, you know, we just work together. You have to. We have to work together, to put on perfor-mances, and, to like, have success, and it's just, just a real learning experi-ence.

In the girls' focus group at Redmount, descriptions of identity as an often contradictory performance, a work in progress, were also omni-present. The performative aspects of the drama classroom had seeped into their social-identity performances:

Isabelle: If you were us asking you questions, what kinds of questions would you ask? And if you had an opportunity to come to Canada and talk to girls taking theatre, what kinds of questions, what would you want to know, what would you be interested in finding more about?

Tanisha (Bi-racial [Black and Hispanic], female, grade twelve student: [I'd ask them,] Are you planning to continue theatre in college? And if not, uh, like if I'm not going to do this in college, I plan to do it on the side, audi-tion or whatever, ... just make it part of my life, it's a part of my life, it's a huge part of my life, because I am who I am because of the classes I've taken here. When I go into job interviews, I'm so like, up there, and they're

*looking at me, like we were expecting this shy little girl to sit in the corner
and just merely answer the questions. No! I'm in theatre, I'm going to
answer the questions, you know, I'm going to elaborate on those questions.
When I'm on the street, and guys are like, 'Hey mommy, how you doin?'
they don't expect how I react ...*

There can, however, be a less affirmative side to the construction of
gender performance in schools too, and that was encountered at St
Bernadette's. Because of Ms G's framing of 'good girls' and 'bad girls'
in her classsroom, much of our research that followed took a particular
interest in examining how these gender performances get reproduced
and resisted in this all-female environment. A subset of literacy research
illustrates how children, from a very early age, use literacy to make
sense of the versions of masculinity and femininity they see in their
lives and imagine themselves as actors of them (Orellana 1995). They
write themselves into different gendered societal categories – like 'good
girl' or 'bad girl' – and effectively try on different gendered practices
and identities:

Isabelle: Do 'good girls' ever break the rules?
Ruby: Yes, good girls do break rules.
Dominique: How often are they caught?
Ruby: Hardly (laughs).
Dominique: Why do you think that is?
*Ruby: Because they're sneaky and they're good (laughs). Because, because,
   because of the way they're perceived. It's not likely for them to look like
   they're going to get into any trouble, but there's girls, like, who will get in
   trouble all the time.*

Many girls reiterated the good girl / bad girl dichotomy in interviews,
something the school had certainly reinforced in our observations, but
in an open focus-group discussion on the topic of gender performance,
there emerged some interestingly different readings of gender-norma-
tive behaviour. There are clear disagreements about 'feminine'
behaviours. In this instance, the differences fall along racial lines:

*Maria (Female, first-generation Canadian, of Italian descent, grade ten
   student): I think that there might be, um ... In a co-ed school, there's
   probably more competition for getting the guy, or whatever.*
Kathleen: Between girls?

Maria [agreeing]: Between girls.
Kathleen: Uh-huh. Bridgit, what were you going to say?
Bridgit (Female, White, first-generation Canadian, of European descent): It's
  more organized because girls are ... easier, to tell what to do ... [Everyone
  laughs, but Sabina says, 'Yeah, okay. What school do you go to?' More
  laughter follows.]
Kathleen: Okay, we have different opinions.
Maria: But if you go to a Drama class with all guys, you say, 'Be quiet!' and
  they'll keep talking. You go into an all girls Drama class, you flip the lights
  on, and they'll, like, shut up.
Kathleen: So you think ... girls are more submissive.
Maria [hesitantly]: Yeah ...
Kathleen: They do what they're told, more.
Maria: They tend to.
Kathleen: Okay. Sabina?
Sabina (Female, Black, of Caribbean descent, first-generation Canadian):
  Okay, I completely disagree with that, but anyway ...

One of the most striking interviews was with a grade eleven student
at Middleview, who had admitted that he'd been bullied quite regularly in grade nine, he thought, because of his gender non-conformity.
Stefan, being a 'sissy boy,' was a very fine example of what McInnes
and Couch (2004) consider a disruption to discursive reproduction. He
was a boy who took 'Fashion' as one of his subjects, which made him an
easy target, in his view. He eloquently explained to us that it was not
about his sexuality, but about his sensibilities. His analysis, subse-
quently, of good-boy performances of masculinity at school was particularly enlightening, taking into account the social contexts in which
such performances occur. This interview speaks once again to the complexities of (and obsessions with) 'discipline' in urban high schools:

Stefan (White, male, Yugoslavian-born, grade eleven student): I have a
  feeling that people take, you know, different approaches to hurting other
  people, which is also a problem ... I think last year is when they expelled
  about 1,200 students or something along those lines.
Isabelle: 1,200? Sorry?
Stefan: Yeah, I think it was around 1,200, and they, if I remember this cor-
  rectly, they had this sort of criteria, whether you skipped so many classes or
  whether you've been called to the office 5 times. And I have to say, since
  that has happened, it's been a lot nicer in the school.

Isabelle: So it has had the overall effect of lessening the hate?

Stefan: It has. But I think there is a problem though because in a way, we are just sort of throwing out the sort of 'problem students,' but then again, a lot of those problem students can't be dealt with. There are issues that are far too deep for the school to go into, you know, it's not an issue, like, you're not doing your homework, or not liking your teacher. There's family issues, there's you know, social status issues, there's financial issues.

Isabelle: You think those issues contribute to making those particular students more aggressive?

Stefan: Oh, completely! I find that a lot of people are, or the majority of the people that have been kicked out, if you look at their background, you go, 'Oh, oh well it wasn't too too great to start with,' and it's unfortunate because you'd like to think of a school as a place where if you're having problems, you can at least come here, or at least that's what they're saying. It'd be GREAT if that were true, but I think with the zero-tolerance policy, and again, I don't know the full extent of how they go about it, but, I have a feeling that they just throw people out. I mean they give them enough chances, I think, but there's always, that, 'Hmm, they treated that person a little bit harshly, they could have maybe organized something with the family to ...'

Isabelle: You mean to find solutions?

Stefan: ... find solutions. I'm not saying to go into therapy or anything (laughs), but working out problems, which is just a major, major part of it. I know that half of the people, when I was in grade 9, I had a pretty rough time in the school, and I sort of realized that part of the problem was not that people had a direct problem with me, but people had a problem with the fact that, you know, I wasn't going through the problem of so-called, 'teenage angst,' and I wasn't rebelling against my parents, you know, and I wasn't saying I was going to run away from home, or I'm going to commit suicide. I'm going home, with a car that my parents bought me, and I'm going ... my mother and I are going out to see a show and then I'm taking my sister somewhere, and I think that, and I didn't realize this when I came here, but I think that a lot of people actually have a lot of family issues here and I think that actually really contributes to a lot of the problems. And I'm sorry to say, but that's part of the problem. And I certainly didn't know that when I came here. I realized that a lot of the people that were sort of against me, the principal would tell me, I remember a couple times, I was talking to the V-P, and they'd say, 'Well, you know, that person comes from a really, really terrible background, and you know, there's abuse.' I mean,

*you know, the worst thing is throwing out a student and they have to go
back into a worse situation.*

We continued talking to Stefan about his experiences of school and his
perception of the challenges of social cohesion. He described those who
don't conform, especially to gender codes, as was his own experience,
to be on the 'outskirts' of school. But for him, drama was a kind of
sanctuary and, as so many of the students had described it, a place
where unlikely people 'bonded':

*Stefan: I have no idea [why drama is like that]. I think, I guess, part of it
would be the whole, the whole exercises in drama, having to teach you to
present yourself and how to work with other people. I think those do more
than we give them credit for, you know? Um, really, I don't know why
because there are other classrooms where it would seem like people would,
would mix well, and they don't.*
Isabelle: Like what kind of class?
*Stefan: Well, sort of the general interest courses, right? Like when people are
taking, you know, auto mechanics, or, or gym, where you're thinking it's a
whole bunch of people doing something that they supposedly like, so why
aren't they talking? I've been in a few of those different classes, and I don't
find that people are as, as interested in, in making friendships as they are in
drama, I'm not really sure why but drama class it's really, I find that by the
end of the year, it's like a well-oiled machine ... yeah. A lot of people who
you didn't think you'd be talking to, and then you're best friends, so hey,
why not?*
Isabelle: Like that 'mingling' that you were talking about earlier.
Stefan:Yeah.

⌐There is much talk of 'border-crossing' in postmodern theories of
schooling, but very little pedagogical practice that lives up to that
promise.⌐ Through the course of this research, we have observed time
and again that in drama classrooms, curriculum and pedagogy come
together, in the best cases, in very potent ways. These experiences are
valued by students precisely because they challenge encounters between the self and the other where impermanence is the only constant.
The persistence of the search, the discovery of a new concept or the
repositioning of an old one, the shaky exploration, that is the pedagogical life of a drama curriculum⌐ I am persuaded now, more than ever,
that drama accomplishes something crucial in the 'global' world that is

the urban school: it resymbolizes the very experiential, intuitive, subcultural, 'home' knowledge that is prized by young people, who work
assiduously at making meaning of their present circumstances and
have the courage to imagine better futures. More often than not, they
tell us, drama class provides them with the laboratory in which to
experiment and work through what they know in their bodies, but
seldom find reflected in their textbooks. Grumet's poetic rumination
(1991, 75) is appropriately insistent:

> The practical knowledge that we bring with us from home remains trapped
> in memory coded in images, sensory associations, stories, and emotions.
> Lodged in intuition, this practical knowledge is rarely extended to our
> work in the public world because it is rarely resymbolized through pro-
> cesses that encode if for reflection and translation to other settings.
>
> The problem with practical knowledge is that we don't know we have it
> until the context where we developed it is changed. Then in a new place,
> seeing again the events, relationships, and configuration of the old, we
> experience *re-cognition*, recognizing the world we know and realizing that
> we know it well. When home and school are dichotomized into the
> private and the public, the female and the male, the infantile and the
> adult, the familiar and the strange, both students and teachers are cut off,
> isolated from the practical knowledge that is our real homework. Instead
> of recognizing what we learned at home and extending it and elaborating
> it in other forms, we deny it and relinquish a usable past.

5 CONSTITUTING CULTURE AND CO-RESEARCH WITH YOUTH

The weight of this sad time we must obey,
Speak what we feel, not what we ought to say
The oldest hath borne most; we that are young
Shall never see so much, nor live so long.
> *Exeunt with a dead march.*
>
> *King Lear*, act 5, scene 3

Despite our claim to be committed to critical ethnographic practice, there is no way to know whether our dialogues with youth and their teachers will result in substantive change in their lives. As in teaching, one never really knows. And what would be the measure of such change? Would it be enduring change? Without the benefit of time, the most we have are our teachers' observations of students they know, in most cases, much better than we do and the periodic comments made by individual young people:

Kathleen: You said something really interesting in your reflections about what you understood about what we were doing as researchers in your classroom and what we were inviting you to do as co-researchers. Can you tell us a little bit about that? What your thoughts are on that?

Sanjeet: (Brown, female, first-generation Canadian, South Asian descent, Middleview grade twelve student): I do remember that I said that – um, what I really like about this research is that it's positive as opposed to other research projects that look for statistics and what's wrong with teenagers. But to make us, as teenagers, really contributive members of society, it's important to realize what it is that makes us productive. And I think this research, you guys are trying to figure out, how the drama setting has influenced the people we've become, and if you ... if you expose teenagers to good conditions, you're not going to get involved in drugs or gangs, or that sort of thing. And, yeah, I think that it's very good that you guys look for, study, the positive rather than the negative.

Kathleen: And what did we do that made you think that we were studying the positive?

Sanjeet: Uh – You guys assumed the best about us, in a lot of ways. You didn't assume – you looked at us in a positive light. You encouraged us to get involved, get to know each other and there were lots of times when we worked with you guys and interacted with you whereas I'm sure that if this was in another classroom, you guys would have been at the back, taking notes, and that's intimidating as – you know. Like Phil would organize games and he'd get right involved and he'd get competitive just like us [laughs].

Kathleen: Right. [laughs]

Sanjeet supports what others have expressed who study participatory forms of research with youth. Goodley and Clough (2004), for instance, found that youth benefited most from participation in research when they felt respected by researchers and when projects gave them new and relevant experiences that they could take with them as they entered early adulthood. But Sanjeet's explanation also confirmed, for us, the importance of studying the category of 'youth' more generally. Driscoll (2002) elucidates:

> The idea of youth has been used to question how people come to be particular kinds of individuals and identifiable selves, how cultures surround and define us individually and as groups, and how cultures are reproduced and challenged by individuals and groups. Youth has been a fascinating object of modernity – identified with an attitude to contemporaneity and change – because of its association with the new, the future, and diverse social changes, and provides an important focus for thinking about how societies work. (204)

We cannot know, nonetheless, whether our work with the youth of our study will lead to tangible social change, a goal we privileged in our methodologies. But our experiences together will, surely, outlive the scope of this research project. In our research practices, we tried to change the direction in which knowledge and authority traditionally flow. We often shared data with the students and would ask them, for instance, to work up scenes from the data and give titles to these scenes. This certainly helped us to see their analyses of the data and also to see whether their 'titles' reflected in any way the themes we had, ourselves, drawn out from the data. On many occasions we were impressed by how much congruity there was. But whether this interrupted, in substantive or lasting ways, the traditional forms of knowledge construction in classrooms, we cannot know. We are, after all, in the institution of the school and like all institutions, schools are ultimately interested in self-preservation; any ideas of real empowerment, then, can only go so far. And as always, the problem in education is that we want immediate results. If, however, we are committed to increasing the democratic distribution of power through classroom cultures, this will take time; it is a research problem for dialectical examination rather than quantifiable analysis. As Brown (2004) articulates: 'It is not an act of analysis but of interpenetration insofar as ethnographic inquiry is doubly sheathed in the experience of the ethnographer and in the lived reality of the participant, which are brought into dialectical contact in this knowledge-making process' (308).

What we do know, definitively, is that our research with youth was uniquely powered by drama. In an interview with Ms S in which we asked her to reflect on the impact, on her students, of our methodological shift towards drama in the second year of the study, she clearly articulated the importance of working physically and collaboratively with youth:

Kathleen: I want to ask you about your ... reflections on what we called the second phase of our research, which, as you know, was methodologically different from the first phase, in the sense that we were less the eyes looking down upon the students, and more about helping them facilitate our seeing; asking them to point to the kinds of things we should be looking at, the kinds of questions we might be asking, or might have asked. That was our goal, anyway, and a lot of how we wanted to make that happen, uh, some of it was predetermined, and other parts of it were very much in response to questions or issues that came forward from students. So, in terms of the research, we wanted this period of time to be different from the first phase, in the sense that we're moving along in our analyses, in our understanding, in our data collection ... We have a fuller knowledge of the place and the people now. Given all of that, we were attempting to figure

out how to tap into the opinions, ideas, structures for meaning-making
that kids have for themselves, that we don't necessarily figure out as ...
researchers. So did you see differences in terms of the ways students
engaged?

Ms S *(White, Jewish, female, Canadian-born, teacher): Um, okay ... there's*
lots in that question, so ... I think that ... One thing that I think is so
important with teenagers, especially with Drama, is that I think that a lot
comes out and they make a lot of meaning when they're on their feet,
working. I think that so much has to come out in the body, or through the
body. The conversations were very rich, and I always love the conversa-
tions that happen when, when you are here, when the researchers are in the
classroom. So, I – I don't mean that part, but I think that, um, when you
did the process drama [the 'employee review' drama], I thought then a lot
of interesting stuff came out, because you were ... that was really success-
ful, that really engaged them. And also, the ones who are usually silent,
right, in the conversation, could, you know, physicalize, and vocalize all of
a sudden. Yeah, so it created a space for them. I think that working impro-
visationally with students is really good. And, I don't feel ... I feel like I'm
learning more about it, and I want to learn even more. I think they respond
to stories ... and fiction.

The business of bringing worlds into being, bringing people together in concerted action, cannot be underestimated in the evolving world of ethnography. Further, the extent to which actual lives become the fodder for new imaginaries, the creative ways in which the drama world can use and manipulate realities, creates a playfulness with potentially serious consequences.

A Problem-Posing Ethnography

The purpose of art is to lay bare the questions which have been hidden by the answers.

James Baldwin, in Lerman and Borstel, *Critical Response Process*, 8

As ethnographers, we have the privilege, unlike most teachers, of entering the classroom and freely admitting that we have no particular plan or expectation of how it will all turn out. Even though the best kind of learning should be spontaneous and unpredictable, increasingly, in the current fervour for accountability, teachers are expected to have it all mapped out in advance. Our asking the students to help us with the research task – to be co-researchers – was thus at odds with much of what students are required to do these days; Loralei openly expressed confusion about some of the 'weird' activities we were asking the students to engage in. Her friend, Ari, responded better than we could have, in this way:

They're researchers, they don't know what answers they want yet. They want to see if they can find it. If they wanted it on acting then they would go straight to the point and say, 'Okay I want to see you act.' But it's about students and how they act in Drama class ... They don't know what they're looking for, that's why they're doing all these activities and exercises, just to see our reaction and how we act towards it ... in Drama class.

With our special status as outside eyes, we were free to imagine ways in which our cumulative work would flow from the students' interests and concerns, an overall shape being suggested not by timelines, course outlines, or assessment needs, but rather by the more intuitive pedagogical practice of following where the students' enthusiasms and insights led us. Ari's comments bear witness to how little room there is, in traditional pedagogy, to provide students with opportunities to engage in open-ended inquiry. This kind of research also requires a flexible teacher who is open to having her curriculum re-imagined, so as to more organically and more thoroughly integrate the research frame.

Despite regularly insisting that we were involved in 'co-research' with a tremendously diverse set of students, we never lost sight of the power dynamics at work in presenting ourselves in this way: owing to our elevated professional status and access to cultural capital (relative to the teacher and the students) we had the luxury of conferring whatever title we wished upon ourselves and upon the students. In other words, simply calling ourselves co-researchers did not make it so. From several informal asides uttered by the students, we were aware that their conception of a researcher was of someone who experiments, uses trial and error; we were thought of as impartial observers, appraisers, highly educated people conducting tests to generate data, with the results and conclusions to be published in a scientific journal they would never read. Given their preconceptions and our desire to establish a trusting relationship with the class, it was a daunting task to (1) genuinely collaborate with them on this research; (2) explicate the subtleties of our critical ethnographic methodology; (3) overturn a built-in self-consciousness that obtains whenever visitors from outside the classroom come to observe; and (4) remain ever vigilant about our raced, classed, gendered translations of *their* ideas. Fine's caveats (1994) about ethics, praxis, and qualitative research rang in our ears: 'Domination and distance get sanitized inside science. Portraits of disdain, pity, need, strength, or all of the above are delivered for public consumption' (79). We do not delude ourselves into thinking that we could ever fully disrupt the power relations from which we gained our elevated status, nor was this our goal. And certainly the framework within which our research was conducted would never dissolve so completely that we could fail to notice that these students still occupied their roles as students, and we as 'the researchers from the university.'

Our persistent interests in engaging our students as co-investigators in this inquiry compelled us to invite them to devise their own final interview protocols. At the end of the first semester at Middleview (February 2004), in the second year of the study, we set up an interesting interview session wherein students, in pairs, could interview one another with three questions they invented. It was our last day with them after a full and intense semester and we'd grown quite close to this group. Two long rows of students, seated in chairs, faced each other, while four researchers wandered on the margins. One pair after another 'conducted' their interview while the rest of us listened in; I particularly wanted all the students to hear each other's questions and answers. There were many extraordinary exchanges between students as we looked on, but our more passive researcher roles and our 'plan' was soon interrupted. Instead of addressing his partner when his turn arrived, Andre turned the gaze on us: Are you satisfied with the research you did at Middleview and other places you've been to?

Kathleen to Andre [confirming]: Is that for the researchers? [Andre nods.]
Phil: Can you repeat the question?
Andre (Male, African Canadian, heterosexual, English, a little Patwa [Jamaican], Christian: Are you satisfied with the research you did at Middleview, and other places you've been to?
Kathleen: More than satisfied is my answer. It's been bigger and more interesting than I ever imagined when I dreamt up the project. So 'satisfied,' for me, is not even an adequate word. I learned more ... I knew I would learn a lot, but I had no idea that it would be this kind of experience: so complex, so interesting, so full of meaning ... amazing people and also working with an incredible team.

Phil: Ditto.

Dominique: What she said.

Phil: I don't have anything to add to that.

Andre: [laughs] 'ditto, ditto, ditto,' do I ask my next question?

Kathleen [nodding]: Sure.

Andre: Do you think we stayed on track with the research, or do you think a lot of the time was wasted and we could have done more?

Phil: I will take that. To say, in every activity whether that's teaching or acting or living, there's 'wasted time' … we have this idea of 'wasted time,' and I think, instead – in a creative project especially – you need 'wasted time'; you need time where things may not be working right or it's not coming together. My feeling is that if there was 'wasted time,' the only time when there was 'wasted time' is, on my part, if I didn't respond to what I was seeing well enough, like maybe I didn't pick up on some things and maybe let other things go, but in terms of the class as a whole, what we did? I don't think any time was wasted. I think we did some really great stuff, and, who knows, maybe we needed it to be that way to do what we did.

Loralei and Sabicca then had an exchange between them that helped us confirm some of what we had been observing in their drama classroom, which further underscores the impact of pedagogical spaces on young people:

Loralei (Black, female, new immigrant, born in the former Congo, moved from South Africa to Belgium, to Canada, grade twelve student): When drama students walk out of this class, why is it that it is a different story when you walk out of that door?

Sabicca (Black, female, first-generation Canadian, Caribbean descent, grade twelve student): Wow. Um – 'cause the atmosphere just changes. It's like, I don't know – it's like livin' downtown and going to the suburbs, the atmosphere is completely different, you know? So once you're in here … this nice friendly atmosphere where, like, everyone's happy, or lying down, and laughing and crack jokes, then you go out to the serious world, and it's like, 'Now I got to stay focused,' and you got to do your work. The atmosphere just changes, that's the only difference. So you have to adjust your atmosphere to where you are.

Sanjeet and Shaylene also have an interesting exchange:

Shaylene (Black, female, first-generation Canadian, of Caribbean descent, grade twelve student): OK Sanjeet, how does drama differ from other classes?

Sanjeet: Um, I think it differs in that you have a lot of opportunities to interact with your fellow classmates a lot more, and it's a freer environment that fosters class discussions, which are always important to have. And it really gives you an opportunity to meet a lot of people whom, otherwise, you wouldn't have a chance to meet. OK, Shaylene, how has the drama class had an impact on your development as an individual?

Shaylene: Like, this is the first time I actually took drama and I've learned quite a bit, actually. I learned a lot and it feels good, and, like, what you're saying about how you get to interact with people so much more, it's really true. And that's how it's helped me, in that sense, the interacting a little more and the turning out more.

Then Ari turned the gaze back on us:

Ari (Bi-racial [Jamaican and French-Canadian], female, grade twelve student): This is a question for an adult, so whoever wants to answer ... Um, as a teenager, you must have felt lost and hoped that you'd find your way when you reached adulthood. But now that you're an adult, do you feel as sure of yourself and the point of life?

Phil: I don't think there's much difference. But just one of the differences though, between high school life compared to my life now, is that I answer to myself. In high school, I'd get frustrated with how many people I'd have to answer to: my parents, the teachers, and blah, blah, blah, blah. Now, I find it harder in a way, because I have high expectations for myself and when I don't meet those expectations, it's very hard to cope with that. If you let somebody else down, you can kind of go, 'Oh, they're a jerk!' but if it's you that you're letting down, it's kind of harder to live with and that gives you a feeling of being lost, because, well, you wonder, 'Are my standards too high, or am I just not measuring up?'

*Kathleen: I think I would say that when I was a teenager ... I liked being a teenager, but I also spent a lot of time thinking that I'd be this really **different** person when I was old and things would be just so. I'm really happy with my life but I realize now that the seeds of who I am were present then. So I didn't morph into this different person, but who I was then – with all my insecurities, and worries and concerns – they're still with me, except I feel that the ground beneath my feet is a little bit more solid.*

I don't know why I hadn't anticipated this, but it was clear that they were building on each other's ideas and had important questions to ask of us. It was the case that they had been 'co-researchers' with us, but they were increasingly aware that the authorial privileges and responsibilities lay with me:

Misha (White, Serbian, new immigrant, male, grade eleven student): OK, I have a question for you guys [looks up to Kathleen, Phil, and Dominique]. What is the ... what was the best idea that you guys got from us so far?
Dominique: The best idea ... They've all been really good ideas. I don't know that there's one that I can sort of say, 'That's it, that's the best thing.' I think, um, what I particularly like about this class – and, maybe, it's the school in general – is the way that the plans that we have for you don't always work out according to our plan but what you do with it is way better than anything we could have come up with anyway, so, it's really good that way. The spontaneous discussions that we've had, the way you engage with the work that we give you, there's no way we could have planned or imagined that, so, I say that's what would be the 'best thing' about this class, about this research.

I would be remiss if I ended this book without, again, acknowledging the contributions of my research assistants. I am all the more aware, as I near the conclusion, of the intellectual community we created over three years. I was aware, especially, as I immersed myself in field notes and interview transcripts, of how tremendously fortunate I was to find a group of students – six of them over the course of three years – each of whom embodied the respect for our research participants that I prized, the pedagogical skills and bravery to leap so completely into our classrooms, and the analytical and theoretical capacity to constantly challenge our ethical, methodological, and dramatic decisions. I regularly demanded of us a self-reflexivity and commitment to the work that was equally valued by them. After the first day of year two, I asked each of us to reflect on this poignant day at Middleview. Phil writes:

My impression of this class, in the end, is that we are luuu-u-ucky to be working on this project with them: I think we are going to get some dynamite stuff. I hope they enjoy it and don't feel like we're taking advantage of their friendliness, their enthusiasm, their youth. I looked around the room at one point and I was just so excited to get to know these kids, to hear from them what they make of the world; to be in conversation with them around how they view themselves and others, and how they would like to be viewed. It's going to be a good year, I think. (12 February 2004)

Over the course of three full years in four exceptional 'urban schools' in two very different cities, we became infected with the humanity of these places. We were humbled by the resilience of young people, angered by institutional incompetence, persuaded over and over again by the intelligence required to teach, fired up by the politics and ideology that marginalize many youth, troubled by our own inability to make swift changes, but strengthened in our conviction that change was necessary. The prescriptive social roles (sometimes strikingly defied by artistic roles) currently afforded young people are not only limiting, but also increasingly dangerous. These ubiquitous negative depictions of youth change our social space in ways that progressively diminish our capacity to cross borders and confront the politics of power and the realities of social malaise in our classrooms, on our streets, and in our imaginaries. Our early impressions of urban schools as security-obsessed spaces, inhospitable to many young people, were not inaccurate, but were, thankfully, countered by the creative work and powerful youth voices of resistance we encountered over the ensuing three years. Upon reflection, it was not so strange after all, to examine – in two great North American cities – the state of social cohesion for youth in urban schools through the telephoto lens of the drama classroom.

Isabelle: So what kinds of stereotypes exist about teenagers?
Kayla: Well, that we steal. I don't know, like, we just have like a bad 'rep.'
  Everyone just thinks ... especially about, like it's, you know, you're a
  teenager, you're still a child, so it's like: oh yeah they don't know anything.
Dominique: Okay. Any thoughts on that, Jin?
Jin: Yeah, just one. Adults tend to think that teenagers are still young and
  they do something and they don't know what they're doing. They don't
  have the responsibility to handle anything they do, so the adults have to be
  responsible for them. But I don't think that's true for all teenagers, so I
  don't like that stereotype. In general, they think of everyone in the same
  way as they would think of, I don't know exactly how you would say it, but
  they don't want to separate the bad from the good, but they just want to
  think of everyone the same way ...
Dominique: They lump everyone together, okay.
Jin: Yeah, save themselves time and save themselves work.

There is a Russian folk tale about a mythical town called Kitezh. The story goes that when Kitezh sensed that marauders were approaching, it encased itself in a mist and shrank into it and vanished from sight. But even as it disappeared, even after it had disappeared, the church bell never stopped ringing and could be heard through the mist and over the whole countryside.

I suppose that like all folk tales this story can be interpreted in whatever way your needs require. But for me the true gift of theatre, the real benediction of all art, is the ringing bell which reverberates quietly and persistently in the head long after the curtain has come down and the audience has gone home. Because until the marauders withdraw and the fog lifts, that sacred song is the only momentary stay we have against confusion. (Friel 1999, 180)

REFERENCES

Ackroyd, J. 2006. *Research Methodologies for Drama Education*. Oakhill, Eng.: Trentham Books Ltd.

Andersen, C. 2004. 'Learning in "As-If" Cognition in Drama in Education.' *Theory Into Practice* 43(4), 281–85.

Angrosino, M., and K. Mays de Perez. 2000. 'Rethinking Observation: From Method to Context.' In N. Denzin and Y. Lincoln, eds, *Handbook of Qualitative Research* (2nd ed.), 673–702. Thousand Oaks, CA: Sage Publications.

Anyon, J. 1997. *Ghetto Schooling: A Political Economy of Urban Educational Reform*. New York: Teachers College Press.

– 2005. *Radical Possibilities: Public Policy, Urban Education, and a New Social Movement*. New York: Routledge.

Apple, M., ed. 2004. *Ideology and Curriculum*. 3rd ed. London, New York: Routledge Falmer.

Apter, E. 1998. 'Harem: Colonial Fiction and Architectural Fantasm in Turn-of-the-Century France.' In H. Nast and S. Pile, eds, *Places through the Body*, 119–32. New York: Routledge.

Arnot, M. 1982. 'Male Hegemony, Social Class and Women's Education.' *Journal of Education* 164(1), 64–89.

Austin, J.L. 1962. *How to Do Things with Words*. Oxford: Clarendon Press.

Ball, S.J., ed. 1990. *Foucault and Education: Disciplines and Knowledge*. London, New York: Routledge.

Barker, H. 1997. *Arguments for a Theatre*. 3rd ed. Manchester: Manchester University Press.

Barry, B. 2005. *Why Social Justice Matters*. Cambridge, UK, and Malden, MA: Polity.

Bayliss, P., and C. Dodwell. 2002. 'Building Relationships through Drama: The Action Track Project.' *Research in Drama Education* 7(1), 43–60.

Becker, C., ed. 1994. *The Subversive Imagination : Artists, Society, and Responsibility*. New York: Routledge.

Berger, J. 2002. 5 March 1992, 'Teachers union, in solid front, authorizes walkouts.' *New York Times*, B4.

Besley, A.C. 2003. 'Hybridized and Globalized: Youth Cultures in the Postmodern Era.' *Review of Education, Pedagogy, and Cultural Studies* 25(2), 153–77.

Best, S., and D. Kellner. 2003. 'Contemporary Youth and the Postmodern Adventure.' *Review of Education, Pedagogy, and Cultural Studies* 25, 75–93.

Bhawuk, D.P.S. 1990. 'Cross-cultural Orientation Programs.' In R.W. Brislin, ed., *Applied Cross-cultural Psychology*. Cross-cultural Research and Methodology Series, vol. 14, 325–46. Thousand Oaks, CA: Sage Publications.

Boal, A. 1979. *Theatre of the Oppressed*. Trans. A. Charles and M.-O. Leal. New York: Urizen.

– 1992. *Games for Actors and Non-Actors*. Trans. A. Jackson. London and New York: Routledge.

Bond, E. 2000. *The Children; and, Have I None*. London: Methuen Drama.

Booth, D. 1994. *StoryDrama: Reading, Writing and Roleplaying across the Curriculum*. Markham, ON: Pembroke Publishers.

Branch, C. 1996 'Lessons (in Identity) Learned from the Competing Curriculum: Some Thoughts.' In E.R. Hollins, ed., *Transforming Curriculum for a Culturally Diverse Society*, 169–78. Mahwah, NJ.: Lawrence Erlbaum Associates.

Brannon, R., and D.S., David, eds. 1976. *The Forty-nine Percent Majority: The Male Sex Role*. Reading, MA, and Don Mills, ON: Addison-Wesley Pub. Co.

Bransford, J., ed. 2000. *How People Learn: Brain, Mind, Experience, and School*. Expanded ed. Washington: National Academy Press.

Britzman, D.P. 1998. 'Is There a Queer Pedagogy? Or, Stop Reading Straight.' In W.F. Pinar, ed., *Curriculum: Toward New Identities*, 211–32. New York: Garland.

– 2000. '"The Question of Belief": Writing Poststructural Ethnography.' In E.A. St.-Pierre and W.S. Pillow, eds, *Working the Ruins: Feminist Poststructural Theory and Methods in Education*, 27–40. New York: Routledge.

– 2001. 'The Arts of Inquiry.' *Journal of Curriculum Theorizing* 17(2), 9–26.

Brooke, R., and C. Hogg. 2004. 'Open to Change: Ethos, Identification, and Critical Ethnography in Composition Studies.' In S.G. Brown and S.I. Dobrin, eds, *Ethnography Unbound: From Postmodern Theory to Critical Praxis*. Albany: State University of New York.

Brown, S.G. 2004. 'Beyond Shock Theory: Ethos, Knowledge, and Power in Critical Ethnography.' In S.G. Brown and S.I. Dobrin, eds, *Ethnography Unbound: From Theory Shock to Critical Praxis*, 299–315. Albany: State University of New York.

Bruner, J. 1986. *Actual Minds, Possible Worlds*. Boston: Harvard University Press.

Burns, K. 1997. *A House for Josephine*. In B.G. Nalbantoglu and C. Wong, eds, *Postcolonial space(s)*, 53–72. New York: Princeton Architectural Press.

Butler, James. 1996. 'The Proof Paradox: Homonegativity and Silencing.' In L. Laskey and C. Beavis, eds, *Schooling and Sexualities: Teaching for a Positive Sexuality*, 131–50. Geelong, AUS: Deakin Centre for Education and Change.

Butler, Judith. 1990. *Gender Trouble: Feminism and the Subversion of Identity*. New York: Routledge.

– 1993. *Bodies That Matter: On the Discursive Limits of 'Sex.'* London: Routledge.

– 1995. 'For a Careful Reading.' In S. Benhabib, J. Butler, D. Cornell, and N. Fraser, eds, *Feminist Contentions: A Philosophical Exchange*. New York: Routledge.

– 1997. *Excitable Speech: A Politics of the Performative*. New York: Routledge.

– 2004. *Undoing Gender*. New York, London: Routledge.

Butler, J., Peter Osborne, and Lynne Segal. 1994. 'Gender as Performance. An Interview with Judith Butler.' *Radical Philosophy* 67 (Summer), 32–9.

Calliste, A., and George J. Sefa Dei, eds. 2000. *Anti-racist Feminism: Critical Race and Gender Studies*. Halifax: Fernwood Publishing.

Çelik, Z. 2000. Excerpts from 'Le Corbusier, Orientalism, Colonialism.' In Rendell, Penner, and Borden, eds, *Gender, Space, Architecture*, 321–31.

Centre for Addiction and Mental Health. 2006. 'One in 50 Ontario High School Students Reports Carrying a Gun.' *CAMH Population Studies eBulletin* vol. 7(1).

Centers for Disease Control and Prevention. 2004. *Surveillance Summaries*, 21 May. MMWR 2004: 53 (no. SS-2).

Chapman, C., and A. Harris. 2004. 'Improving Schools in Difficult and Challenging Contexts: Strategies for Improvement.' *Educational Research* 46(3), 219–28.

Cole, E.B. 1993. *Philosophy and Feminist Criticism*. New York: Paragon House.

Colomina, B., ed. 1992. *Sexuality and Space*. New York: Princeton Architectural Press.

Comer, J.P., and N. Hayes. 1991. 'Parent Involvement in Schools: An Ecological Approach.' *Elementary School Journal* (Special Issue: Educational Partnerships: Home, School, & Community) 91(3), 271–7.

Connell, R.W. 1995. *Masculinities*. Berkeley, Los Angeles: University of California Press.

Crowhurst, M. 2002. 'Heteroprivilegism: Three Layers of Discriminatory Practices That Target Non-Heterosexual Subjects.' *National Drama* 26(2).

Cummins, J. 2001. *Negotiating Identities: Education for Empowerment in a Diverse Society*. 2nd ed. Ontario, CA: California Association for Bilingual Education.

Daiutte, C. 2000. 'The Narrative Sites for Youths' Construction of Social Consciousness.' In L. Weis and M. Fine, eds, *Construction Sites: Excavating Race, Class, and Gender among Urban Youth*. New York and London: Teachers College Press.

de Certeau, M. 1984. *The Practice of the Everyday Life*. Trans. S. Rendall. Berkeley: University of California Press.

Delpit, L. 1988. 'The Silenced Dialogue: Power and Pedagogy in Educating Other People's Children.' *Harvard Educational Review* 58(3), 280–98.

Denzin, N.K. 1997. *Interpretive Ethnography: Ethnographic Practices for the 21st Century*. Thousand Oaks, CA: Sage Publications.

Dovey, K. 1999. *Framing Places: Mediating Power in Built Form*. London, New York: Routledge.

Driscoll, C. 2002. *Girls: Feminine Adolescence in Popular Culture & Cultural Theory*. New York: Columbia University Press.

Dunbar, C., Jr, and F.A. Villaruel. 2004. 'What a Difference the Community Makes: Zero Tolerance Policy Interpretation and Implementation.' *Equity & Excellence in Education* 37(4), 351–9.

Duncan-Andrade, J.M.R. 2004. 'Your Best Friend or Your Worst Enemy: Youth Popular Culture, Pedagogy, and Curriculum in Urban Classrooms.' *Review of Education, Pedagogy & Cultural Studies* 26(4), 313–37.

Ellsworth, E.A. 1997. *Teaching Positions: Difference, Pedagogy, and the Power of Address*. New York: Teachers College Press.

Emerson, R.M., R.I. Fretz, and L. Shaw. 1995. *Writing Ethnographic Fieldnotes*. Chicago: University of Chicago Press.

Ennis, C.D., and T.M. McCauley. 2003. 'Creating Urban Classroom Communities Worthy of Trust.' *Journal of Curriculum Studies* 34(2), 149–72.

Fasset, D.L., and J.T. Warren. 2005. 'The Strategic Rhetoric of an "At-Risk" Educational Identity: Interviewing Jane.' *Communication & Critical/Cultural Studies* 2(3), 238–56.

Fine, M. 1994. 'Working the Hyphens: Reinventing Self and Other in Qualitative Research.' In N.K. Denzin and Y.S. Lincoln, eds, *Handbook of Qualitative Research*, 70–82. Thousand Oaks, CA: Sage Publications.

– 2003. 'Silencing and Nurturing Voice in an Improbable Context: Urban Adolescents in Public School.' In Fine and Weis, eds, *Silenced Voices and Extraordinary Conversations*, 13–37.

Fine, M., and L. Weis, eds. 2003. *Silenced Voices and Extraordinary Conversations: Re-imagining Schools*. New York and London: Teachers College Press.

Fine, M., L. Weis, and L.C. Powell. 1997. 'Communities of Difference: A Critical Look at Desegregated Spaces Created for and by Youth.' *Harvard Educational Review* 67(2): 247–84.

Finn, P.J. 1999. *Literacy with an Attitude: Educating Working-Class Children in Their Own Self-Interest*. New York: State University of New York Press.

Fishman, S.M., and Lucille McCarthy. 2005. 'Talk about Race: When Student Stories and Multicultural Curricula Are Not Enough.' *Race, Ethnicity and Education* 8(4), 347–64.

Foucault, M. 1977. *Discipline and Punish: The Birth of the Prison*. Trans. A. Sheridan. New York: Pantheon Books.

– 1978. *The History of Sexuality: An Introduction*. Vol. 1. Trans. R. Furley. New York: Vintage Books.

– 1980a. 'What Is Enlightenment?' In P. Rabinow, ed., *The Foucault Reader*, 32–50. New York: Pantheon Books.

– 1980b. *Power/Knowledge: Selected Interviews and Other Writings, 1972–1977*. New York: Pantheon Books.

– 1997. 'Of Other Spaces: Utopias and Heterotopias.' In N. Leach, ed., *Rethinking Architecture: A Reader in Cultural Theory*. New York: Routledge.

Friel, B. 1999. *Brian Friel: Essays, Diaries, Interviews: 1964–1999*. Ed. Christopher Murray. London, New York: Faber & Faber.

Gallagher, K. 2000. *Drama Education in the Lives of Girls: Imagining Possibilities*. Toronto: University of Toronto Press.

– 2004. 'The Art and Politics of Qualitative Research in Drama Education: Creating Culture, Representing "Reality."' *Drama Research* 4(1): 3–18.

– 2006. 'Sexual Fundamentalism and Performances of Masculinity: An Ethnographic Scene Study.' *International Journal of Gay and Lesbian Issues in Education* 4(1).

Gallagher, K., and D. Riviere. 2004. 'Pink ... with Shades of Grey: Mediating Moments of Diversity in Urban Secondary Classrooms.' *Westminster Studies in Education* 27(2), 127–41.

Gaudio, R.P., and S. Bialostok. 2005. 'The Trouble with Culture: Everyday Racism in White Middle-Class Discourse.' *Critical Discourse Studies* 2(1), 51–69.

Gearing, F.O. 1995 (1979). *Toward a Cultural Theory of Education and Schooling*. The Hague and New York: Mouton.

Gee, J.P. 2004. 'What Video Games Have to Teach Us about Learning and Literacy.' *International Review of Education* 50(5–6), 574–6.

Geertz, C. 1973. *The Interpretation of Cultures: Selected Essays*. New York: Basic Books.

Gilman, S.L. 1985. *Difference and Pathology: Stereotypes of Sexuality, Race, and Madness*. Ithaca: Cornell University Press.

Giroux, H.A. 2003. *The Abandoned Generation: Democracy beyond the Culture of Fear*. 1st ed. New York: Palgrave Macmillan.

– 2005. *Border Crossings: Cultural Workers and the Politics of Education*. 2nd ed. New York and Milton Park, Abingdon: Routledge.

Godley, A.J. 2003. 'Literacy Learning as Gendered Identity Work.' *Communication Education* 52(3–4), 273–85.

Goffman, E. 1959. *The Presentation of Self in Everyday Life*. Oxford, Eng.: Doubleday.

– 1961. *Asylums: Essays on the Social Situation of Mental Patients and Other Inmates*. Oxford, Eng.: Aldine.

Goodley, D., and P. Clough. 2004. 'Community Projects and Excluded Young People: Reflections on a Participatory Narrative Research Approach.' *International Journal of Inclusive Education* 8(4), 331–51.

Gordimer, N. 2000. *Selected Stories*. London: Bloomsbury.

Gordon, L.R. 2005. 'The Problem of Maturity in Hip Hop.' *Review of Education, Pedagogy & Cultural Studies* 27(4), 367–89.

Grossberg, L. 1994. 'Bringin' It All Back Home – Pedagogy and Cultural Studies.' In H.A. Giroux and P. McLaren, eds, *Between Borders: Pedagogy and the Politics of Cultural Studies*. New York: Routledge.

Grosz, E.A. 2001. *Architecture from the Outside: Essays on Virtual and Real Space*. Cambridge, MA.: MIT Press.

Grumet, M. 1991. 'Curriculum and the Art of Daily Life.' In G. Willis and W. Shubert, eds, *Reflections from the Heart of Educational Inquiry: Understanding Curriculum and Teaching through the Arts*, 74–89. Albany: State University of New York Press.

– 1990. 'On Daffodils That Come before the Swallow Dares.' In E. Eisner and A. Peshkin, eds, *Qualitative Inquiry in Education: The Continuing Debate*. New York, London: Teachers College Press.

Hall, S. 1990. 'Cultural Identity and Diaspora.' In J. Rutherford, ed., *Identity: Community, Culture, Difference*. London: Lawrence and Wishart.

– 1991. 'Old and New Identities, Old and New Ethnicities.' In A.D. King, ed., *Culture, Globalization and the World-System: Contemporary Conditions for the Representation of Identity*, 41–68. Basingstoke and Binghamton, NY: Macmillan in association with Department of Art and Art History, State University of New York at Binghamton.

Hatch, A.J. 2002. *Doing Qualitative Research in Education Settings*. New York: State University of New York Press.

Hattam, J., and R. Smyth. 2001. '"Voiced" Research as a Sociology for Understanding "Dropping Out" of School.' *British Journal of Sociology of Education* 22(3), 401–15.

Henry, M. 2000. 'Drama's Ways of Learning.' *Research in Drama Education* 5(1), 45–62.

Hollier, D. 1992. *Against Architecture: The Writings of George Bataille.* Cambridge, MA: MIT Press.

hooks, b. 1992. *Black Looks: Race and Representation.* Boston: Sound End Press.

– 1994. *Teaching to Transgress: Education as the Practice of Freedom.* New York: Routledge.

Hursh, D. 2005. 'The Growth of High-Stakes Testing in the USA: Accountability, Markets and the Decline in Educational Equality.' *British Educational Research Journal* 31(5), 605–22.

Ibsen, H. 1992. *A Doll's House.* New York: Dover Publications Inc.

Ingraham, C. 1992. 'Initial Properties: Architecture and the Space of the Line.' In B. Colomina, ed., *Sexuality & Space*, 255–71. New York: Princeton Architectural Press.

Jung, C. 1933. 'On the Relation of Analytic Psychology to Poetic Art.' In A. Rothenberg and C. Hausman, eds, *The Creativity Question*, 120–6. Durham, NC: Duke University Press.

Kimmel, M.S. 1994. 'Masculinity as Homophobia: Fear, Shame, and Silence in the Construction of Gender Identity.' In H. Brod and M. Kaufman, eds, *Theorizing Masculinities*, 119–41. Thousand Oaks, CA: Sage Publications.

Kobayashi, A. 2003. 'GPC Ten Years On: Is Self-Reflexivity Enough?' *Gender, Place and Culture* 10(4), 345–9.

Kumashiro, K.K. 2001. *Troubling Intersections of Race and Sexuality: Queer Students of Color and Anti-Oppressive Education.* Lanham, MD: Rowman & Littlefield.

Kvale, S. 1996. *InterViews: An Introduction to Qualitative Research Interviewing.* Thousand Oaks, London, New Delhi: Sage Publications.

Lahiji, N., and D.S. Friedman, eds. 1997. *Plumbing: Sounding Modern Architecture.* New York: Princeton Architectural Press.

Lather, P. 1991. *Getting Smart: Feminist Research and Pedagogy with/in the Postmodern.* London: Routledge.

– 2004. 'Scientific Research in Education: A Critical Perspective.' *British Educational Research Journal* 30(6), 759–72.

Lefebvre, H. 1991. *The Production of Space.* Oxford: Blackwell.

Lerman, L., and J. Borstel. 2003. *Critical Response Process.* Takoma Park, MD: Liz Lerman Dance Exchange.

Lesko, N. 2001. *Act Your Age!: A Cultural Construction of Adolescence.* New York: Routledge Falmer.

Lincoln, Y.S. 1993. 'I and Thou: Method, Voice and Roles in Research with the Silenced.' In D. McLaughlin and W.G. Tierney, eds, *Naming Silenced Lives*, 29–47. New York: Routledge.

Lippi-Green, R. 1997. *English with an Accent: Language, Ideology, and Discrimination in the United States*. London: Routledge.

Luhman, S. 1998. 'Queering/Querying Pedagogy? Or, Pedagogy Is a Pretty Queer Thing.' In W.F. Pinar, ed., *Queer Theory in Education*, 141–56. Mahwah, NJ: Erlbaum.

Lyman, S.M., and M.B. Scott. 1975. *The Drama of Social Reality*. New York: Oxford University Press.

Lyotard, J.-F. 1984. *Phenomenology*. Albany: SUNY Press.

– 1988. *The Differend: Phrases in Dispute*. Trans. G.V.D. Abbeele. Manchester: Manchester University Press.

MacDonald, A.-M. 2005. *Belle Moral: A Natural History*. Niagara-on-the-Lake: Playwrights Canada Press and the Academy of the Shaw Festival.

MacLeod, J. 1987. *Ain't No Makin' It: Leveled Aspirations in a Low-Income Neighborhood*. Boulder, CO: Westview Press.

Mahiri, J. 1998. *Shooting for Excellence: African American Youth Culture in New Century Schools*. New York: Teachers College Press.

Markus, T.A. 1993. *Buildings & Power: Freedom and Control in the Origin of Modern Building Types*. New York: Routledge.

McCormick, J. 2003. '"Drag Me to the Asylum": Disguising and Asserting Identities in an Urban School.' *The Urban Review* 35(2), 111–28.

McGrath, J.E. 2004. *Loving Big Brother: Performance, Privacy, and Surveillance Space*. New York, London: Routledge.

McInnes, D., and M. Couch. 2004. 'Quiet Please! There's a Lady on the Stage: Boys, Gender and Sexuality Non-conformity and Class.' *Discourse: Studies in the Cultural Politics of Education* 25(4), 431–43.

McNeil, L.M. 2000. *Contradictions of School Reform: Educational Costs of Standardization*. New York: Routledge.

Minwalla, O., B.R. Simon Rosser, J. Feldman, and C. Varga. 2005. 'Identity Experience among Progressive Gay Muslims in North America: A Qualitative Study within Al-Fatiha.' *Culture, Health & Sexuality* 7(2), 113–28.

Morrell, E., and J. Duncan-Andrade. 2003. 'What Youth Do Learn in School: Using Hip Hop as a Bridge to Canonical Poetry.' In J. Mahiri, ed., *What They Don't Learn in School: Literacy in the Lives of Urban Youth*, 247–68. New York: Peter Lang.

Nakagawa, G. 1987. 'Why Must You Reopen Old Wounds? Disfiguration, Refiguration and Healing in Stories of Japanese American Internment.' Paper presented at the Western Speech Communication Association Annual Convention, Salt Lake City, UT.

Nalbantoglu, G.B., and T. C. Wong, eds. 1997. *Postcolonial Space(s)*. New York: Princeton Architectural Press.

Nayak, A., and M.J. Kehily. 1996. 'Playing It Straight: Masculinities, Homophobias and Schooling.' *Journal of Gender Studies* 5(2), 211–30.

Neelands, J. 2004. 'Miracles Are Happening: Beyond the Rhetoric of Transformation in the Western Traditions of Drama Education.' *Research in Drama Education* 9(1): 47–56.

Neelands, J., and T. Goode, eds. 1990. *Structuring Drama Work: A Handbook of Available Forms in Theatre and Drama*. Cambridge: Cambridge University Press.

Ngo, B. 2003. 'Citing Discourses: Making Sense of Homophobia and Heteronormativity at Dynamic High School.' *Equity & Excellence in Education* 36, 115–24.

Nicholson, H. 2002. 'The Politics of Trust: Drama Education and the Ethic of Care.' *Research in Drama Education* 7(1), 81–91.

– 2003. 'Acting, Creativity and Social Justice: Edward Bond's The Children.' *Research in Drama Education* 8(1), 9–23.

– 2005. *Applied Drama: The Gift of Theatre*. Basingstoke and New York: Palgrave Macmillan.

Noddings, N. 2003. *Happiness and Education*. New York: Cambridge University Press.

Omi, M., and H. Winant. 1994. *Racial Formation in the United States: From the 1960s to the 1990s*. New York: Routledge.

O'Neill, C. 1995. *Drama Worlds: A Framework for Process Drama*. Portsmouth, NH: Heinemann.

Orellana, M.F. 1995. 'Good Guys and "Bad" Girls: Gendered Identity Construction in a Writing Workshop.' Paper presented at the annual meeting of the American Educational Research Association, San Francisco, CA, April.

Orfield, M. 2002. 'American Metropolitics: The New Suburban Reality.' Washington, DC: The Brookings Institution.

Osler, A., and H. Starkey. 2005. 'Violence in Schools and Representations of Young People: A Critique of Government Policies in France and England.' *Oxford Review of Education* 31(2), 195–215.

Paechter, C. 2006. 'Reconceptualizing the Gendered Body: Learning and Constructing Masculinities and Femininities in School.' *Gender and Education* 18(2), 121–36.

Paterson, J. 1995. *Students at Risk Program: Training and Development Materials*. Adelaide: Department for Education and Children's Services South Australia.

Phelan, P. 1993. *Unmarked: The Politics of Performance*. London, New York: Routledge.

Pronger, B. 1999. 'Fear and Trembling: Homophobia in Men's Sports.' In
P. White and K. Mark, eds, *Sport and Gender in Canada*, 182–96. Toronto:
Oxford University Press.

Quantz, R.A. 1992. 'On Critical Ethnography (with some postmodern consid-
erations).' In M.D. LeCompte, W.L. Millroy, and J. Preissle, eds, *The Handbook of Qualitative Research in Education*, 447–505. New York: Academic Press.

Rabinow, P., ed. *The Foucault Reader*. New York: Pantheon Books.

Raby, R. 2004. 'There's no racism at my school, it's just joking around': Ramifi-
cations for Anti-Racist Education.' *Race Ethnicity and Education* 7(4), 367–83.

Radford, M. 2000. 'Emotion and Creativity.' *Journal of Aesthetic Education* 38(1):
53–64.

Rajchman, J. 1985. *Michel Foucault: The Freedom of Philosophy*. New York: Columbia University Press.

Rampton, B. 1995. *Crossing: Language and Ethnicity among Adolescents*. London:
Longman.

Razack, S. 2004. *Dark Threats and White Knights: The Somalia Affair, Peacekeeping,
and the New Imperialism*. Toronto: University of Toronto Press.

Redman, P. 2005. 'Who Cares about the Psycho-Social? Masculinities, Schooling and the Unconscious.' *Gender and Education* 17(5), 531–8.

Rendell, J. 1998. 'West End Rambling: Gender Architectural Space in London
1800–1830.' *Leisure Studies* 17(2), 108–22.

Rendell, J., B. Penner, and I. Borden, eds. 2000. *Gender, Space, Architecture: An
Interdisciplinary Introduction*. London, New York: Routledge.

Rich, A. 1978. *The Dream of a Common Language: Poems, 1974–1977*. 1st ed. New
York: Norton.

– 1993. *What Is Found There: Notebooks on Poetry and Politics*: New York:
Norton.

Rich, M.D., and A.C. Cargile. 2004. 'Beyond the Breach: Transforming White
Identities in the Classroom.' *Race Ethnicity and Education* 7(4), 351–65.

Riele, T.K. 2006. 'Schooling Practices for Marginalized Students: Practice-with-
Hope.' *International Journal of Inclusive Education* 10(1), 59–74.

Rizvi, F. 2005. 'Representations of Islam and Education for Justice.' In C.
McCarthy, W. Crichlow, G. Dimitriadis, and N. Dolby, eds, *Race, Identity,
and Representation in Education*. 2nd ed. New York, London: Routledge.

Rodriguez, N. 1998. '(Queer) Youth as Political and Pedagogical.' In W.F.
Pinar, ed., *Queer Theory in Education*, 173–86. Mahwah, NJ: Erlbaum.

Rose, N. 1996. *Inventing Ourselves: Psychology, Power, and Personhood*. London:
Cambridge University Press.

Samovar, L.A., and R.E. Porter, eds. 2001. *Communication between Cultures*.
Belmont, CA: Wadsworth/Thomson Learning.

Sartre, J.-P. 1960/2000. 'Beyond Bourgeois Theatre.' Trans. R.D. Reck. In C. Martin and H. Bial, eds, *Brecht Sourcebook*, 50–7. London, New York: Routledge.

– 1962. *Huis Clos (No Exit)*. New York: Appleton-Century-Crofts.

– 1965. *The Philosophy of Jean-Paul Sartre*. Ed. R. Cumming. New York: Random House.

– 1973. *Un théâtre de situations. Textes rassemblés, établis, présentés et annotés par Michel Contat et Michel Rybalka*. Paris: Gallimard.

Sawicki, J. 1991. *Disciplining Foucault: Feminism, Power, and the Body*. New York: Routledge.

Sedgwick, E.K. 1990. *Epistemology of the Closet*. Berkeley: University of California Press.

Seelye, N.H. 1996. *Between Cultures: Developing Self-identity in a World of Diversity*. Lincolnwood, IL: NTC Business Books.

Shakespeare, W. 1964. *The Falcon Shakespeare*. Toronto: Academic Press Canada.

Shlasko, G.D. 2005. 'Queer (v.) Pedagogy.' *Equity & Excellence in Education* 38(2), 123–34.

Simons, J. 1997. 'Drama Pedagogy and the Art of Double Meaning.' *Research in Drama Education* 2(2): 193–201.

Skelton, C. 2001. *Schooling the Boys: Masculinity and Primary Education*. Buckingham: Open University Press.

Sleeter, C.E. 2005. *Un-standardizing Curriculum: Multicultural Teaching in the Standards-Based Classroom*. New York: Teacher College Press.

Smith, A.D. 1994. *Twilight, LA. 1992*. New York: Anchor Books / Doubleday.

– 2001. 'Anna Deavere Smith.' In M. Luckhurst and Chloe Veltman, eds, *On Acting: Interviews with Actors*, 131–8. London, New York: Faber and Faber.

Smith, D.E. 1999. *Writing the Social: Critique, Theory, and Investigations*. Toronto: University of Toronto Press.

Smith, L.T. 1999. *Decolonizing Methodologies: Research and Indigenous Peoples*. London, New York: Zed Books Ltd.

Sontag, S. 2001 (1966). *Against Interpretation*. London: Vintage.

Spivak, G.C. 1990. *The Post-colonial Critic: Interviews, Strategies, Dialogues*. New York, London: Routledge.

– 1988. *In Other Worlds: Essays in Cultural Politics*. New York: Routledge.

Spry, L. 1994. 'Structures of Power: Toward a Theatre of Liberation.' In M. Schutzman, and J. Cohen-Cruz, eds, *Playing Boal: Theatre, Therapy, Activism*, 171–84. London, New York: Routledge.

Staiger, A. 2005. 'Recreating Blackness-as-Failure through Educational Reform? A Case Study of a California Partnership Academy.' *Equity & Excellence in Education* 38(1), 35–48.

Swadener, B.B., and S. Lubeck, eds. 1995. *Children and Families 'At Promise': Deconstructing the Discourse of Risk*. Albany: State University of New York Press.

Tatum, B.D. 1997. *'Why are all the Black kids sitting together in the cafeteria?' and Other Conversations about Race*. New York: Basic Books.

Tavernise, S. 2004. 'Watching Big Brother; on this tour, hidden cameras are hidden no more.' *New York Times*, 17 January, B1.

Taylor, K. 2005. *Globe and Mail*, 22 October, R5.

Tedlock, B. 1991. 'From Participant Observation to the Observation of Participation: The Emergence of Narrative Ethnography.' *Journal of Anthropological Research* 47(1), 69–94.

Thomson, P. 2002. *Schooling the Rustbelt Kids: Making the Difference in Changing Times*. Melbourne: Allen and Unwin.

Trinh, T.M.-H. 1989. *Woman, Native, Other: Writing Postcoloniality and Feminism*. Bloomington: Indiana University Press.

Turner, V. 1982. *From Ritual to Theatre: The Human Seriousness of Play*. New York: Performing Arts Journal Publications.

Valenzuela, A. 1999. *Subtractive Schooling: US-Mexican Youth and the Politics of Caring*. New York: SUNY Press.

Warren, D., and P. Adler. 1977. 'An Experiential Approach to Instruction in Intercultural Communication.' *Communication Education* 26(2), 128–34.

Weaver-Hightower, M.B. 2003. 'Crossing the Divide: Bridging the Disjunctures between Theoretically Oriented and Practice-Oriented Literature about Masculinity and Boys at School.' *Gender and Education* 15(4), 407–23.

Weis, L. 2003. 'Constructing the "Other": Discursive Renditions of White Working-Class Males in High School.' In Fine and Weis, eds, *Silenced Voices and Extraordinary Conversations*.

Weis, L., and M. Fine, eds. 2000. *Construction Sites: Excavating Race, Class, and Gender among Urban Youth*. New York: Teachers College Press.

Whiteman, J., J. Kipnis, and R. Burdett, eds. 1992. *Strategies in Architectural Thinking*. Cambridge, MA.: MIT Press.

Wigley, M. 1992. 'Untitled: The Housing of Gender.' In B. Colomina, ed., *Sexuality and Space*, 326–89. Princeton, NJ: Princeton Architectural Press.

Williams, K.L. 2003. 'Mirrored Images: The Impact of Stereotypes on Black Learners in Ontario High Schools.' Unpublished Master's thesis, University of Toronto, Toronto.

Willis, P.E. 1981. *Learning to Labor: How Working Class Kids Get Working Class Jobs*. New York: Columbia University Press.

Wilshire, B.W. 1982. *Role Playing and Identity: The Limits of Theatre as Metaphor*. Bloomington: Indiana University Press.

Wilson, M. 1998. 'Dancing in the Dark: The Inscription of Blackness in Le Corbusier's Radiant City.' In Heidi Nast and Steve Pile, eds, *Places through the Body*, 133–52. London: Routledge.

Winston, J. 1998. *Drama, Narrative and Moral Education*. London, Washington: The Falmer Press.

Woods, P. 1994. Book Review: *Critical Incidents in Teaching: Developing Professional Judgement*. *Educational Research* 36, 308–9.

Yon, D.A. 2000. *Elusive Culture: Schooling, Race, and Identity in Global Times*. Albany: State University of New York Press.

Yosso, T.J. 2005. 'Whose Culture Has Capital? A Critical Race Theory Discussion of Community Cultural Wealth.' *Race Ethnicity and Education* 8(1), 69–91.

NAME INDEX

Note: Italicized names are pseudonyms for research participants. Names listed in full are those of research team members (i.e., research assistants and principal researcher).

Ackroyd, J., 88
Adeline, 131
Adler, P., 147
Adrianna, 29, 121
Alessandra, 67, 104–5, 134, 150
Alissa, 163
Andersen, C., 159
Andre, 103–5, 107, 108, 136, 139, 149–53, 163, 177–8
Angelina, 98, 103–5
Angrosino, M., 11
Antonio, 67
Anyon, J., 74
Apple, M., 33
Apter, E., 27
Ari, 1, 10, 38, 152–3, 176, 179
Arla, 145–6
Arnot, M., 94
Austin, J.L., 129

Baldwin, J., xiii, 175
Ball, S.J., 57
Barker, H., 1, 91, 110, 140
Barry, B., 74

Bayliss, P., 86
Becker, H., 129
Berger, J., 27
Besley, A.C., 131
Best, S. 131
Bhawuk, D.P.S., 147
Bialostok, S., 36
Bloomberg, M., 21
Boal, A., xii, 84, 152–4
Bond, E., 78
Booth, D., 88
Borden, I., 27
Borstel, J., 175
Branch, C., 126
Brannon, R., 116
Bransford, J., 158
Brent, 110, 113
Brian, 69
Brianny, 81
Bridgit, 168
Britzman, D., ix, 54, 59–60, 61, 71, 85, 128
Brooke, R.W., 55
Brown, S.G., 174

Bruner, J., 161
Burdett, R., 27
Burns, K., 27
Bush, G.W., 33, 73, 150–4
Butler, James, 121
Butler, Judith, 62, 118, 129, 164

Calliste, A., 122
Calvin, 144
Cargile, A.C., 149, 151
Carlin, 62–3, 68
Carlos, 68
Carm, 20, 21, 22, 23, 24, 117–20
Carter, 131
Çelik, Z., 27
Chapman, C., 76
Charlie, 136, 155, 160
Clough, P., 173
Cole, E.B., 55
Colomina, B., 27
Comer, J.P., 149
Connell, R.W., 164
Couch, M., 168
Crowhurst, M., 118
Csuka, M.E., xii, xiii
Cummins, J., 157

Daiutte, C., 4
Damien, 131
David, D.S., 116
De Certeau, M., 70
Dei, G.J.S., 122
Delpit, L., 22
Denzin, L., 130
Dion, xi, 34–5, 66, 79, 110–11, 113–15,
    122–3, 142, 163
Dodwell, C., 86
Doug, 138
Dovey, K., 27
Driscoll, C., 145, 173

Dunbar, C., Jr, 33
Duncan, 95
Duncan-Andrade, J., 157
Dwayne, 142

Eliza, 80
Ellsworth, E., 81
Ely, 92–6
Emerson, R.M., 55
Ennis, C.D., 21

Fanny, 121
Fassett, D.L., 75
Faye, 145–6
Feldman, S.J., 27, 126
Felicia, 93
Fine, M., xiv, 32, 96, 102, 130, 177
Fishman, S.M., 149
Foucault, M., 14, 26–9, 31, 32, 54, 109
Freire, P., 55
Fretz, R.I., 55
Friedman, D.S., 27
Friel, B., 78, 97, 182

Gallagher, Kathleen, ix, x, xi, xiii, 21,
    22, 27–8, 29, 55, 62–71, 66, 68, 89,
    92, 103–5, 110–15, 117–21, 124,
    133–9, 143–4, 145–6, 162–3, 168,
    172–5, 177–9
Gaudio, R.P., 36
Gearing, F.O., 61
Gee, J., 157
Geertz, C., 12
Gilman, S.L., 154
Giroux, H., 29, 75, 102
Godley, A.J., 156–7
Goffman, E., 1, 26
Goode, T., 98
Goodley, D., 173
Gordimer, N., 61

Gordon, L.R., 95, 147
Gramsci, A., 164
Grossberg, L., 155
Grosz, E.A., 27
Grumet, M., 60, 73, 171
Guzkowski, Adam, 6, 62, 82, 93–4,
    105–6, 110–15, 123–5

Hachiya, Masayuki, 6
Hall, S., 102, 164
Harris, A., 76
Hatch, A.J., 54
Hattam, J., 155
Hayes, N., 149
Heathcote, D., 56
Henry, J., 60, 131
Hessa, 80
Hitler, Adolf, 113
Hogg, C., 55
Hollier, D., 27
hooks, bell, 135, 154
Hursh, D., 74

Ingraham, C., 27
Isaius, 62
Iver, 70

Jake, xi
James, H., 60
Janeen, 152
Janus, 110–14
Jehovah, 15
Jeremy, 62–3, 67–8
Jerome, 94
Jesus Christ, 15, 17
Jin, xi, 157–60, 181
Joseph, 22, 166
JP, 110–13
Juliet, 94
Jung, C., 128

Kayla, 133, 150, 181
Kehily, M.J., 116
Kellner, D., 131
Kim, Isabelle, 6, 13, 22, 157–8, 166–7,
    181
Kimmel, M.S., 102, 116–17
Kipnis, J., 27
Kumashiro, K.K., 127
Kvale, S, 11, 59

Lahiji, N., 27
Lather, P., 5, 76
Lefebvre, H., 11
Lenna, 110–11
Lerman, L., 175
Leroy, 13, 86, 166
Lesko, N., 130, 148
Lila, 62
Lina, 70
Lincoln, Y., 8
Lippi-Green, R., 157
Liza, 85–6
Loralei, xi, 137, 146–54, 178
Lortie, Philip, 6, 10, 13, 16, 34–5,
    63, 64, 79, 82–3, 85–7, 96, 110–15,
    122–5, 126, 131, 133–9, 142, 150,
    152–3, 155, 158–60, 165–6, 173
Lubeck, S., 75
Luhman, S., 128
Lydia, 37
Lyotard, J.-F., 35, 132

MacDonald, A.-M., 6
MacLeod, J., 155
Mahiri, J., 157
Mahler, G., 78
Maniqua, 161
Mara, 121
Marahai, 145–6
Marcus, 93

Marcuse, H., 129
Margo, 82
Maria, 168
Markus, T.A., 27
Marley, 80
Marlow, 95
Martina, 22
Marvin, 69, 91
Mays de Perez, K., 11
McCarthy, L., 149
McCauley, T.M., 21
McCormick, J., 27, 30
McGrath, T., 33, 37
McInnes, D., 168
McLung, N., 93
McNeil, L.M., 75
Minwalla, O., 126
Misha, 36, 81–2, 160–1, 180
Miyamoto, K., 6
Mohammed, 67, 107
Morrell, E., 157
Mr M, 13, 27–28
Ms G, 16, 17
Ms S, 62–71, 91–6, 107–9, 110–15,
    124–7, 135, 139, 141, 155–6, 175

Nakagawa, G., 150
Nalbantoglu, G.B., 27
Natalie, 110–11, 113–14
Nate, 62, 67–8, 103–6, 110–14, 162–4
Nayak, A., 116
Neelands, J., 88, 98
Ngo, B., 127
Nicholson, H., 78, 88, 105, 153
Niela, 88, 98, 103–5, 110–15
Noddings, N., 20

Omi, M., 34
O'Neil, C., 88
Orellana, M.F., 167

Orfield, M., 74
Osborne, P., 129
Osler, A., 37

Paechter, C., 119
Paterson, J., 75
Paula, 110, 113
Penner, B., 27
Perry, 110–11, 114–15
Peter, 126
Peters, M., 131
Phelan, P., 61
Plato, 78
Porter, R.E., 147
Powell, L.C., 96
Pronger, B., 119

Quantz, R.A., 58
Queenie, 64

Raby, R., 142
Radford, M., 161
Rajchman, J., 26
Rakamena, 82–3
Rally, 91–6
Rampton, B., 157
Razack, S., 102
Redman, P., 129
Rendell, J., 27
Rich, A., 77, 79, 88
Rich, M.D., 149, 151
Ricky, 13, 86–7, 129–30, 165
Riele, K., 20
Rina, 124
Rivière, Dominique, 6, 9, 10, 63, 66,
    80–1, 89, 110–15, 124–5, 167, 177,
    180–1
Rizvi, F., 125, 127
Rodriguez, N., 9
Romeo, 94

Rosaria, 110, 115
Rose, N., 32
Rosser, B.R.S., 126
Ruby, 167
Ruck, M., ix

Sabicca, 36, 134–9, 146, 150, 178
Sabina, 168
Salvador, 22
Samovar, L.A., 147
Samuel, 62–3, 68
Sanjeet, 57, 138, 143–4, 172–5, 178–9
Sartre, J.-P., xiv, 84–5, 88
Sawicki, J., 5
Sedgwick, E., 127
Seelye, N.H., 147
Segal, L., 129
Shahbib, 110–15, 126
Shakespeare, W., 13, 89–90, 91–6, 99,
   172
Shaw, L., 55
Shaylene, 179
Shlasko, G.D., 116, 127
Simons, J., 88
Skelton, C., 157
Sleeter, C.E., 97
Smith, A.D., 86, 106
Smith, D.E., 131–2
Smith, L.T., 7, 8
Smyth, R., 155
Sontag, S., 137
Sonya, 81
Spike, 66
Spivak, G., 57
Spry, L., 88
Staiger, A. 34, 109
Starkey, H., 37
Stefan, 168–70
Steven, 13, 165
Swadener, B.B., 75

Tanisha, xi, 166
Tanya, 95
Tatum, B.D., 149
Tavernise, S., 32
Taylor, K., 81
Tedlock, B., 54, 61
Tenisha, 94
Thompson, J., 107
Thompson, P., 130, 154
Torrie, 22
Trinh, T. M-H., 57, 98
Turner, V., 90

Valenzuela, A., 156
Varga, C., 126
Venus, 163
Villaruel, F.A., 33
Viviana, 110, 114

Wardeker, W.L., 86
Warren, D., 147
Warren, J.T., 75
Weaver-Hightower, M.B., 157
Weis, L., 96, 102, 130
Whiteman, J., 27
Wigley, M., 27
Williams, K.L., 149
Willis, P.E., 155
Wilshire, B.W., 128–9
Wilson, M., 27
Winant, H., 34
Winston, M., 88
Wong, T.C., 27
Woods, P., 11

Yon, D.A., 36, 130
Yosso, T.J., 35

SUBJECT INDEX

ability, 6

Aboriginal, x

academic: Academic and Technological study programs, 12; advisor, 25; conflict, 5; excellence, 18; institutions, 15

academics, x; academically disengaged, 156

accountability: Education Quality Accountability Office, 77; movement in public education, 74

acting, 13; 'Black,' 10; material subject vs. imagined one, 85; and metaphor, 86; 'real' and 'acted' performances, 103–5; roles, 11, 117; role-playing, 91–8, 117–18; 'scriptive acts,' 98; 'urban,' 10

action research, 55–56

actor, 86; 'actorship,' 86

'adolescence,' 90; 'adolescent development,' 148; and popular culture and the media, 147–8; study of adolescent girls, 142

adult, xi; prisons, x

aesthetic: experience, xii, and engagement, 161–2; representation, 163; sociology of aesthetics, 155–61; space, 57

aesthetics, Western formal, 27

Afghanistan, 107; Afghanis, 108

African: A. American(s), x, 22, 81, 166; A. Canadian, 103, 152; African History Awareness Month, 146–54; Black African, 99; culture, 149; students, 89; Students' Association, 147

agency: spaces for, xii

alternative: Amor Alternative, 19; discourses, 20; literacies, 155–61; program, 24; space and masculinity, 164–6

American, 4; A.-born, 10, 64, 85, 110, 133, 142, 152, 158; congressional and public protest, 33; history and racism, 146–54; school survey on guns and students, 31; students, 89 (*see also* African); 'Zero Tolerance' concept, 33–4

Amor Alternative School, 19, 20, 21, 24–5 (official story); Amor Mid-Town, 25; Amor school group, 24; blackboard in drama classroom (photo), 45; fieldnote excerpt (Jan. 2004), 19–20; parent account, 26; resource room service, 25; 'SINI' (School In Need of Improvement),

26; students, 81, 117–20; teachers,
19–24, 119–21
anti-racist feminism, 122
architecture: architectural designs
of schools, 26–8, 32, 62; cultural
studies of, 27; institutional,
14
Arguments for a Theatre (Barker), 1,
91, 109, 140
arrest rates, x
art, xiii; art/theatre project, 98;
Canadian arts critic, 81; and cultural contexts, 128–9; and ethics,
85; inquiry, qualitative research,
60; kinaesthetic art form, 98; and
learning, 77; performance artist,
31; as practice of freedom, 129;
programs, 13; purpose of, 175;
quality of work, 76–7; and teaching, 77
'art of distributions' (Foucault), 31–2
artefacts, 7, 97
artistic practices, 7
artistic theatre, 3
Asian, 24, 91, 96, 108, 160; East, 16;
South-East, 16
Asperger's syndrome, 92
asylums, 26; architecture of, 27
atheist, 162
'at risk' label, 33
audience, xiii
Australia, ix; population, x; school
policies, 74; studies of schooling,
154; urban, x

background checks, 14
'Be My Baby,' 64–71
behaviour as performance, 26
beige youth, 156
Belgium, xi, 137, 147, 178

bi-racial, xi, 10, 13, 22, 152, 157, 165,
166, 179
Black, ix, xi, 9, 10, 13, 14, 16, 21, 22,
24, 30, 33, 36, 66, 79, 91–6, 106,
107–10, 110, 133, 137, 142, 147, 150,
156, 165, 166, 178; 'acting Black,'
10; Black African parents, 99;
children, 33; culture, 149; magazine, 149; meanings of blackness,
33; sociocultural characteristics of
Black students, 149; television,
149; youth, 147–8, 156
Bleeding between the lines (playscript),
99–102
Bloomberg administration, 21
'border-crossing,' 170–1, 181
bourgeois, bourgeoisie, 84–5
Britain, 37; closed-circuit television
cameras, 37
'breakfast club,' 13
British Broadcasting Corporation, 37
British descent, 82, 85, 104, 145
Brooklyn, 23
Brown, 82, 110, 172; youth, 156
bullying in schools, 168–70; interventions 140
Bush administration, Terrorist
Information Awareness System, 33

California Partnership Academy, 108
Canada, ix, xi, 3; first massacre,
fourteen women in Montreal, 115;
'Oh Canada,' 68; urban, x; urban
school policies, evaluation of, 73–
7; —, Zero Tolerance policy, 33–4
Canadian, 4; African Canadian, 103,
177; arts critic, 81; C.-born, 110,
133, 135, 176; descent of, British,
82, 85, 104, 145; —, Caribbean, 66,
110, 133, 134, 137, 142, 150, 152,

156, 168, 177, 179; —, East Asian, 155, 157; —, Eastern European, 126, 168; —, Estonian, 110; —, European, 80–81, 144, 168; —, Filipino, 16, 145; —, Greek, 110; —, Italian, 29, 110, 121, 168; —, Polish, 17, 62, 105, 110; —, Portuguese, 103, 110, 121, 145, 162, 163; —, Spanish, 110; —, Scottish, 22, 68, 110, 143, 156; —, South Asian, 57, 138, 143, 172; first generation, 9, 10, 66, 68, 80, 81–2, 105, 110, 121, 134, 137, 138, 143, 144, 145, 150, 152, 155, 156, 163, 168, 172, 178; French-Canadian, 10, 13, 64, 152, 157, 179; schools, 31, 32; second generation, 80, 82, 85, 104, 121, 126, 145, 156; third generation, 121; version of U.S. Emergency Preparedness Program, 33; visitors, 14

Caribbean born/descent, 66, 110, 133, 134, 137, 150, 152, 156, 168, 177, 178, 179; Jamaican-born, 142

Catholic publicly funded schools, 16, 18. See also St Bernadette's High School

Centers for Disease Control and Prevention, 31

Centre for Addiction and Mental Health, 30

Chinese-born, 157

Christian, 103, 152, 177; faith, 18; Jesus Christ, 15, 17

chronic absenteeism, 31; student perspective, 34–5

city: City Hall (NYC), 25; CUNY (City University of New York), 25; North American, xii

class(es), xi, xiii

class/classrooms, 14, 16; atmosphere, 37; communities, 5; competitive, 5; and creativity, 79–83; cultures, 174; democratic, 5; drama, x, xi, 6, 36, 45 (photo), 46 (photo), 48 (photo), 54; —, expression of 'Self' and 'Other,' 102–5; —, improvisation, 90, 162–4; —, reading, 99–105; —, student complaints, 83; —, whole class discussions, 110–15, 146–54; dynamics of, 5, 90, 97; English, 31, 104, 106, 156–7; and essentialism, 122; and expression, 79–83; fashion, 161, 168; humane, 31; lateness, 70; as a 'Location of Possibility,' 146–54; progressive, 23; relationships, 91; research, 88; 'safe,' 126; spaces, 28; traditional accounts of, 58

class (social), 6, 9, 85; anxieties, 29; bourgeoisie, 84–5; descriptors, 9; lower, 9; lower-middle, 9; middle, 9, 76; proletariat, 85; representations of, 27; rich/poor, 10; working, 9, 103

closed-circuit television cameras, 37

coding: analysis software (N6), 71; qualitative data, 71

colonization: of African people, 146–54; colonizing minds, ix; decolonizing methodologies, 8; effects of, 7; history of, 146–54; ideologies of empire, 27; material effects of, 8; 'uncolonized imagination,' 129

'colourblind' vocabulary, 33

communities: Black, 148; classroom, 5; of colour, 35; urban, 8, 11

competing cultural models, 35;

curriculum, 126; identities, 126;
narratives, 9
conflict(s): academic, 5; between
dominant and subjugated parties,
35; bullying interventions in
schools, 140–1; creative, x; —,
exploration of, 140; cultural, 5;
drama writing and performing,
88; mediators, 18; pedagogies of,
140–6, 152–4; perspectives on
conflict and drama, 143–6; political, 5; productive power of,
152–4
conservative: 'common sense,'
'modernization,' 33
*Constant Comparison Grapho-Linear
Imaging Matrix Coding Apparatus*
(CCGLIMCA), 72
construction of social consciousness,
4
context 11, 88; post-foundational, 5
criminalization: ideology of crime,
33; of youth, x, 33, 90
critical: citizens, 96; critical-humanist paradigm, 22; critical race
theorists, 35; epistemology, 56, 58;
ethnography, 54–6, 58; —, methodologies, 59, 172–5; gaze, 8;
inquiry, x; interrogation of difference, 96; literacy, 159–60; scholars,
x; social research, 58; students'
critical imagination, 97; theorists,
11, 27; theory, 58; —, and drama
pedagogy, 87
cultural: adaptation, 35; assimilation, 35, 149; beliefs, 105; competing cultural models, 35; conflict, 5;
contested terrain, 58; hegemony,
109; and human capital, 154, 163;
narratives, 86; participation, 155–

6; 'poverty disadvantages,' 35;
ruptures, 89
culture: African, 149; Black, 149;
Black students, sociocultural
characteristics, 149; creating, 58;
culturally relevant pedagogy, 21;
'culture clash,' 34; documentation,
27; dominant, 149; global, 81;
heterosexual, 111; hip hop, 95–6;
'home' culture, 35, 59; ideologies,
27; insiders, 54; 'intercultural
training,' 146–7; 'knowledges,' 36,
83; local, 81; multicultures, 36;
'peer,' 59; popular culture, and
the media, 147–8; —, and social
cohesion, 89; productions of
youth, 4; 'security obsessed,' 90;
strategies of culture, 161; studies,
studying, 27, 58; 'sub'-cultural
knowledges, 36, 59; values, 35;
White, 34, 142
curriculum, 11, 83; choices (in
drama), 23; co-curricular programs, 13; competing, 126; curricular constraints, 84; curricular
constructions, 89; drama, 80, 89;
formal, 36; hidden, 7; and ideology, 33; informal, 126; jointly
constructing, 22; official, 90;
realist-technicist, 22; 'rigorous,' 73

danger: colour-coded levels of
'alert,' 29; criminality and, 28, 37;
dangerous class of youth, 33;
'dangerous times,' 28; Emergency
Preparedness Program, 33; ideology of fear, 28; public school
space, 28; in schools, 28–9; Terrorist Information Awareness System, 33

'dark dramas,' 128–39
data coding and analysis; coding decisions, 71–3; *Constant Comparison Grapho-Linear Imaging Matrix Coding Apparatus* (CCGLIMCA), 72; data management, 71; software (N6), 71–3; technologically assisted, 71–3; thematic data coding, 71–2
decolonizing methodologies, 8
democracy, 5; democratic classroom spaces, 5; discourses of, 74; and Islam, 125–6; and participation, 96
dialectics, 59; of self, other, 5
'différend,' 35
difference, 36; categories of, 122; conceptualizing of, 125; critical interrogation, 96; and drama, 88, 105
discipline: 'disciplinary measures,' 15, 18; 18th- and 19th-century European bourgeois concerns, 28; maintenance of, 31; and society, 109; techniques; 109; technologies of, 32
discourse, 9; of 'care,' 20; as conceptual terrain for knowledge production, 26; levels of, 97; neo-liberal, 74; race-free, 34; risk and safety, security, surveillance, 28–9, 36; school-effectiveness, 20
discourses: in aesthetic and social spaces, 57; alternative, 20; of commonality and racial transcendence, 89; pedagogical, 5, 74–7
discursive: cohesion, 4; consistency, 4; space, 10, 26
diversity, 5, 10, 142; diverse student body, 15
Dominican, 13, 86, 166

'do rag,' 92
downtown: school, 9; Toronto, 10
drama, xii; aesthetic engagement, experience, 161–2; artistic space, 23; atmosphere, 37; audience experience, 102; and border crossing, 84, 170–1; choices in fictional contexts, 129; class(es)/classroom(s), xi, 1, 6, 7, 16, 23, 45 (photo), 46 (photo), 48 (photo), 54, 58; —, chair exercise (photo), 53; —, changes, 34; —, improvisations, 131–9; —, research, 58, 97–8; —, student complaints, 83; —, whole class discussions, 110–15, 146–54; club, 70; collective experience, 78; conventions, hot seat, 62–71, 81–3, 162–4; —, improvisations, 97, 162; —, tableau, 93; —, whole class improvisation, 90–6, 151–4; —, writing in role, 97; curricular choices, 23, 80, 89; difference, 88; distance from, xii, 163; dramatic pieces around religious holidays, 89; dramatic writing, 88–90, 97–109; —, by students, 98–109; ethnodrama, 130; and freedom, 137–9; identification with, xii, 163–4; kinaesthetic art form, 98; 'lessons' from Middleview, 90; and literacy, 155–61; metaphorical and sub/unconscious work, 129; movement exercises (photo), 51; narrative modes of drama education, 58, 88–90; the 'Other' in drama class, 102; pedagogy, 23, 54, 82, 84, 86–8, 152–4; —, emancipatory, 89, 145–6; and personal change, 177–80; physical nature of, 8–83; praxis, 83; rela-

208   Subject Index

tionships, 66; research, 56; as a
research method, 4, 56, 79, 128–39;
resources, 69; school subject, 6;
and self-esteem, 137–9, 157–9, 165–
8; and self-expression, 80–3, 99–
105; and self-representation, 86;
social art, 102; space, xi, 36; space
for, 21; space of many chances, 23;
student performances, 49 (photo),
50 (photo); students' perspectives,
37, 80–3; —, on conflict and
drama, 143–4; —, on process
drama, 131–7; —, at Redmount,
27; —, on teacher, 22; —, on work
in role, 58; —, on writing, 88–90;
and trust, 105, 119–20
drug use: cocaine, 63; teenage, 103
dynamics, of classrooms, 5, 90

East Asian, 16, 155, 157
Eastern European, 16, 126, 168
education: critical tradition in, 58;
drama, 3; —, narrative modes of,
58; and economic productivity,
74; educational achievement, 74;
failure in, 75; educational community, 15; global, 5; —, forces of, 84;
Japanese education system, 75;
knowledge about, 7; and liberal
notions, 90; mis-education, xi;
policy, 21; 'quality,' 74, 77 (Education Quality Accountability
Office); —, of art work, 76–7; —,
of learning, teaching, 77; reforms,
74; and social disadvantage, 154;
'social force for good,' 4; space, 28;
special education students, 25;
standards, Office for Standards in
Education (OfSTED), 76; statistics,
National Center for Educational

Statistics (NCES), 75; Theater and
Education Award for Excellence,
14; trust, 21; under-funded, xi
educational ethnography, 55
educators, xi, xii, xiii, xiv
effects of colonization, 7
emancipatory drama pedagogy, 89
embodied experiences, 59
'empathy,' 89
empirical: inquiry, 10, 11; research, 6;
study, 11
empowered individuals, 32
England, 76, 150
English: class, 104, 106; ESL (English
as a Second Language) students,
16; playwright, 78; proficiency, 75;
Regents exam, 16; subject, 76
epistemology, critical, 57, 59
equity, 74, 96
essentialism: in the classroom, 122–3
ethics: and art, 85; 'ethic of care,' 20;
ethical clearance, 7; feminist, 55;
language of in schools, 31
Ethiopian-born, 98, 110
ethnicity: Amor Academy High
School students, 24
ethnographer(s), xi, 11, 54; critical,
57; gender/race of, 57; privilege/
status of, 175–6
ethnographic: critical practice, 172;
critique, 54; contextuality, 11;
fieldwork, 54; generalizability, 11;
methods, 11, 58; research, 11, 58;
study, 3, 71
ethnography: critical, 55–6; educational, 55; ethnodrama, 130;
(inter)disciplinary practices and,
58; multi-site, 4; new, 58; phenomenological approach, 59; problem-
posing, 175–82; qualitative

research, 54; 'situated,' 7; traditional, 8; and 'truth,' 60; writing
of, 11, 54
European descent, 80–1, 144, 168
excellence, academic, 18
'excitable speech,' 118

family group, 22
feminism/feminist: anti-racist, 122;
and drama pedagogy, 87; ethics,
55; frameworks, 55; take on
Shakespeare, 94
feudal society, 93
field notes, 6; analysis of, 71–3;
excerpts from, 16–17 (St Bernadette's High School, 19
(Amor Alternative), 61–72, 180
(Middleview); re whole class
discussion on homosexuality,
123–5
field research, 8, 54
Filipino, 16, 145
fingerprinting, 14
first-generation Canadian, 9, 10, 66,
68, 80, 81–2, 105, 110, 121, 134, 137,
138, 143, 144, 145, 150, 152, 155,
156, 163, 168, 172, 178
focus group (interviews), 11
France, 37; surveillance, 37; youth
riots (winter 2005), 37
French-Canadian, 10, 13, 64, 152,
157, 179
French philosophers: Michel Foucault, 14, 26–9, 31, 32; Jean-
François Lyotard, 35

gay(s), xi, xiii, 13, 22, 86, 109–15,
117–27, 129, 155, 165; anti-homophobia policy, 117; Muslims,
125–6; role, 163; school-based

initiatives on lesbian/gay/bi-
sexual/transgendered issues, 127
gender, 6, 85, 90; analysis, 30; codes,
conformity, 168–70; counter-
hegemonic gender expressions,
164; crossing, 70; erotic violation
of gender, 118; ethnographer's
gender, 57, 61; femininity, 115–27,
164; 'girlhood,' 145, 167–8; and
hegemony, 164; masculinity,
performance of m., 115–27, 164–6;
—, 'hyper' masculinity, 117; per-
formance(s), 164–6; and reading/
literacies, 157; representations of,
27; strategies of gender, 162;
whole class discussions, 110–27
'ghetto,' 117–18
General Certificate Secondary
Education, 77
geopolitics: geopolitical dynamics, x;
strategies of, 14
God, 111; Allah, 126
global: culture, 81; economics, 4;
education, 5, 84; politics, ix, 4;
world, 171
'gold-diggers,' 93
graduate research assistants, 6
grafitti, 15, 16, 45 (photo)
Greek: descent, 110; words, xii
guidance counsellor, 19, 37; laying
off of, 124

Halifax, Nova Scotia, 103
hall pass, 16
hatred, xii; hate speech, 118
hegemony: counter-hegemonic
gender expressions, 164; cultural,
109; and masculinity, 164; and
normalization, 142
hero narrative, 8

heterogeneity of knowledge, 11
'heteroprivilegist,' 118
heterosexual masculinities, 116;
    normativity, 90
hidden curriculum, 7
high school(s), 3; graduation from,
    24
high-stakes testing, xi, 74
hip hop: culture, 95–6; and literacy,
    156–7; orthography, 156
Hispanic, xi, 21, 24, 80, 166; students,
    89
history: historical contexts, 26;
    historico-political problem, 14; of
    powers, 14; of spaces, 14
HIV/AIDS, 90; theatre presentation,
    110–15
homophobia, xi, xiii, 90, 110–15; anti-
    homophobia policy, 117; 'hetero-
    privilegist,' 118; homophobic
    version of masculinity, 118
homosexuality, 90, 110–27
hot seat, 62
Human Rights Commission, 33
Hungarian, 103

identity/identities: calcification, x,
    126; competing identities, 126;
    descriptors of, 9; difference, 5; and
    drama pedagogy, 87–8; elastic, xii,
    160; ethnic/racial, 75; experimen-
    tation, 86; fixing, 9; hyphenated,
    xii; identification cards, 14, 32;
    'Identity-Representation-Surveil-
    lance,' 131–7; invisible marker of,
    9; 'lessons in identity,' 126; mal-
    leable, xii; multiple, x; 'passing,'
    123–4; polarized, xii; politics, 5;
    reconstructing, 3; religious, 125–7;
    scholarly understanding of, 75;

social, 156–7; social identity
    performances, 166–8; 'spoiled,'
    36; unitary categories of, 9;
    'White Identity Transformation,'
    149
ideologies: 'conservative common
    sense,' 33; 'conservative modern-
    ization,' 33; of crime, 33; and
    curriculum, 33; of empire, 27; of
    fear, 28; liberal humanist values
    and education, 89–90
ideological: frameworks, 23; spaces,
    11
immigrants; immigration status, 37;
    new, xi, 137, 161, 178, 180; recent,
    81; youth, xi
imperialism, 7
'improvised worlds,' 58
inclusion/exclusion, 26; school
    policies of, 118–27
Indian-born, 82
industrial boom, 12
informal conversations, 11
informal curriculum, 126
informal learning, 7
informed consent, 7
inner-city: 'challenges,' 5; children,
    74
institutional: architecture, 14; racism,
    30; sexism, 30
institutions: state-sponsored, ix
'intercultural training,' 146–7
interview(s), 10, 11, 22, 79–83, 85–7,
    103–7, 117–21, 122–3, 126, 155,
    156–9, 160–1, 167, 168–70, 172–5,
    181; all-boy focus group, 164–6;
    all-girl focus group, 121, 145–6,
    168; focus groups, 11, 102–5, 142–
    3; in-role, 62–71, 133–9; interview-
    ing, 58–9; as open-ended 'speech

event,' 54; qualitative, 54, 71–3, 119–21; students interviewing each other, 177–80
Iraqi-born, 110
Islam: Allah, 126; and democracy, 125–6; faith, 122; gay Muslims, 125–6; identity, 126; Muslim girls, 16, 122; Nation of Islam, 114; Qur'an, 114, 125; representations of Islam in the West, 125–6
Italian: Canadian, 29, 110, 121, 168; descent, 21; Irish, 20

Jamaica, 35, 142; bush tea, 34–5; Jamaican-born, 34, 110, 122, 142; patwa, 103, 152, 177
Japanese: education system, 75–6; internment of in Second World War, 150–1
Judaism: Jewish, 110, 156, 175; Jews, 113, 114; Torah, 115
justice system, x
juvenile justice system, x

kinaesthetic art form, 98
knowledge(s): of the body, desire, emotion, 81; cultural, 83, 171; about education, 7; embodied, 83, 153–4; experiential, 154; 'home,' 171; knowledge-making process, 174; nature of, 59; production of, 7; situated, 55
Korean, 13, 157

Lady Macbeth, 93–6
language; body, 66, 70; 'colourblind' vocabulary, 33; 'contemporary,' 66; English, 103, 152, 177; —, ESL (English as a Second Language) students, 16, 157; —, proficiency,

75; —, Regents exam, 16; —, subject, 76, 156–7; of ethics, 31; and ethnography, 60; French, 103; 'hate speech,' 'excitable speech,' 118; Hungarian, 103; issues, xi, 82; Jamaican patwa, 103; linguistic construction of reality, 59; linguistic discrimination, 157–8; literacies, 155–61; of multiculturalism, 89; 'official,' 67; patwa, 103, 152, 177; second-language acquisition, 157; Shakespearean, 93–6; slang, 67; of social justice, 31; Spanish, 103; 'speech event,' 54; verbal abuse, 116–27
Latin, 103, 162, 165; Latin dance, 103
Latina, 22, 163
Latino, 13, 22, 86, 129
'Lazy Boy Syndrome,' 23
learning: cooperative, 25; and drama, 81–3, 158–9; 18th- and 19th-century European bourgeois concerns, 28; informal, 7; lifelong, 18; quality, 77; somatic, 153–4
lesbian, 121: school-based initiatives on lesbian/gay/bisexual/transgendered issues, 127
liberal: humanist values, and schools, 89; themes of colour blindness and equality, 149
liminal space, 58
literacy: alternative literacies, 155–61; approaches with urban and minority-language children, 157; critical literacy, 159–60; deficit model, 157; multi-literate, 157; research, 167; school literacy programs, 157; tests, 13; —, Ontario grade 10, 83, 157

Manhattan, Midtown, 19, 24, 45 (photo)
marginality: of the body, desire, emotions, 81; positions of, 8
marginal practices, 6; pedagogical marginalization, 81
media, 15; productions of youth, 4
methodologies, 17; coding decisions, 71–3; data management, 71; decolonizing, 8; drama, 79–83; —, process, 131–9; ethnographic methods, 58–9; N6 qualitative software, 71; porous methodology, 7, 55–6; problem-posing ethnography, 175–82; and risk, 134; students interviewing each other, 177–80; video, 132
Middle East, 126
Middleview Technical High School, 8, 9, 13; academic and technological study programs, 12; African Students' Association, 147; bullying intervention, survey, 140–1; fieldnotes, 61–1; official story, 12; principal, 34; students, 31, 36, 62–1, 79–83, 98, 109–27, 146–54, 157–9; teachers, 62–71, 98
mission statements: St Bernadette's, 18
morbidity, xiii
mortality, xiii
multicultural, 10; classroom communities, 5; languages of multiculturalism, 89; services, 12; student population, 12; 'unofficial multicultural doctrine,' 89
multi-ethnic: services, 12; student population, 12
Muslim, 16. See also Islam

narrative: coherence, 4; hero, 8; knowledge, 132; modes of drama education, 58; sites, 4
narratives: competing, 9; counter, 36; cultural, 86; of individual schools, 6
National Center for Educational Statistics (NCES), 75
National Literacy Strategy (NLS), 76
native, ix
New York: Brooklyn, 19, 23; City, ix, 3, 19, 20, 21, 29, 32; City Hall, 25; CUNY (City University of New York), 25; Department of Education, 15, 29; —, colour-coded levels of 'alert,' 29; guide to public schools (online), 24; Midtown Manhattan, 19, 24; Performance Standards Consortium, 24; police department, 19; Queens, 13, 14; School Standards and Regents Diploma Requirement, 15; State Homeland Security System for Schools, 30; schools, 27; School of Excellence, 14; State, 30; state schools, 30
'new racism,' 149
'nigga,' 107–9
No Child Left Behind Act, Public Law 107-110 (George W. Bush), 73–4
'no hat rule,' 20
North American, x, xi, 3; schooling, 4; urban landscape, x; urban schools, 37
numeracy: tests, 13; National Numeracy Strategy, 76

'occupied space,' xi, 90
Office of Security and Discipline, 14

Office for Standards in Education
(OfSTED), 76
Ontario, 12; Education Quality
Accountability Office, 77; grade 10
literacy test, 83; Ministry of Education, 76; Safe Schools Act, 33;
standardized tests, 76–7; students
and handguns, 30
Operation Clear Sweep, 13, 15
oppressed: classes, 85; theatre of the,
xii
oppression: dramatic representations of, 118–27; gendered-racist,
122; oppressive effects, 8; oppressive practices (educational settings), 22; and research practices,
57; slavery, 146–54
'Other,' the, xiii; dialectics of, 5, 8;
the Gay Other, 109–28; in drama
class, 102

Pakistanis, 108
paradigms: critical-humanist, 22;
technical-instrumental, 22
parent(s): absent, distant fathers, 65;
account re Amor, 26; Black African, 99; conference, 18; divorced,
99, 106; foster mom, 20; letter to,
18; parental permission, 18; parent
body, 15; parenting and homosexuality, 112; single mother, 17;
'smart mom,' 23; step-mom, 20;
teenage, 62–71, 162–4
participant observation(s), ix, 11,
58–61
participation: peripheral, xi, 159
participatory research, x; p. action
research, 55–6
pedagogical: challenges, 5; constraints, 84; discourses, 5; institu-

tions, 28; pedagogical/peer
relationship, 79–80
pedagogy: and critical, feminist
tradition, 87; culturally relevant,
21; drama, 23, 54, 82, 84, 86–8,
152–4, 170–1; emancipatory, 89,
145–6; models of articulation and
risk, 155–6; pedagogies of conflict,
140–6; theatre, xi
peer(s): against drugs, 18; committee
of (at Amor), 25; conflict-media-
tors, 18; ministers, 18; pedagogi-
cal/peer relationship, 79–80;
relations, 36; surveillance, 109;
tutors, 18, 69
performances: acted, 97; —, vs 'real,'
103–5; of adolescents/adoles-
cence, 85; artistic, 5; collaborative
dramatic, 97; co-performers, 58;
and 'excitable' speech, 118; fictional, 56; gay, xi; gender expression in, 164–9; improvising, 6;
originally written playscripts,
97–109; 'performatives,' 129;
professionally written playscripts,
97; social, 5; spaces of, xii; as
students, 6, 95; students in drama
class, 85; subject positions,
subjectivities, 88–90
peripheral participation, xi, 159
phenomenology, 59
philosophy: dialectics, 59; French,
Michel Foucault, 14, 26–9, 31, 32;
—, Jean-François Lyotard, 35; —,
Jean-Paul Sartre, 87–8; German,
Herbert Marcuse, 129; phenomenology, 59; political, Brian Berry,
74; postmodern, 59
pluralism, radical, 5
police, x, 14

policies: of inclusion/exclusion, 118–27; policy analysis framework, 33; school, anti-homophobia, 117; —, post-9/11, 33, 34; —, 'zero tolerance,' 33, 117 (homophobia); race as critical variable in social policy, 34; race-neutral, 34; towards surveillance, 'universalist' vs 'targeted' policy responses, 37; trends, 74
policing measures, xi
Polish, 17, 62, 105, 110
political: anatomy, 109; conflict, 5; correctness, 23; ideology, 27; moment (of homeland safety and security), 14
politics: of being known, 7; 'conservative common sense,' 33; of knowing, 7; of representation, 122; of science, 74
porous methodology, 7, 55–6
Portuguese descent, 103, 110, 121, 145, 162, 163
positions of marginality, 8
postcolonial theories, 8
post-foundational context, 5
postmodern: frameworks, lens, 59; moment, 56; theories in education, 170–1
post-9/11 school policies, 33
poststructural: frameworks, 55; theory, 88
poverty, ix, 9
power: demonstrations of, 154; in educational institutions, 29; history of, 14; and issues of privilege, race, class, and gender, 97, 118–27, 142; mechanisms of, 109; relations, 90, 131; state, x; status quo, 84

'practice-with-hope,' 20
practices: artistic, 7; discursive, 7; of inclusion and exclusion, 26; marginal, 6; spatial, 7; state-sponsored, ix
praxis, 16; drama praxis, 83; ethical consequences, 5; of schooling, xii
pregnancy, teenage girl, xi
principal(s), 10, 15; conference, 18; of Amor Alternative, 19, 25; of Middleview, 34–5; —, meeting with, 69; of St Bernadette's, 17
principal researcher, 7
prisons: adult, x; Foucault's study of, 31; state, x
problem-posing ethnography, 175–82
process drama, 131–7
production of knowledge, 7
program: alternative, 24; art, 13; English as a second language, 17; gifted, 17; individualized, mini-school, 15; resource assistance, 17
progressive classrooms, 23
proletariat, 85
pseudonyms, 9
public: address system, 15; authorities, x; education, US accountability movement, 74; imagination, 33; institutions, 31; protest, 33; publicly funded Catholic school, 16; responsibility, xii; school communities, 38; school spaces, ix; —, and danger, 28; —, transgression of, 32

Qualitative analysis, 71–3
Queens (New York), 3, 13
'question of belief,' 61
Qur'an, 114; readings of, 125–6

race, 6, 85, 89; 'acting Black,' 10; anti-racist scholars, 34; 'background,' 89; children, students of colour, 33–4; 'colourblind,' race-neutral vocabulary, 33, policies, 34; 'Communities of Colour,' 35; critical race theorists, 35; critical variable in social policy, 34; and democracy, 149; discourses of racial transcendence, 89; and equity, 149; ethnographer's race, 57, 61; meanings of blackness, 33; multiracial groups of youth, 96; over-represented as a 'problem,' 34; 'people of colour,' 108; 'race-free' discourse, 34; representations of, 27; and sexuality, 116–17; and slavery, 146–54; whole class discussions, 110–15

racial: anxieties, 29; categories, 34; inequity, 34; injustice, 149; meanings, 33; statistics, 34

racism: anti-racist feminism, 122; apartheid, 107–9; arguments for 'colour-blindness,' 107–9; everyday, 36; hidden effects of, 33; and homosexuality, 111–27; and identity, 108–9; institutional, 31; internment of Japanese in Second World War, 150–1; 'new racism,' 149; and privilege, 152–4; racist attitudes, 107; racist slurs, 'nigga' vs 'nigger,' 108–9; slavery, 146–54; stereotypes, xii, 29, 108; systems of, 107; and Whiteness, 142–9; whole class discussion, 107–9, 117–27

radical pluralism, 5

reactionary times, 84

realist-technicist curriculum, 22

Redmount Public School, 13; drama teacher, 27; microcosm of New York City, 15; New York School of Excellence, 14; official story, 15; 'Operation Clear Sweep,' 32; photos, 43, 44; scanning process, 28, 30, 33; students, 15, 86–7, 164–9; theatre, 27–8; Theater Institute, 15; —, mission; —, student perspectives, 165–8; Theater and Education Award for Excellence, 14

'reflexive analyst,' processes, 57; self-reflexivity, 180

Regents-based school, 21; (standardized) exams, 21; requirements for graduation, 24, 25

religion: atheism, atheist, 103, 162; and culture, 122–3; and homosexuality, 110–23; and race, 122–3; religious identities, 125–7; religious tensions, 90; Seventh-Day Adventist, 122. See also Christian, Islam, Judaism, St Bernadette's High School

representation(s): aesthetic, 163–4; of class, 27; of gender, 27; 'Identity-Representation-Surveillance,' 131–7; ideologies of empire, 27; issues of, 7; legitimacy of, 58; politics of, 122; of race, 27; of reality, 154; self-representation and drama, 86, 160–1; of sexuality, 27; toxic, xii; Western formal aesthetics, 27

research: act, 151–4; action research, 55–6, 130–1; activity, 8; adolescent participants, 56; analysis, 54; a. software, 71; anti-racist scholarship, 34; and art, 60, 131; assistant(s), 6, 9, 10, 13, 61, 62, 66, 89,

122–6, 180; consuming nature of, 7; and creativity, 78; critical, approach, 55–6; —, ethnography, 58; —, social, 58; data collection, 54; with a diverse population, 8; drama as research method, 4, 56, 79, 128, 131–9; educational, 58; empirical, 6, 11; ethnographic, 11, 54; field, 8, 54; grounded theory research, 55; with human subjects, 7; humble, humbling activity, 8; improvisation, 151–4; introduction to research team, 6, 61–2; on literacy, 167; meetings, 6; methods: participant observation, interviewing, 58–9; participants, 7, 9; participatory, x; philosophical dimensions, 130; policy analysis framework, 33; qualitative inquiry, 60; questions, 72; 'reality syndrome,' 130; school-based, 8; sites, 3–4, 11; social science, 7; student perspectives, 57, 70, 172–5; surveillance space, 37; systems of oppression, 57; teacher perspectives, 174–5; on teenagers, 57; traditional modes, 56; on youth and urban classrooms, 11, 156
researcher(s), 6, 10, 16, 22, 32, 68; adult, ix; anti-racist, 34; co-research, 172–5; commitment to doing emancipatory work, 7, 130; in drama classes, 175–6; as engaged inter-actor, 61; immersion, 12; impact on context of the study, 57; introduction to research team, 6, 61–2; as 'outside eyes,' 96, 176; qualitative, 60, 71; reflexivity, 57, 180; of urban schools spaces, 7, 31, 32, 54; youth, ix, 137–9, 177–80

rhetoric of urban schools, 10
risk, xi; anticipation of 'risk' in schools, 31; and drama, 134; metaphor, 75; and methodology, 134; minimizing, 90; pedagogical models of articulation and risk, 155–6
roles, 11; role-playing, 91–8, 131–7, 163
Russian folk tale, 181–2

safety, ix; challenges to, 109; discourses of, 36; homeland safety and security, 14; issues of, 84; New York State Homeland Security System for Schools, 30; police/security guards in schools, 29, 31; 'safe classrooms,' 126; 'safe space,' 32, 96; 'safety officers,' 27; scanning process, 28, 36; school safety, 27, 29, 36; —, bullying interventions in schools, 140; —, colour-coded levels of 'alert,' 29; —, 'Operation Clear Sweep,' 32; —, Safe Schools Act (Ontario), 33; —, 'safe school policy (Toronto), 33; —, shooting deaths, 27
St Bernadette's High School for Girls (Toronto), 16, 19, 29; chaplaincy team, 18; Christ-centred community, 18; drama classroom, 48 (photo); dramatic pieces around religious holidays, 89; field note excerpt, 16–17; mission statement, 18; motto, 17; official story, 17; semestered system, 17; students, 80–3, 85–6, 120–1, 144–6; uniform, 17
scanning system, 15, 26–8, 36
scholars, critical, x

school(s), 8, 15; all-girl, 28, 29; alternative, 19; architectural designs, 26–9; bullying interven-‑ tions in schools, 140; Canadian, 32; —, linguistic discrimination, 157–8; Catholic, 17, 18; clubs, drama, 70; codes of conduct, 26; contradictions of, 7; dances, 63; 'downtown,' 9; d. Toronto, 61; effectiveness discourse, 20; environment, 36, 77; evaluation, 73–7; of excellence, 14; 'high security,' 33; inner-city, 61, 76–7; inner suburbs, 3; as institutions, 26; last resort, 21, 22; and liberal humanist values, 89; life, 89; literacy programs, 157; mission statements, 26; New York schools, 27; NY School Standards and Regents Diploma Requirement, 15; parents, 15, 33; philosophies, 26; physical space of, 11; policies – see under policies; practices, 'Operation Clear Sweep,' 32; —, 'scanning,' 27, 32; primary, 77; profiles, 26; publicly funded Catholic, 16; Regents-based, 21; school-based initiatives on lesbian/gay/bisexual/transgendered issues, 127; safety – see under safety; secondary, 77; 'second chance' school, 21, 22, 23; secular vs religious, 90; security procedures, 28, 33; semestered, 12, 17; shooting deaths, 27; signs from school hallways, 41, 42 (photos); 'SINI' (School In Need of Improvement), 26; sociological study of, 5; space(s), xi, 27–8; —, analyses, 26; standards-driven, 15, 74–7; student perspectives, 34, 38; studies of, 26, 73–7; —, American survey (student violence), 31; —, Foucault's, 31; suburban, 9–10, 146–7; surveillance, 36–7; traditional, 16; uniforms, 16, 17; urban, 5, 30, 181; —, challenges, 36, 75; —, and discipline, 168–70; —, problems of communication, 36; —, and safety, 109; —, systemic barriers, 36; violence, 15, 20; youth avenues of recourse in schools, 31. See also Amor, Middleview, Redmount, and St Bernadette's

schooling: big city, 4; emotional dimensions of, 20; micro-relations, x; North American, 4; social world of, 11; urban, 73–7

scleroderma, xii

Scottish descent, 22, 68, 110, 143, 156

'scriptive acts,' 98

second-generation Canadian, 80, 82, 85, 104, 121, 126, 145, 156

security, ix, 26; discourses of, 36; Emergency Preparedness Program, 33; guards, 15, 19, 30; —, increased presence in schools, 31; 'high security' school, society, 33; homeland, 14; measures in schools, 14, 28; —, sweeps, 30, 33; —, scanning, 15, 26–8, 36; new norms of, 33; New York State Homeland Security System for Schools, 30; police, x; priority of, 14; security obsessed culture, spaces, 90, 181; surveillance, 26, 31, 36; —, video, 37; unchallenged assumptions, 33; 'zero tolerance' policy, 33

self/selves: dialectics of, 5; hyphenated, x; expression in drama class, 102–5; performances of, xi; representation, 86; spectatorship, 102–3; reflexivity, 57, 180; understanding, 102–3

September 11th, ix, 33; post-9/11 school policies, 33

Serbia, 160; Serbian, 81, 161, 180

sexism, 117; abuses, 30; heterosexism, 127; institutional, 31; sexualization of the female subject, 30

sexuality, 6; and parenting, 112; and race, 116–27; and Shakespeare, 94–6; children's, 28; 18th- and 19th-century European bourgeois concerns for, 28; heteronormativity, 90; heterosexual, 103; —, culture, 111; —, heterosexism, 127; —, masculinities, 116; homosexuality/phobia, 90, 110–15; —, 'homosocial' experience, competition, 116; —, lesbian, 120; —, on television, 111; 'passing' as straight, 123–4; performance of masculinity, 116–27, 164–6; premarital sex, 111; prostitution, 93; representations of, 27; researcher's, 61; school-based initiatives on lesbian/gay/bisexual/transgendered issues, 127; sexual orientation, 85; spectrum of sexualities, 127; values in schools, 90; whole class discussions, 110–15, 122–4

SFCC (Schools Facing Challenging Circumstances), 76

Shakespeare: feminist take on, 94; King Lear, 172; Macbeth, 92–6; Romeo and Juliet, 94; student monologues, 89–90; Twelfth Night, 13

single mothers, 17

Sisters of St Bernadette, 18

situated ethnography, 7

situated knowledges, 55

slavery, 146–54

'smart mom,' 23

social: actions, 11; alienation, xi; being, 11; change, and research, 173; 'closure,' 74; cohesion, 3, 170, 181; —, in literature and popular culture, 89; consciousness, 4; constructs, 11; construction of reality, 59; contexts, of schooling, 4; of research sites, 11; crises, 4; critical social research, 58; descriptors, 9; divides, 4; drama, 90; —, as social art, 102; and educational disadvantage, 154; growth, 13; 'homosocial' experience, 116; identities, 156–7; ideology, 27; importance of theatre, 81; injustice, 74; investment in youth, 31; justice, 31, 127; life, xii; locations, 98; malaise, 4; markers, 9; milieu, 88; neglect, xii; norm-governed social interactions, 90; performance, 136; policy, 11; radical movements, xiv; scientists, 11; social-science research, 7; —, applied, 76; social identity performances, 166–8; space, 11, 28, 57; theory of knowledge, 131–2; unrest, 4; workers, 124; world of schooling, 11

sociology: 'established,' 131; sociological studies, 26; —, of asylums, 26; —, of schools, 5

society: 'colourblind,' 34; feudal, 93;

'high security,' 33; surveillance, 37; trends, 36

somatic learning, 153–4

Soulpepper Theatre, 69

South Africa, xi, 137, 147, 178; South African, 107

South Asian, 57, 138, 143, 172

South-East Asian, 16

space(s): aesthetic, 57, 135; for agency, xii; alternative, 19; for border-crossing, 84; discursive, 10, 26; drama, xi, xii, 79–83; education, 28; history of, 14; ideological, 11; imagined, 135; liminal, 58; occupied, xi, 90; 'our,' xiii; of performance, xii; physical, 10; problem of, 14; public, 14; public school, 4, 14; 'safe,' 32, 96; school, 27; security-obsessed spaces, 181; social, 57; and subjects, 26; surveillance space, 37; urban schooling, xii; virtual (websites), 26

Spanish descent, 110

spatial: techniques, 31; texts, 11; theorists, 11

'speech event,' 54

'spoiled' identities, 36

stabbings, 13

standards; movement, 22; New York School Standards and Regents Diploma Requirement, 15; Office for Standards in Education (OfSTED), 76; s.-driven school, 15; standardized testing, 21, 74

state: power, x; s.-sponsored democratic institutions, ix; violence, xi

statistics: racial, 34; National Center for Educational Statistics, 75; student population, Middleview Technical High School, 12

stereotypes: linguistic, 157–8; racist, xii; stereotyping of students by teachers, 146, 181

storytelling, 5

'Strat,' 22

Stratford Festival, 69, 89

student(s), 9, 14; African Students' Association, 146–54; at Amor, 23, 26, 89, 117–20; —, ethnicity, 24; apathy, 31; 'at risk,' 5; 'behaviour,' 5, 80, 103–5; body, 15; chronic absenteeism, 31, 34–5; clubs, 13; —, co-instructional, 18; —, peer-helper, 18; of colour, 34; complaints, 83; conversations/ interviews with, 79–83, 89; as co-researchers, 11, 55, 131–9, 172–82; council, 13; critical imagination, 97; cultural values, 34–5; curfew on, 32; 'esl,' 16; expectations, 22; with handguns in Ontario, 30; and handgun violence, 29–30; 'hard to teach,' 5; health, 34–5, 37; home culture, 35; identities, identification tags, 32; as interviewers, 62–71, 177–80; life, 89; life histories, 68, 79; —, and historical frameworks, 149; marginalization, 36, 155–6; at Middleview, 31, 34, 57, 62–71, 79–83, 89, 98, 99–105, 109–27, 146–54, 157–9; minoritized, 89; monologues, 107–9; needs, 18; perspectives, on conflict and drama, 143–4; —, on racism, 142–4; —, on research, 57, 70, 172–5; —, on school, 34–5, 37; profiling, 23; programs, guidance, 18; at Redmount, 15, 86–7, 89, 164–6; at St Bernadette's, 16, 80–3, 85–6, 89, 120–1, 144–6; as socially responsible citizens, 18; sociocultural characteristics of Black students, 149; special education, 25; student-led discussion, 25, 146–54; suspension, 14, 18; 'voices' in research, 130; work in role, 58; writing, 159; —, analysis of, 71–3; —, in role, 71; theory-building, 130

subject: credits, 18; teachers, 18

suburban, 9, 10; schools, 146–7

surveillance, ix, xi, xii; classed, x; closed-circuit television cameras in Britain, France, 37; electronic, 29; Emergency Preparedness Program, 33; 'Identity-Representation-Surveillance,' 131–7; increased in schools, 31, 36; institutional, 109; peer, 109; racialized, x; studies of, 37; 'Surveillance Camera Performers,' 32; targeted, x; Terrorist Information Awareness System, 33; tools, 62; 'universalist' vs 'targeted' policy responses, 37; video surveillance camera (photo), 40

surveys: American school survey, 31; school, ix; street, ix

symbolic violence, xi, 31

Syrian, 16

tableau, 93

tactics of the habitat, 14

teacher(s), 7, 10, 14, 15; as adviser, 20; at Amor Alternative, 19, 21, 23, 25, 26, 89; as co-researchers, 55; drama, 22, 27; education student, 70; as friend, 20; as good cop/bad cop, 20; at Middleview, 31, 34–5, 62–1, 89; perspectives on research, 174–5; at Redmount, 86, 89; at St

Bernadette's, 16, 89; as step-mom, 20; stereotyping of students, 146; student complaints, 83; work in role, 58

teaching, 8, 11; as a career, 26; as a caring profession, 20; choices, 96, 126–7; craft of, 7; quality, 77; techniques (directed instruction, student-led discussion, cooperative learning), 25

technical-instrumental paradigm, 22

technical training, 12

teenagers: drop-out rates, 57; drug use, 57, 63, 99–105; involvement in gangs, 57; pregnancy, 64–71, 99–105, 162–4; research issues, 57; stereotypes, 181; violence, 99–105

terrorism, 126; Terrorist Information Awareness System, 33

testing: high stakes, xi, 74–7, 83

tests/exams: English Regents, 16, 21, 77; 'falling test scores,' 73–7; literacy, 13; National Literacy Strategy, 76; National Numeracy Strategy, 76; numeracy, 13; Ontario literacy, 83

theatre: activism, 84–5; art/theatre project, 98; craft, skills, 89; embodied theatrical context, 151–4; metaphor, 26, 58, 86, 88, 128–9; pedagogy, 90; practitioners, 128; production, 89; at Redmount, 27–8; school competitions, 89; of situations, 87–8; social importance of, 81; Soulpepper Theatre, 69; Stratford Festival, 69; studios, traditional accounts of, 58; Theater and Education Award for Excellence, 14; theatrical imagination, 128–9; travelling theatre company, 90

'theoria,' 132
theory, theories; critical, 58; critical
race theory, 35; critical theorists,
11; dialectics, 59; feminist frameworks, 55; Foucault, 26; grounded
theory, 55; post-colonial, 8; postmodern, 8; —, and 'performatives,' 129; post-structural, 55, 88;
social, knowledge, 131–2; spatial
theorists, 11; students challenging,
130; theoretical framework of
educational trust, 21; theorizing in
ethnographic research, 54
'thick description,' 12
third-generation Canadian, 121; of
Caribbean descent, 66, 110, 133,
134, 137, 142, 150, 152, 156, 168,
177, 179; of East Asian descent,
155, 157
Toronto, ix, x, 3, 16; city of, 12; downtown, 10, 61; north-east end, 16
Toronto District School Board, 12,
124; 'safe school policy,' 33
Total Information Awareness System, 33
traditional ethnography, 8
traditional schools, 16; accounts of
classrooms, 58

United Kingdom, educational
policies, 74–6
United States, ix, 3; accountability
movement in public education,
74–7; schools, x, 31, 73–7; zero-
tolerance policy impacts, 34
University of Toronto, 76
urban, 3, 9, 10; 'acting Black,' 10;
Australia, x; Canada, x; challenges, 36, 75; communities, 8;
contexts, 3; and discipline, 168–70;

landscape, x; problems of communication, 36; researchers of, 7;
rhetoric of, 10; school(s), 5, 10, 11,
14; s. policies, 73–7; studies of, 33;
systemic barriers, 36; theorists of,
7; United States, x; urban/subur-
ban, 10; —, schools, 146–7; youth,
ix, xi, 22; —, cultural and media
productions of, 4

video cameras, 37
violence: abuse, 65; against women,
115; bullying, 168; emotional, 145–
6; family, 65; in schools, 15, 168–
70; state-enacted, xi; structural, 31;
students and handguns in Ontario,
30, 31; symbolic, xi, 31; terrorism,
126; weapons in schools, 30–1; and
youth, 99–102
'virtual schoolbag,' 154

wand scanner, 14
White, xi, 10, 13, 16, 21, 22, 24, 27, 29,
62, 68, 76, 80–2, 85, 91, 92, 105, 107,
109, 110, 133, 135, 142, 143, 144,
145, 150, 152, 156, 158, 163, 168,
172, 180; 'acting White,' 108–9;
culture, 34, 142; suburban school,
144–7; 'White Identity Transformation,' 149; 'white liberal guilt,'
24; 'whiteness,' decentring of, 36
witness, 6
wit(h)ness, ix, xiv
witnessing, burden of, xiii
working class, 9
working poor families, 9
working in role, 58
worldviews, 151–4

xenophobia, xii

youth: academically disengaged, 156; and 'at risk' label, 33, 36; avenues of recourse in schools, 31; Beige, 156; Black, ix, 147–8; Brown, 156; of colour, ix, 156; construction of social consciousness, 4; criminalization of, x, xi, 90; 'dangerous,' 33; developmental notions, 147–8; disenchanted, 73; identities, stakes, 86; —, threatening identities, 29; immigrant, ix, xi, 5; in role, 90; less privileged, 8; minoritized, 108–9; multiracial groups, 96; Native, ix; non-indigenous, x; popular culture, 155–6; riots, 37; researchers, ix, 11, 55, 131–9, 172–82; stereotypes, 86, 147–8, 181; 'talk back,' 36; 'taken-for-granted assumptions,' 36, 172–5; targeting, x; social investment in, 31; urban, ix, xiv, 22; violence, 99–2

Yugoslavian-born, 168

'zero tolerance,' 26, 33

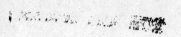